WITHDRAWN

Do Babies Matter?

Families in Focus

Series Editors

Anita Ilta Garey, *University of Connecticut*

Naomi R. Gerstel, *University of Massachusetts, Amherst*

Karen V. Hansen, *Brandeis University*

Rosanna Hertz, *Wellesley College*

Margaret K. Nelson, Middlebury College

Anita Ilta Garey and Karen V. Hansen, eds., *At the Heart of Work and Family: Engaging the Ideas of Arlie Hochschild*

Mary Ann Mason, Nicholas H. Wolfinger, and Marc Goulden, *Do Babies Matter? Gender and Family in the Ivory Tower*

Jamie L. Mullaney and Janet Hinson Shope, *Paid to Party: Working Time and Emotion in Direct Home Sales*

Markella B. Rutherford, *Adult Supervision Required: Private Freedom and Public Constraints for Parents and Children*

Do Babies Matter?

Gender and Family in the Ivory Tower

MARY ANN MASON
NICHOLAS H. WOLFINGER
MARC GOULDEN

RUTGERS UNIVERSITY PRESS

NEW BRUNSWICK, NEW JERSEY, AND LONDON

LIBRARY OF CONGRESS CATALOGING-IN-PUBLICATION DATA

Mason, Mary Ann.
    Do babies matter? : gender and family in the ivory tower / Mary Ann Mason,
Nicholas H. Wolfinger, Marc Goulden.
      p. cm.
    Includes bibliographical references and index.
    ISBN 978-0-8135-6081-6 (hardcover : alk. paper) — ISBN 978-0-8135-6080-9 (pbk. :
alk. paper) — ISBN 978-0-8135-6082-3 (e-book)
    I. Sex discrimination in higher education—United States. 2. Women in higher
education—United States. 3. Mothers—Employment—United States. I. Wolfinger,
Nicholas H., 1966– II. Goulden, Marc. III. Title.

    LC212.862.M33 2013
    378.082—dc23   2012033357

A British Cataloging-in-Publication record for this book
is available from the British Library.

Visit our website: http://rutgerspress.rutgers.edu

Manufactured in the United States of America

Mary Ann Mason dedicates this book to the many women
graduate students at UC Berkeley who have asked her,
"When is a good time to have a baby?"

Nicholas Wolfinger thanks his parents, Ray and Barbara Wolfinger, for
their love, inspiration, and support

Marc Goulden thanks his wife, Regan Rhea, and mother,
Nancy Goulden, for their unceasing support

CONTENTS

FIGURES AND TABLES

ACKNOWLEDGMENTS

The "Do Babies Matter?" project has spanned more than ten years and has benefited from the contributions of numerous colleagues.

At the University of California, Berkeley, Karie Frasch participated in our research on the careers and lives of graduate students and scientists. She also helped to develop our policy recommendations. This would not be same book without her input. Many other Berkeley colleagues provided valuable assistance, including Carol Hoffman, Sharon Page-Medrich, Angelica Stacy, and Sheldon Zedeck. We would also like to thank Executive Director Ann O'Leary and the Berkeley Law Center for Health, Economics and Family Security for promoting our research on women in science.

Special thanks go to Sheila O'Rourke and Ellen Switkes, then at the UC Office of the President, for helping to successfully support, implement, and sustain the UC Family Friendly Initiative, and to Berkeley Chancellors Robert Berdahl and Robert Birgeneau for supporting and promoting our research, and helping to implement the resulting policies. The UC Council of Graduate Deans was also instrumental in obtaining permission to survey graduate students and postdoctoral fellows and in promoting new family-friendly initiatives.

At the University of Utah, we benefited from discussions with Carrie Byington, Kathleen Digre, Joanne Yaffe, Cathleen Zick, and the Utah Demographic Network. Sonja Anderson, Jackie Griffith, Bin Emma Liang, and Alta Williams provided expert research assistance, while Cindy Brown, Marilyn Cox, Sandra Earl, and Sandy Stark furnished able administrative support.

At the National Science Foundation, we thank Maurya Green, Kelly Kang, Nirmala Kannankutty, Adrian McQueen, and Keith Wilkinson for their assistance with the Survey of Doctorate Recipients. The use of NSF data does not imply NSF endorsement of research methods or conclusions contained in this book.

Korey Capozza served as our editor over the past eight years. She worked tirelessly and cheerfully to make our often murky prose more readable. Without her help, our work might never have come to fruition. We owe her a great debt of gratitude.

Andy Roth kindly read the entire manuscript. His comments produced a clearer and more logically consistent book. Other colleagues who provided valuable suggestions over the years include Richard Ingersoll, Jerry Jacobs, Matthew McKeever, Phil Morgan, Benita Roth, Sharon Sassler, and Ann Marie Wood.

Generous extramural funding made this research possible. Both the Association for Institutional Research and the Alfred P. Sloan Foundation provided multiple years of funding, and we are grateful. At Sloan, Kathleen Christensen deserves much credit as our long-term supporter.

At Rutgers we thank our editor, Peter Mickulas, and our series editor, Karen Hansen, for their enthusiasm for this project. It goes without saying that this book wouldn't exist without their support. Romaine Perin also deserves great thanks for her astute copyediting.

Nick Wolfinger owes a special debt to two mentors. Bill Mason taught him to think carefully and creatively about quantitative data, providing lessons that will inform a lifetime of scholarship. Paul Sniderman has been a constant source of wise professional counsel, instrumental for navigating the rocky shoals of academia. Finally, Nick thanks Eric Magnuson, a debt long past due, for a very different sort of academic advice.

Do Babies Matter?

Introduction

Today, women receive slightly more than half the doctoral degrees granted in the United States.[1] With women and men now feeding the academic pipeline in equal numbers, is it just a matter of time before we see gender parity in the professoriate? Regrettably, the answer is no. In two important measures of gender equality, the representation of women in academe and the family characteristics of women who do become professors, we see a serious imbalance. Put simply, there are far fewer women than men at the top of the academic ladder, and these women are much less likely to be married or have children than are the men at the top. In contrast, at the bottom of the academic ladder, among the ranks of contingent and part-time faculty, there are disproportionately more women, and these women are almost as likely as the men to have children. Mothers are more likely to sink to the second tier of academia or leave higher education altogether.

This book draws on over a decade of research to offer the first broad examination of the effects of family formation on the academic careers of men and women across their professional lives.[2] The story begins with graduate students and postdocs; moves to the critical assistant professor years, when careers advance or founder; continues with the midcareer years, in which some academics take on leadership roles, while others experience professional stagnation; and finally, looks at retirement. It is important to note that this story is not just about women. Although family formation plays a more dramatic role in women's academic careers, it does affect the choices that men make and how they manage to balance career and family. In particular, the status of fathers as equal caretakers is seriously challenged by many of the same professional obstacles that hold back mothers. Our research on the lives and careers of male and female academics, built on a multitude of rich data sets, describes these challenges at length.

The "Do Babies Matter?" research project began at the University of California, Berkeley, in 2001. The previous year had been a milestone for graduate education at Berkeley: for the first time more than 50 percent of the incoming class were women. This landmark event reflected the national trend; the percentage of women among U.S. citizens receiving doctorates in the United States rose from 12 percent in 1966 to 49 percent in 2000 (today it stands at 51 percent).[3] Still, in 2000 women composed only 23 percent of tenure-track faculty (pre- and post-tenure) at Berkeley, and in higher administrative posts they were scarcely visible. This was not simply a chronological lag. In 2000, women received 39 percent of all doctorates granted at Berkeley, but they represented only 28 percent of the new faculty hires. This disparity between the gender breakdown of the available pool and of hired faculty has been the norm for decades at American universities. The numbers may have changed somewhat, but the pattern has not: the gap between women's Ph.D. receipt and faculty hiring has only grown at Berkeley and other universities in recent years.[4]

When our Do Babies Matter? project began in 2001, Mary Ann Mason was the first woman dean of the Graduate Division of the University of California, Berkeley, and Marc Goulden served as a senior research analyst. Nick Wolfinger, a family sociologist at the University of Utah, joined the team the next year.

We began to investigate the effect of family formation on the academic careers of both men and women. To address this question we first turned to the Survey of Doctorate Recipients (SDR), a national data set sponsored largely by the National Science Foundation, with contributions from the National Endowment for the Humanities and other agencies. This ongoing biennial longitudinal survey, begun in 1973 and continually replenished with new respondents, tracks more than 160,000 Ph.D.s across the disciplines throughout their careers, until age seventy-six. It is arguably the best employment data set in the United States. Using the SDR we were able to examine the experience of Ph.D. recipients in the sciences, including engineering and mathematics, as well as in the social sciences and humanities.[5] The SDR includes faculty members at liberal arts schools, community colleges, and research universities, as well as Ph.D. recipients working in the private sector or government.

Our initial inquiry, funded by the Association for Institutional Research, produced intriguing results.[6] Women who had children within five years of receiving their Ph.D. were much less likely than men with early babies to acquire tenured professorships. This pattern persisted across the disciplines, from the bench sciences to the humanities, and held across different types of four-year institutions, from liberal arts colleges to major research universities. Moreover, mothers often fell into the second tier of adjunct faculty or instructors at two-year colleges.[7] Marriage in and of itself and older children had different effects on women's careers, underscoring the complexity of gender equity in the academy. Also, we had not yet identified the stage in the academic life course where mothers dropped out. Do they leave academia right after graduate school, or do they fail to get tenure? Our subsequent research would address these questions.[8]

Concerned by our finding of a strong relationship between family formation and professional success in academia, we turned the question on its head and asked: What is the effect of career on family formation? Do men and women who achieve their goals and become tenured professors have similar family configurations? Here the results were equally alarming.[9] The familial gap between men and women professors was far larger than the career gap: only one in three women who takes a tenure-track university job before having a child ever becomes a mother, and women who obtain tenure are more than twice as likely as their male colleagues to be single twelve years after earning their Ph.D. Women are also much more likely to be divorced than men in similar career circumstances.

This analysis suggested that a full consideration of gender equity in the academy needed to be measured in two ways.[10] Comparing the number of tenured men professors with the number of tenured women professors only told part of the story; equally important were the family configurations of those who had obtained tenure. True parity could only be achieved when men and women realized the same professional *and* familial goals.

Our research led to another surprising finding. Using the 2000 United States Census we compared the frequency of childbirth for academic women and men with workers in two other time-demanding, fast-track professions, law and medicine.[11] Not only did academic women have fewer children than did women doctors and lawyers, but academic men experienced a similar gap. Compared with other fast-track professions, the academy is less family friendly for both men and women.

Our Do Babies Matter? findings offered compelling evidence of a phenomenon that had previously been noted only anecdotally. Universities could no longer ignore the problem. They were losing some of their best and brightest students, and those who stayed in the academy often did so at a familial disadvantage. Attracted by our work, the Alfred P. Sloan Foundation, long involved with work and family issues, sponsored us to promote real change in academia. We developed the UC Faculty Family Friendly Edge (http://ucfamily edge.berkeley.edu/) project as a vehicle to implement reform at the entire ten-campus UC system.

Our first step was a baseline survey of the more than eight thousand tenure-track faculty members in the nine-campus University of California system (a tenth campus, UC Merced, was added in 2005). We wanted to know what their work and family lives were like. What were their greatest challenges? What did they perceive to be the best solutions? Ironically, the UC system had been an early pioneer in offering family-friendly policies in the late 1980s, but our findings showed that more than half the faculty did not know many of these policies existed. Of those that did know, too few used them. Clearly, just creating new policies would not change the culture.

The political work of enhancing the existing family accommodation policies at the huge UC system has taken many years and remains ongoing. Administrators from top to bottom had to be convinced that developing strong policies was important for the future of the UC system. The university spent months working out the thorny details, such as how to evaluate research productivity for faculty who had stopped the clock for tenure. Furthermore, the department chairs, the on-site managers of the faculty, had to be trained in the new policies.

Ultimately, our faculty family-friendly package included innovative policies for both mothers and fathers. We aspired to create a new climate in which families were integrated into all stages of men's and women's academic careers. It was clear that culture change would not occur unless men were equally invested. Several of the reforms focused on the early faculty years, for both men and women the time of greatest demands both professionally and at home. These years, which we call the "make or break" period, occur roughly between the ages of thirty and forty and are when most academics get tenure-track jobs and many receive tenure. These are also the years when most babies are born. We promoted a pre- and post-tenure part-time track for both mothers and fathers with the right to return to full-time work. We advocated for options to stop the tenure clock and provide relief from teaching for one semester for fathers and two semesters for mothers. The part-time tenure-track also offered a more flexible way of managing work and family over the course of a career, including the midcareer years when elder care—for parents and, later on, for spouses or partners—can become time consuming. Recognizing that department chairs were often the most critical link in encouraging or discouraging personnel policy, we developed a set of guidelines for academic administrators, "Creating a Family-Friendly Department: Chairs and Deans Toolkit," which provided specific instructions on how administrators should handle family matters and improve family friendliness across their institutions.[12]

Our research did not stop with the implementation of these family-friendly policies. Over time we learned that many women (and some men) had already made up their minds in graduate school to abandon an academic career. Others made the decision while they were postdoctoral fellows. To discover why men and women doctoral students were turning away from academic research careers and heading instead to four-year teaching colleges or jobs in industry and government, we surveyed students in their second year or beyond at nine of the ten campuses in the UC system (UC Merced had too few graduate students to participate). We learned that many of our young graduate students become disenchanted with academia during the course of their studies, as they become aware of the challenges of balancing family with a career in the professoriate.[13]

To address these concerns we proposed a new set of family-friendly policies for graduate students in order to change the culture for them as well. The message we sought to convey through these policies is that it is possible to pursue an academic career and still maintain balanced family and personal lives. We wanted students to feel that families are welcome at any time, including in graduate school. The new policies included paid maternity leave for graduate students, help with child care, and a stop-the-clock option so that men and women doctoral students who became parents could take a year longer to complete their degree without being penalized.

Initially our research had focused on the early years, when careers are made or broken and family formation has the most dramatic consequences. We extended our inquiry to the midcareer years and investigated the rank and salary lag for women. Women are more likely to remain as associate professors than are men. Women professors make less money than their male colleagues. Furthermore, women are not ascending to the major academic leadership roles—deans, provosts, presidents—commensurate with their numbers.

We learned that the story regarding family formation in the midcareer years is both more hopeful and more complex than it is in the make-or-break years. The effect of family on midcareer advancement is smaller but still noteworthy. Children don't affect promotion to the rank of full professor, but they do reduce women's salaries. Taken together our findings show that marriage and children affect men and women in different ways at different stages in the academic life course.

A different kind of family issue becomes imperative for many women and men in the mature heart of their careers, around age fifty, as parents become dependents and husbands and wives must care for each other in times of failing health.[14] Although the average time requirements of later-life caregiving are less predictable than during family formation, they nevertheless affect many academics. As is the case in the make-or-break years, it is women who often bear the lion's share of the burden. Our research looks at family and career in these later years and explores when and why professors retire and what role family plays in that decision.

More recently our research has focused on the scientific disciplines, including the physical and biological sciences, mathematics, and engineering. These disciplines present unique challenges for work-family balance, especially for women. In the physical sciences, the low enrollment of female graduate students and the paucity of tenured female scientists perpetuate a culture that is decidedly unfriendly toward women. In the biological sciences, women are thriving at the graduate school level, yet they face huge obstacles in sustaining their postgraduate careers with the support of funding from federal agencies. In many cases, the family demands experienced (or anticipated) by young women scientists are a key reason for their failure to continue.

We also discovered that federal granting agencies may contribute to this problem by making few allowances for family needs. We surveyed the thirteen major federal agencies that support scientific research to identify their family-friendly policies and practices.[15] This was followed up with a survey of the Association of American Universities schools—the top sixty-one research universities and where most scientific research takes place—to determine the extent of their family-friendly policies for graduate students, postdocs, and faculty. But the problem isn't limited to research universities. At the numerous conferences where we have shared our findings, we have learned that the need for family-friendly policies is similar across all types of higher education institutions, including liberal arts colleges and junior colleges.

Equipped with these many strands of research, we present a comprehensive picture of how career and family intersect over the course of an academic career. We can pinpoint the key junctures where families derail careers. The story is complex; family formation can also have professional benefits for both men and women. For men, marriage and children appear to have a positive effect at most career stages. For women, marriage and older children have benefits at certain stages. Although there are clearly nuances to this story, overall we see large discrepancies between men and women faculty regarding marriage and children—a finding that cannot be ignored. With this knowledge we can begin to understand what interventions are necessary at different stages of an academic career to allow academics, male and female, to live balanced lives.

The following chapters describe the relationship between gender, work, and family at each stage of the academic career path: the graduate student years, looking for the first job, the probationary pre-tenure years, midcareer, and retirement. Specific strategies and interventions are outlined for achieving work-family balance at each career stage; many of these interventions are already best practices at some universities and federal agencies. Broader issues, such as the future of tenure and the reach of Title IX in restructuring the academic workplace, are addressed. The frustration of fathers in their emerging role as equal caretakers and the regrets of tenured women without children are carefully examined. As often as possible, we present the voices of the men and women who are living the challenge of balancing work and family. These voices emanate from comments in the many surveys we have undertaken over the years; from online accounts such as in blogs; and from the interviews we have conducted, some of them in conjunction with Mary Ann Mason and Eve Ekman's book, *Mothers on the Fast Track*.[16]

This is a turning point for universities. Many of our best and brightest young people are rejecting careers at research universities. According to our research, the lack of accommodations for family obligations is a key reason the new generation of scholars views an academic career as unappealing. This is costly in many ways. The United States cannot afford to lose many of its best researchers and thinkers, scholars who will eventually train the next generation. And these talented young scholars should not have to forsake careers for which they have already invested many years of their lives.

We are arguing for a new model for the academic workplace that's more in line with the actual experience of men and women scholars. This model must take into account that many couples have dual careers, and that children, spouses, and parents are an integral part of most scholars' lives. This dramatic shift is needed to attract and retain the women who are now nearly the majority of Ph.D. recipients, but who are often not able to achieve their full career potential and still have a family. Change is also needed for men, who are committed to active family participation but feel thwarted by career pressures.

Spurred in part by our research and the progressive model now in place at the University of California system, family-friendly policies are getting serious national attention. Giant steps towards family friendliness have been taken at many colleges and universities. At the University of California we have seen tremendous shifts in the past few years, since we developed the UC Family Friendly Edge program. Women assistant professors are more than twice as likely to have children as they were in 2003. Faculty are making use of accommodations for childbirth at an unprecedented rate, and graduate students are routinely stopping the clock and taking paid maternity leave. Many other universities and colleges have important success stories to tell. Long the epitome of workplace inflexibility, academia is gradually becoming a benchmark for progress. The following chapters will show why this transformation is needed, and how it might be implemented.

I

The Graduate School Years

New Demographics, Old Thinking

The graduate student and postdoc years are the proving ground for future academics. Many students enter with clear plans to become professors, but end up changing their minds. There are many reasons to reject an academic career, but family considerations—marriage and children—are most prominent for women and a serious concern for men as well. How concerns about family affect these young scholars' decisions is complex. Some students lack the role models that might otherwise demonstrate that work-family balance is possible in academia. For others, encountering intense professional hostility after having a baby weakens their commitment to an academic career. Sometimes marriage presents a barrier to developing two careers. The scientific disciplines, which foster a nonstop competitive race to the top, offer a particular challenge. The academy has recently focused attention on the work-family concerns of faculty, but it has largely ignored graduate students and postdoctoral fellows. This chapter considers how these young scholars confront family issues, and how a few universities are beginning to remake the academic workplace in order to retain graduate students and postdocs in the career pipeline.

The New Face of Graduate Students

The new generation of doctoral students is different in many ways from that of just thirty or forty years ago. Academia was once composed largely of men in traditional single-earner families. Today, men and women fill the doctoral student ranks in nearly equal numbers, and most will experience both the benefits and the challenges of living in dual-earner households. This generation also has different expectations and values from previous ones; most notably, the desire for flexibility and balance between their careers and their other goals. But changes to the structure and culture of academia have not kept pace with this major shift in students' priorities. The outdated notion of the "ideal worker" prevails, including in a de facto requirement for sole devotion to the academy and a linear, lockstep career trajectory that permits no interruptions. Senior faculty and administration, still largely men, are not role models for the new generation of scholars when it comes to demonstrating the work-family balance and flexibility that these students desire.[1]

The most significant change in the graduate student body is that women are now as numerous as men. Indeed, gender parity in graduate education is one of the remarkable accomplishments of the past forty years. In 1966, just 12 percent of all American doctorates were awarded to women.[2] By 2008 that number had soared to over 50 percent.[3] There have also been impressive gains for minority students, particularly minority women, but they still are by no means proportionally represented. Moreover, the gender balance remains more uneven in some disciplines than in others. In 2008, women received only 28 percent of the doctorates awarded in the traditionally male-dominated physical sciences, including computer science and math, and just 22 percent of those awarded in engineering.[4] Although these are lower proportions than seen today in the more human-centric disciplines such as biology and psychology, they nonetheless represent extraordinary progress. As figure 1.1 shows, over the past four decades the proportion of women Ph.D. recipients has increased more than a hundredfold in engineering, twelvefold in the geosciences, and sevenfold in the physical sciences. Since these trends appear unabated and women are outperforming men at the baccalaureate and master's levels, it seems reasonable to assume that further gains will occur.[5]

In addition to being notably more female than they were three decades ago, today's doctoral students are a bit older: The median male Ph.D. recipient is now thirty-two and the median female doctorate recipient is now thirty-three.[6] Students in the natural and physical sciences often finish their Ph.D. at a somewhat younger age but are increasingly likely to spend time as postdoctoral fellows.[7] They may hold these positions for years before acquiring a tenure-track job. Most women faculty will therefore be at or near the end of their childbearing years by the time they achieve tenure. Postponing a family until tenure, the old wisdom offered to women graduate students, remains bad advice for purely biological reasons.[8] But what about having children during graduate school, when women are more fertile? As we shall see, few students view this as a good option.

A Bad Reputation

Work-family balance weighs heavily on the minds of graduate students as they ponder their careers; in our landmark 2006–2007 survey of about eight

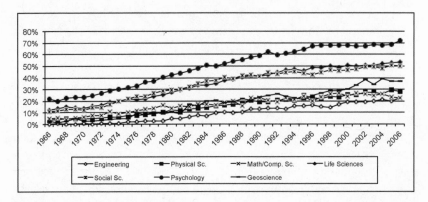

FIGURE 1.1 Women Doctoral Recipients in the United States in the Sciences, 1966–2006

Source: National Science Foundation, Division of Science Resources Statistics "Survey of Earned Doctorates," WebCASPAR, http://webcaspar.nsf.gov/; Marc Goulden, Mary Ann Mason, Karie Frasch, and the Center for American Progress, "Staying Competitive: Patching America's Leaky Pipeline in the Sciences," Berkeley Center on Health, Economic, and Family Security, University of California, Berkeley, 2009, figure 4, http://www.american progress.org/issues/2009/11/women_and_sciences.html.

Note: Data are for U.S. citizens only.

thousand doctoral students at the University of California, 84 percent of women and 74 percent of men registered the family friendliness of their future workplace as a concern. Yet more than 70 percent of women and over half of all men doctoral students surveyed consider faculty careers at research universities not friendly to family life.[9]

Most doctoral students begin their careers with the same hopes and dreams as generations before them: they want to become professors. About two-thirds of doctoral students at the University of California said this was their objective when they began graduate school. The majority aspired to faculty positions at major research universities, and most of the others to jobs at four-year teaching colleges. But graduate school frequently causes them to change their minds about careers at research universities. About 30 percent of the women and 20 percent of the men we surveyed turn away from their goal of becoming a professor at a major research university, and instead intend to pursue careers in nonacademic settings.[10]

Men and women offer somewhat different explanations for their apprehensions about academic careers. Both men and women are more likely to report dissatisfaction with the unrelenting work hours. As one male student at the University of California complained, "[I'm] fed up with the narrow-mindedness of supposedly intelligent people who are largely workaholic and expect others to be so as well."[11] Women, however, are especially likely to focus on family concerns. "I could not have come to graduate school more motivated to be a research-oriented professor," one female student related. "Now I feel that can only be a career possibility if I am willing to sacrifice having children."[12]

Our one-on-one interviews with doctoral students yielded similar findings. Carolyn, a fifth-year Ph.D. student in engineering at a major research university and mother of a three-month-old son, faced a series of challenges when she considered starting a family during her graduate studies.[13]

Carolyn grew up in a working-class neighborhood in Texas. Neither of her parents attended college, but her father worked with engineers at a power plant, and he strongly encouraged Carolyn's interest in an engineering career. She was an outstanding student in both science and the liberal arts and earned a double degree, a BA and a BS, from the University of Texas. Soon after graduation Carolyn married her high school sweetheart. She planned to work for four or five years, then start a family.

But Carolyn was soon drawn back to academia. "I realized I could do much more real research with a Ph.D.," she related. Carolyn's husband, Ken, was already pursuing a doctorate, so she waited her turn and supported his studies. She began her own graduate program at the age of twenty-seven, but realized that the time commitment and work environment probably wouldn't allow for children in the near future. "We were already very ready to have a family, but I didn't see how we could make it work," she said. Only 20 percent of the students in Carolyn's department were women, and none had ever had a baby. The demands of graduate school had upended Carolyn and Ken's plans, and they abandoned their intention to start a family anytime soon.

Doctoral Student Parents

According to our survey of University of California Ph.D. students, only 14 percent of men and 12 percent of women are parents.[14] Yet over two-thirds of the women claim that between twenty-eight and thirty-four would be the optimal age to have a first child.[15] Why do most women avoid having children during graduate school? After all, it's a time of flexible schedules and the possibility of a community with which to share the experience of parenting. The most common reason provided by our University of California respondents is the workload, as table 1.1 shows. Sixty-eight percent of male students and 76 percent of female students cite graduate school work requirements as the most important reason to hold off on children; women are also far more likely than men to believe that graduate school and parenthood are fundamentally incompatible.

It is worth noting that women are more likely than men to put off having children for the same reasons that one of the authors of this book, Mary Ann Mason, did more than thirty years ago: they fear that they will not be taken seriously and that their professors and future employers will disapprove. One

TABLE I.I.

University of California Ph.D. Students' Reasons for Not Having a Child or Uncertainty about Having One

Reason cited as "very important"	Total (%)	Men (%)	Women (%)
Time demands of current Ph.D. program/ employment	72	68	76
Current level of personal/household income	. 64	67	61
Anticipated demands of future program/career	54	48	59
Stress of raising a child as a Ph.D. student	53	48	58
Concerns re affordability/availability of quality child care	53	49	56
Concerns re affordability/availability of quality housing	51	51	52
Uncertain future employment situation	50	48	51
Concerns re affordability/availability of health insurance	47	47	48
Worry Ph.D. program and caregiving are incompatible	46	36	54
Concerns regarding degree progress	43	34	51
Concerns about availability of pregnancy leave	43	32	50
Uncertain current employment situation	38	35	40
Concerns re future career advancement/success	36	27	43
Anticipated future level of personal/household income	33	32	33
Uncertainty regarding future spouse/partner (not married)	30	27	33
Limited interest in becoming parent as a Ph.D. student	29	31	28
Spouse/partner does not want child at this time	28	32	24
Time for leisure or social activities	23	23	23
Effects of a(nother) child on my marriage/relationship	17	17	17
Worry advisor would take my work less seriously	15	8	21
Worry possible employers might take my work less seriously	15	6	23
Worry other faculty might take my work less seriously	13	6	19
Medical or health reasons (including age)	13	8	17
Worry peers would take my work less seriously	9	4	14

Note: Boxed items represent statistically significant (p < .001) gender differences.

N = 3,880–4,353

Source: University of California Doctoral Student Career and Life Survey, 2006–2007.

student at the University of California commented on her department's attitude toward pregnant students: "There is a pervasive attitude that the female graduate student in question must now prove to the faculty that she is capable of completing her degree, even when prior to the pregnancy there were absolutely no doubts about her capabilities and ambition." According to table 1.1, two to three times more women than men were concerned that having a child would be negatively perceived by their professors or future employers.

The bench sciences offer additional challenges for student parents, particularly mothers. Would-be scientists have far less flexible schedules than do graduate students in the humanities and many of the social sciences. Most of the bench sciences require long hours spent in campus labs. Moreover, the competitive race to achieve scientific breakthroughs and prove oneself offers little respite for childbirth or childrearing.[16] This is reflected in the blog of a postdoc at the Washington University School of Medicine, *Academic Aspirations*: "In science especially, research fields move very quickly. The maternity leave time could be just enough for you to be scooped and lose months or years' worth of work. It's a frustrating thing to think about."[17]

None of this is a secret to female scientists. Jennifer, a neuroscience postdoc, had her first child soon after finishing her Ph.D. "I don't think I'll ever be able to do a tenure-track job, and people were very upfront with me about that when I had my child. Looking around me, I see that people are completely shut out of positions because of family."[18] Not surprisingly, the message is different for men. Men who marry and have children are considered more mature and better able to handle their work, while women are considered less serious.[19] The assumption is that women with children do not get work done—and with limited grant funding available, research positions should go to those who have the most promising futures. Marriage, as we will see in the following chapter, limits a woman's flexibility to seek the best jobs, and pregnancy anytime prior to tenure is seen as evidence that she is not seriously dedicated to her career. And the density of men, as in many professions, reinforces the male status quo. At present, too many students agree with one UC woman student's appraisal: "Don't get a Ph.D.! Just don't do it: there are so many other things in life that you could do for a living that are as intellectually challenging, pay more, and where women having children is not a big deal. Academia is stuck in the 1970s at best on this issue."

Financial Constraints

The graduate student years are typically a period of limited incomes and modest lifestyles—the years of the Ramen noodle diet—and finances are clearly a concern for student couples considering parenthood. Raising a child brings many new expenses: health care costs, child care, housing, diapers, and clothing. All told, American parents now spend more than eleven thousand dollars a year on expenses for a baby or toddler.[20] In our survey of Ph.D. students at the University of California, the second most cited reason for delaying having children was money: 67 percent of men and 61 percent of female graduate students cited their paltry incomes as a reason for not starting a family (see table 1.1). It's not surprising that men are more likely to invoke financial justifications for waiting on parenthood: they are more likely than women to have partners who aren't working, or are working only part time.[21] As one zoology Ph.D. candidate recounted in an anthology of personal accounts, *Motherhood, the Elephant in the Lab*, child care costs can be a particular challenge for cash-strapped students: "Student life means working long hours and receiving little money for your efforts. Childrearing means working long hours and receiving no money for your efforts. Therefore, if you are busy in the lab and have little money, how can you pay the high costs of child care?"[22]

Would-be parents are unlikely to receive much help from their universities. According to a 2008 survey of over one hundred institutions conducted by *The Chronicle of Higher Education*, annual Ph.D. student stipends ranged from three thousand to twenty-eight thousand dollars.[23] Most students probably receive less than twenty thousand dollars. Only 42 percent have health insurance through their universities, obviously a crucial resource when considering parenthood.[24] Just 13 percent of Association of American Universities schools (sixty-one top-ranked research universities) offer graduate students six weeks of paid maternity leave without notable limitations.[25] Students who wish to take more than six weeks of maternity leave face many barriers. Such was the case for Carolyn, the engineering Ph.D. student from Texas introduced earlier. Toward the end of graduate school, Carolyn finally decided to become a mother. She wanted to take twelve weeks of maternity leave, which she felt would be the minimum necessary to establish a close relationship with her baby. She thought she was entitled to this much time off under the FMLA (Family and Medical Leave Act), which allows all American workers twelve weeks of unpaid parental leave. To her dismay, Carolyn found that as a student she was not covered by the FMLA. Her federal granting agency by law could allow only what the university allowed: six weeks. Only with a great deal of complaining within her university was she granted permission to extend her leave.

Role Models and Mentors

Carolyn's decision to have a child stemmed in part from encouragement she received from a role model, a junior faculty mother. Across all disciplines, a personal mentor is often a key influence in the work and family decisions of today's graduate students. As traditionally conceived, mentors provide academic support, teach analytic and other technical skills, guide student research, and provide career advice.[26] But faculty mentors also serve as role models on a more personal level: they provide a model for work-family balance.[27] As Carolyn's story illustrates, the presence of a successful faculty mother can be a powerful source of encouragement for students. Conversely, a faculty mentor can discourage graduate students by exhibiting a lifestyle seemingly incompatible with parenthood. Life-changing mentors are not always women. Many senior faculty men provide encouragement and serve as role models for flexibility for family life; sometimes they have wives or daughters in academia or other professions. Some women faculty are neither helpful nor good role models as mothers. Still, the living example of a senior faculty member, especially a woman who successfully balances a demanding career with a satisfying family life, is an important beacon for graduate students.

Apprehension about the ability to balance an academic career with a family often begins in graduate school. Doctoral students cannot help but notice that their advisers are far more likely to have families if they are men. Of tenured women faculty who received their Ph.D.s between 1978 and 1984, 45 percent were childless twelve years after completing graduate school. The comparable figure for men is much lower, on the order of 26 percent. There is a similar difference in marriage rates. Eighty-five percent of the men are married, compared with 63 percent of the women.[28] Tenured academics from this cohort are now senior scholars and the mentors of today's graduate students. According to our nine-campus University of California survey, students frequently observe that women have more difficulty balancing academic careers and families. For some graduate students, the reality seemed painfully clear. "I can recall no female faculty getting tenure in our department while raising children," one women in the STEM (science, technology, engineering, and math) fields pointed out. This sentiment was echoed by a female doctoral student in the physical sciences: "Most importantly, I can't think of an example of a (perceived [to be]) successful female professor at our (or any other) top research university who has a 'normal' family situation. The only time these women appear successful both personally and professionally is if a spouse dedicates his (or her) career to helping his (or her) wife succeed."

For other women graduate students the issue is not so much whether to have children, as when. This dilemma, exacerbated by the absence of role model mothers, plays out at different times in women's professional lives, most commonly when they go on the academic job market or when the tenure clock runs up against the biological clock later in their careers. One female graduate student studying math at the University of California evidently devoted considerable thought to this question:

> My most pressing concern is that I do not have enough information about *when* to have children. There are not enough women (especially

in math) whom I have encountered to have enough information about when/how having children affected their career. At a recent dinner with other (female) math graduate students, we recognized that we know of no female math grad student who has successfully had a child in grad school (except for one in the 1970s who is now a professor at [another school in the University of California system]). I acknowledge that . . . [because] our program is shorter (than, say, English) it might make more sense to finish one's degree first, but the years of one's post-doc do not seem optimal either, nor the years of a tenure-track position, but who wants to wait until she is 35?

Across all disciplines, graduate student women in particular indicate that having a female role model in their department is critical to whether they perceive academia to be a family-friendly workplace. The fewer faculty mothers they see, the less likely women students are to feel that tenure-track faculty careers at research universities are family friendly—and the less likely they may be to continue on that track. According to our University of California survey, only 12 percent of women doctoral students who said they were in departments devoid of faculty mothers viewed research universities as family friendly, compared with 46 percent of women students in departments where women faculty more commonly had children.[29]

Faculty mentors are not always helpful, and women can be at a disadvantage if they get stuck with a sexist advisor.[30] This was the case for Sue. Just after receiving her Ph.D. in chemical engineering from a prestigious university in four years (near record speed for a doctorate), Sue related to us that her advisor not only failed to offer her help in finding a job, but didn't even ask about her career plans. In the lab, Sue's advisor picked clear favorites and marginalized female graduate students. "I took my qualifying exams early, and his only remark was, 'I'm surprised you passed!'" Sue recounted. "I wasn't sure if he was surprised because I am a woman, or because I am Black." (Sue was born in Ghana and came to the United States at seventeen.) On campus, she was known as the extremely effective and articulate president of her university's graduate student assembly. She seemed self-assured and focused, but clearly her advisor's lack of interest had eroded her confidence. Discouraged, Sue turned away from an academic research career and took a position on the business side of an engineering company.[31]

Scientific Challenges

Concerns about work-life balance are particularly pronounced among doctoral students in the bench sciences. This may help explain why relatively few women obtain Ph.D.s in most scientific fields and ultimately contribute to the gender imbalance among faculty at research universities. A recent report by the National Research Council of the National Academy of Sciences discusses at length the underrepresentation of women in many of the scientific disciplines at academic institutions across the country, particularly in the faculty ranks.[32] The report confirms that women who receive Ph.D.s in the sciences are less likely than men to seek academic research positions, often the path to cutting-edge scholarship, and they are more likely to drop out before attaining tenure if they do take on a faculty post. Data from both the National Institutes of Health (NIH) and National Science Foundation (NSF), the two agencies providing the bulk of research funding to American universities and colleges, tell a similar story. Women compose a much larger proportion of the total number of predoctoral fellowships awarded by these agencies than they do postdoctoral fellowships and competitive faculty grants. The drop-off in relative proportion is dramatic, with women receiving 63 percent and 54 percent of NIH and NSF's predoctoral awards in 2007, respectively, but just 25 percent and 23 percent of the competitive faculty grants awarded in the same year.[33] This winnowing out of women scientists is depicted in figure 1.2. The recent surge in the number of women Ph.D.s may account for some of this dramatic disparity in federal funding. Equally likely, the rapid decline in funding between graduate school and the professoriate results from women leaving the academy due to concerns about work-family balance.

The fund-raising requirements of a scientific career soon become apparent to graduate students and postdoctoral fellows. As one established woman scientist commented:

> We are required in most cases to produce 65% or more of our salary and benefits from research grants. In addition, we often also pay anywhere from 50–90% institutional overhead from our research grants. In order to do this successfully, we must on the average have at least two active research grants every year. The success rate of a grant application at the NIH is now about 10%. This coupled with the fact that one needs at least 2–3 publications per year to be competitive for a grant and graduate students typically take 4 years to produce one publication, combines for a stressful situation. Lastly, scientists are also required to pay 100% of salary and benefits for technical staff, students and post-docs.[34]

Graduate students are not often fully aware of these fund-raising duties. They represent one more burgeoning challenge for scientists in training who may already be concerned about work-family balance.

And there are continuing concerns about gender bias in science. Often this bias relates to motherhood. Elga Wasserman, author of *The Door in the Dream: Conversations with Eminent Women in Science*, notes that many of the obstacles

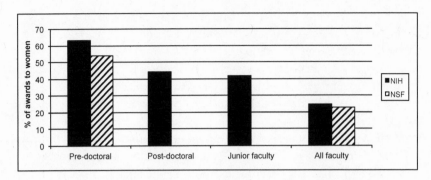

FIGURE 1.2 NIH and NSF Awards Received by Women, by Level of Award Recipient

Source: NIH and NSF Accountability Reports, 2008; Marc Goulden, Mary Ann Mason, Karie Frasch, and the Center for American Progress, "Staying Competitive: Patching America's Leaky Pipeline in the Sciences," Berkeley Center on Health, Economic, and Family Security, University of California, Berkeley, 2009, figure 5, http://www.americanprogress.org/issues/2009/11/women_and_sciences.html.

Note: The postdoctoral award information for NSF is missing significant data (39 percent of awards were to women, 47 percent were to men, and 14 percent of the sample was unknown in 2007). We chose not to include the data point because it is not comparable with the others. Information is from Fae Korsmo, senior advisor, Office of the Director, National Science Foundation.

that contemporary women scientists encounter stem from stereotypes about motherhood and the notion that women can't succeed as professionals while also having a family life.[35] Some scientists may believe that mothers cannot be serious professionals because academic science demands exclusive attention to research. Yet men are not victims of bias against parents and parenthood, even though male scientists are far more likely to have children than are women scientists; two years after earning their Ph.D.s, nearly 50 percent of men have children under age six, compared with just over 30 percent of women.[36] Motherhood, but not fatherhood, is seen as a mark against a young scientist's career. Because of these ingrained stereotypes, the precious few women who do receive their Ph.D. in the physical sciences or engineering may be less likely to be invited to join the teams that perform the cutting-edge research that leads to professional distinction, or like Sue, the chemical engineer from Ghana, they are marginalized within their research group.

Female graduate students may feel pushed in this direction by the unfriendly climate of science departments.[37] Alice Agogino, a mechanical engineering professor at UC Berkeley, believes the male-dominated culture is a deterrent to many prospective female applicants. "There is a perception that mechanical engineering is for 'gear heads.' The field is not set up for women and [even] looks unattractive to women; it needs to look more humanistic to entice further participation from women."[38] This unwelcoming culture creates an environment where women feel ill at ease. Claudia Henrion, author of *Women in Mathematics: The Addition of Difference*, notes that the women mathematicians she interviewed for her book were accomplished scholars but "still feel like outsiders in the math community."[39] Another female scientist, author of a blog called The *Prodigal Academic*, says that a department's culture and its inclusion or exclusion of women can serve as a powerful recruiting tool—or a deterrent to talented female scholars:

> When I was interviewing for faculty positions, I noted the number of women and underrepresented minorities on the faculty and in the student body. Several departments had just one woman and no visible underrepresented minorities. This was hugely unattractive to me, especially after working in my diverse division at National Lab. My current department has almost 20% women and several underrepresented visible minorities on the faculty. This was an important secondary consideration (after research fit and startup package, and on par with location and salary). . . . The presence of women in positions of leadership in the department and at the university is an important signal, as I learned at my National Lab. As an example, in my department, faculty meetings start at 2, not at 4 or 5 so people who need to be home by 5:30 can see to both work and home obligations.[40]

Making the scientific climate more amenable to women is not easily accomplished. The smallest details matter, as Alice Agogino noted: "I fought for 15 years to take down these photographs of 50 men that were on the walls of the department. I did not make a stink the first year, but those photos really did get to me. I started working with student groups and got $70,000 worth of money to help graduate women and to get the photos taken down; to create an environment and a climate appropriate for women."[41]

Faculty and graduate students aren't the only people who may pick up on atmospheric clues, such as the photographs hanging in Alice Agogino's department. Attracting female students to the sciences early on is important, as grooming for science careers begins in the undergraduate years. Unlike in most other fields, men and women in the physical sciences and engineering must pursue a rigorous, focused curriculum as undergraduates. Young women students may not be interested in a field populated by the hoary white men depicted in Alice Agogino's departmental photos. Women in the physical sciences often take themselves out of the running for doctorates in science early on. Even by 2006, women were a third more likely to pursue a master's degree than a Ph.D.[42]

Robert C. Nicholson, Nobel laureate in physics and chair of the National Science Board panel that investigated why the brightest American students aren't pursuing advanced degrees in science, believes part of the problem is the culture of the laboratory, which requires punishingly long hours in an extremely hierarchical structure. His conclusion was a nod toward greater family friendliness: "To get more women, we probably need to re-structure work environments in labs and universities so that they're more responsive to them in their childbearing years."[43]

The biological sciences are different, with women receiving about half the Ph.D.s.[44] Still, most do not go on to academic research careers. In addition to the other challenges described here, today's young scientists have to clear yet another hurdle: several more years as postdoctoral fellows. The significant extension of the scientific training period represented by postdocs has clear implications for career paths and family formation.

Postdoctoral Delays

Postdocs are a burgeoning phenomenon in the sciences, particularly in the biological disciplines. According to the National Science Foundation, the number of postdocs in the sciences doubled between 1975 and 2007, and there is no end in sight.[45] Indeed, there are now more postdocs than there are doctorate recipients in any given year.[46] This protracted training period, a kind of limbo between the Ph.D. and a real job, creates a class of highly trained young scientists working for lower salaries and few benefits. This assessment is buttressed by some of the only research on the subject, in which Curtiss Cobb and Jon Krosnick suggest that postdoctoral fellows have more in common with graduate students than with faculty.[47] Yet many are already productive scientists, as judged by the fact that they are first authors on a large share of the research articles published in *Science*.[48]

The postdoctoral period of extended training comes directly during academic women's prime reproductive years, the fertile thirties. A scientist will then be in his or her late thirties or early forties before taking a position at a university or other research venue. Nevertheless, relatively few women postdocs have children. According to a recent survey of over seventy-six hundred postdocs conducted by Sigma XI, a science and engineering research society, 29 percent of the women and 37 percent of men are parents.[49] These numbers are substantially higher than the comparable figures for graduate student parenthood at the University of California, but still reflect a large gender difference. Men, less likely to be the primary caretakers, are more likely to have children.

Parenthood dramatically influences postdoctoral women's (and many men's) decisions to abandon academic research careers. Among University of California postdoctoral scholars with no children and no future plans to have them, we found that women and men are almost equally likely, about one in five, to indicate that they shifted their career goal away from "professor with research emphasis." Plans to have children affect the career goals of women and men postdoctoral scholars differently, with women more likely to reject the goal of a tenure-track professorship (28 percent of women versus 17 percent of men). Actually having a child or children prior to entering a postdoctoral position at the University of California, or having a new child since entering the position, appears to ratchet up the pressure on women (and some men) to reject the professoriate as a career goal—these parents now realize what combining parenthood and science will entail. Forty-one percent of women and 20 percent of men postdoctoral scholars who had children after becoming a postdoctoral scholar in the University of California system eschew plans of a research professorship.[50] There is a smaller but still noteworthy gender gap for scholars who began their postdoctoral fellowships with children, while men are equally likely to change their career goals whether or not they have children. Notably, women with no plans to have children look like men, with only 20 percent turning away from an academic research career. These results are summarized in figure 1.3. They are corroborated by the Sigma XI postdoc survey, which found that women were more likely than their male colleagues to say that being a postdoc had affected their plans for children.[51]

For some postdocs, the fear that motherhood will derail their careers is instantly realized. Sherry Towers, a particle physicist described in a *Chronicle of Higher Education* story penned by Robin Wilson, was effectively blacklisted by her advisor when she became a mother. During her pregnancy, her advisor warned that he would not write her a letter of recommendation unless she returned to work almost immediately after having her baby. Even though she did return quickly, he still refused, and she received no interviews for any of the positions she applied for.[52]

Postdocs are vulnerable because their careers depend so much on the faculty supervisor who accepts them in his or her laboratory. Jennifer, a neuroscience postdoc, watched her cohort of elite scientists grapple with these issues: "Mine was the first class that was a 50/50 gender balance. I totally believed I

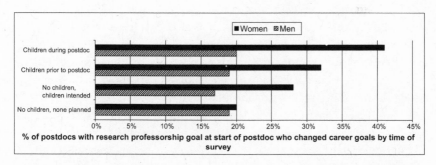

FIGURE 1.3 University of California Postdoctoral Career Goal Shift from Research Professorship, by Gender and Family Status

Source: University of California Postdoctoral Career Life Survey, 2009; Marc Goulden, Mary Ann Mason, Karie Frasch, and the Center for American Progress, "Staying Competitive: Patching America's Leaky Pipeline in the Sciences," Berkeley Center on Health, Economic, and Family Security, University of California, Berkeley, 2009, figure 8, http://www.american progress.org/issues/2009/11/women_and_sciences.html.

N = 1,323

could have it all as a female going into the sciences, but that doesn't help you when it comes time for family. Most of the women have to make a decision when they hit their late twenties or early thirties. They either have to quit or take a breather. If you take a breather, it's hard to get back on [track]. Of the female students in my starting class, none . . . became faculty and two dropped out."[53]

A 1999 study of more than eight hundred postdocs at UC Berkeley revealed that postdoc mothers worked many fewer hours in the laboratory, attended fewer conferences, and published fewer papers than their male colleagues, including men with children.[54] Postdoc mothers were relatively dissatisfied with their mentors, whom they often perceived as unlikely to recommend them for university research positions. These women believed they had already lost the race. They spoke of their decision to leave their career track as a choice, but in the rat race of science, the choice was not entirely their own.

Making the Student Years Work for Parents

Are the student and postdoc years fundamentally incompatible with starting a family? They shouldn't be; with the advantages of a flexible schedule and strong community, this period offers many benefits for young parents. So what needs to happen for women to be able to start families during their student years? The experience of Anna Westerstahl Stenport, a Swedish graduate student at UC Berkeley, provides some insight.[55] Anna had a daughter, Courtney, while working on her doctorate in Scandinavian studies. Her decision to start a family was strongly influenced by the benefits available to graduate student researchers at Berkeley, which include subsidized child care and family housing, evening and weekend child care to support study time for parents, free healthcare for graduate student researchers and instructors, and breastfeeding support.

Anna believed that her student schedule worked fairly well with motherhood. She worked forty-five to fifty hours a week, but as a scholar in the humanities these hours were flexible. Having a committed partner willing to share the burden of parenting was crucial for Anna; her husband's work schedule permitted him to take care of Courtney when she couldn't. Anna's experience with her faculty advisor was also very positive. The advisor herself had a five-year-old daughter and completely supported Anna's maternity. We asked if Anna thought her family might be an impediment on the academic job market. She replied that she felt secure at Berkeley, but still worried that other institutions might not be as progressive. "Not right now, right here, but when I went to the job fair for the Modern Language Association [for job interviews] last November I did not wear my wedding band, nor did I bring up my family."

Time passed. We heard from Anna again about a year after her interview at the annual meeting of the Modern Language Association. "You will be happy to know," she said triumphantly, "that I got a job at [a major research university], and I was pregnant [with my second child] at the time of the interview. Guess what? They offered me my first semester off for parental leave!" This was indeed a happy outcome for this student parent, and a hopeful sign that the culture is inching forward toward family friendliness.

Student life, as Anna relates, can offer a nurturing environment for young mothers, particularly if they are not in the sciences. Moreover, there are signs that the climate is improving. The University of California, like many other universities, stops the time-to-degree clock for student parents. Students are allowed to leave for a semester and return without penalty. The University of California also offers a substantial grant to help student parents with their child-raising expenses. Elsewhere, Yale University has pioneered a five-year medical school plan for student parents who wish to withdraw for a year.[56]

These are positive signs, but there is still a long way to go. Unless the old academic culture, which discourages family formation at all levels but is particularly unfriendly to graduate student parenthood, and especially to women, radically changes to welcome families, we are in danger of losing many of our best and brightest minds. There has been a serious movement to accommodate new faculty parents, but by then it is too late to help disaffected graduate students who have already found careers elsewhere. What might universities do to help? For starters, some of the policies now offered to many faculty could be extended to graduate students and postdoctoral scholars:

- Organized mentoring systems that address work-family balance as well as professional advice
- Affordable child care, including drop-in care
- Family housing
- Paid parental leave for employed graduate students and postdocs
- Health care for dependents
- Stopping the normative time clock for childbirth
- Parent centers and lactation rooms

At best, today's universities offer only one or two of these accommodations, most likely family housing and parent centers.

Title IX

An important argument for offering family accommodations to graduate students and postdoctoral fellows is compliance with the letter and spirit of federal law. Title VII, which outlaws gender discrimination in the workplace, has dramatically changed the work world for employees. Title IX could potentially accomplish the same transformation for graduate students and postdoctoral fellows, who are usually considered "trainees" rather than employees and are not covered by Title VII. We usually think of Title IX, renamed in 2002 as the Patsy T. Mink Equal Opportunity in Education Act, as helping to level the playing field for women in high school and collegiate sports. Less well known is the fact that Title IX covers all forms of sex discrimination in federally funded educational programs, including discrimination against mothers.[57] Graduate students and postdocs are clearly engaged in educational programs according to the actual language of Title IX: "No person in the United States shall, on the basis of sex, be excluded from participation in, be denied the benefits of, or be subjected to discrimination under any education program or activity receiving Federal financial assistance."

Every major federal granting agency has identical Title IX regulations that include some form of family leave for employees of educational institutions. Most colleges and universities receive federal funds and fall under the jurisdiction of these regulations. The agencies require, for example, that universities and colleges treat pregnancy as a temporary disability, and provide unpaid, job-protected leave to birth mothers "for a reasonable period of time" if the institution does not maintain a leave policy for its employees.

What makes these regulations significant is that if properly enforced they fill gaps in university policies for graduate students and postdoctoral fellows supported by federal grants who are facing pregnancy and caregiving responsibilities. But it is not clear whether these legal requirements are being met at all universities. When asked about the provision of unpaid leave to postdoctoral scholar mothers in our survey of the Association of American University schools, one AAU university indicated that it does not provide it, and six others indicated that they did not know whether or not it was provided.[58] Moreover, only 23 percent of schools offer unrestricted paid maternity leave to postdocs. It is therefore unclear whether all these young scientists are receiving the job-protected, twelve-week unpaid leave stipulated by the Family and Medical Leave Act. Faculty mothers fare much better, but by then many women have decided against academic research careers. All universities and colleges should have in place a clear policy regarding leave for employed graduate student and postdoctoral scholar mothers. Title IX reviewers should consult these policies to ensure that universities are in compliance.

Conclusion

About half of all doctoral students are now women, but a far smaller proportion will become tenure-track faculty members.[59] This chapter has documented some of the challenges women graduate students and postdocs face. Despite their large (and growing) numbers, women students find themselves in a male world. In many disciplines, few of their advisors are women, and even fewer are mothers. The top administrators are likely to be men as well. This leaves women graduate students with few role models and with profound doubts about how to go about combining families with high-powered research careers. These problems tend to be particularly vexing in the bench sciences, because of both a male research culture and the exigencies of scientific discovery.

At the same time that they are having doubts about an academic career, many women graduate students are getting married or forming lasting relationships, and a small but notable minority are becoming mothers. Men graduate students also marry and become parents, and in somewhat greater numbers than women. Both marriage alone and marriage with children raise serious doubts for both men and women as they ponder academic careers. Some, women more than men, will start turning away from the goal of an academic career. They do not anticipate being able to balance career and family.

Toward the end of their graduate school years, perhaps around age thirty, most women, married or not, consider their career choices in light of present or future family obligations.[60] It may not be the first time they have considered these issues, but now the matter is of some urgency. They know their biological clock has limits. They must make choices that will determine their life's work, and they must evaluate how, and when, having children will fit into the picture, if at all. Many women at this point do not stick to their original career goals.[61] Nor do many men. Sometimes this reflects their concerns about money. Men, more than women, see academia as less likely to provide a family wage than other career choices.[62]

As noted in our survey of University of California graduate students, the great majority of both men and women registered the family friendliness of the future workplace as a serious concern, and as graduation approaches most women and nearly half of all men consider research universities hostile to family life. When our colleague Karie Frasch finished her Ph.D. at Berkeley and started to think about having children, her career plans suddenly looked less appealing: "I went into graduate school thinking a faculty position would be a great way to have kids, that there is flexibility and open summers. Then as I began to see professors who had kids totally strung out and stressed out I began to realize, wait, I am not going to do that!"[63] For many woman graduate students like Karie, thoughts about work and family loom large as graduation approaches. Looking forward, reality sets in as students see the challenging road leading to tenure. What they know about the academic career path is that the next ten years of their lives, the "make or break" years between the ages of thirty and forty, will be the most demanding. The hours are long, perhaps longer than they experienced as a student, and there is often limited flexibility.

How do women respond to these challenges? This will be addressed in the following chapters of this book.

2

Getting into the Game

Should women get special conditions? I come from a European country with a lot of protection for mothers. What's the effect? Impossible to get hired, unless you put your uterus in a jar of alcohol on the desk.

—A forum post at the *Chronicle of Higher Education*

Perhaps the most important turning point in a young scholar's life is the decision to pursue employment after graduate school. Given that the average doctoral student takes eight years to finish, this decision is a long time coming.[1] As we saw in the previous chapter, many doctoral students, women more often than men, decide during their student years that a research professor's life is not for them. Both men and women worry about having balanced lives in the academy, but for women, concern about combining a family with the demanding life of a tenure-track professorship is the overriding factor. Nevertheless, many students will view a tenure-track job as the normal outcome of doctoral training, the goal expected by their advisors and many of their peers, if not always the most common result (about one in three graduate students gets a tenure-track position after graduate school and, sometimes, a postdoc).[2]

Those who do seek tenure-track employment will find that the job hunt is an involved process. An aspiring professor must assemble an application dossier, typically comprising a cover letter, a vita, sample dissertation chapters or publications, and letters of recommendation from several faculty mentors. The job seeker then embarks on a national search—only the hottest candidates can be choosy about location—that culminates in a move to an unfamiliar town or city. This geographical upheaval occurs in few other professions. But first the candidate must likely pass a preliminary screening at the annual meeting of a professional association (this varies by field), and in all cases undergo an on-campus interview. The academic interview is a uniquely protracted affair, generally lasting at least one and a half days. In a few fields, job candidates will have to make more than one visit. If all goes well, the applicant will be offered a job that he or she could potentially hold until retirement.

Getting into the academic game is a complex process that bears little similarity to job searches outside the ivory tower. As we will see, the outcome of this critical professional transition is strongly influenced by gender, marriage, and children. This chapter also considers which young scholars fall into the second tier of contingent professorships, and whether faculty in this second tier manage to make it back to the tenure track.

The experience of Anna Westerstahl Stenport, the Swedish humanities scholar introduced in the previous chapter, illustrates some of the issues women confront when seeking their first academic position.[3] Despite an extensive track record of publications, Anna declined to wear her wedding band while interviewing for faculty positions at an academic meeting—she didn't want to signal to prospective employers that her family relationships might compromise her ability to relocate, or to perform once hired. By the time she was ready for on-campus interviews, she was visibly pregnant with her second child. This was ultimately not held against her, and she landed a tenure-track faculty position at a good school.

Anna, as we will see, was fortunate. She had a few busy years combining motherhood with graduate school and, later on, her assistant professorship. Many married women, especially mothers, never get that far. Jackie faces a less certain future in academia.[4] Like Anna, she obtained her Ph.D. from a top research university. Jackie's degree is in the life sciences. Her husband, Grayson, has a Ph.D. in the same field and the two are now postdoctoral fellows together. Two years into her postdoc, Jackie is weeks away from giving birth to her first child. A couple of years down the road, she will confront the academic job market with a toddler. Perhaps more daunting, Jackie and Grayson face the "two body" problem: having to get two academic jobs in the same metropolitan area.[5] As the mother, Jackie will probably spend more time caring for their child. This will make it difficult for her to travel to job interviews. Unless she and Grayson are lucky enough to land two jobs in the same region, one of them will likely leave academia, or at least forego a tenure-track position. Despite changing attitudes toward working mothers, stay-at-home moms still vastly outnumber stay-at-home dads.[6] This means that Grayson will probably get the coveted tenure-track job while Jackie cares for their child. Perhaps she will teach a class or two as an adjunct faculty member. Because she will lack a laboratory and the other perquisites of a tenure-stream position, her research will suffer, ultimately making it harder to get back into the game as a tenure-track professor. When she says, somewhat nervously, "I don't know what to expect," she could easily be talking about either incipient motherhood or her professional prospects. With a young child in the picture she may have to chart a new career course, more than likely one that will take her off the tenure track.

How Marriage and Children Affect Academic
Hiring out of Graduate School

In this book we describe two kinds of family formation: marriage and children. Family formation has the largest effects at the beginning of academic careers, when young scholars are first trying to secure postdoctoral employment—and often, at the same time, starting families. Marriage and children present different challenges for male and female academics. The age of the children in question also makes a difference.

Survey of Doctorate Recipients (SDR) data based on all academic disciplines indicate that women in general are 7 percent less likely to obtain tenure-track assistant professorships in comparison with men.[7] This predictable finding accords with previous scholarship on the career prospects of men and women doctorate recipients.[8] However, this overall gender difference conceals even greater disparities: both marriage and children have substantial negative effects on women's job market prospects. Compared with her childless female counterpart, a woman with a child under six is 21 percent less likely to land a tenure-track position. This same mother is 16 percent less likely to get a tenure-track job than is an otherwise comparable father. As we will see, young children make it extremely difficult for women to go on the academic job market. Many mothers forego tenure-track positions and the arduous probationary periods they entail for less demanding employment.

Marriage has a smaller but still noteworthy adverse effect on women's job market prospects. A married woman is 17 percent less likely to get a tenure-track job than is her unmarried female peer. Compared with a married man, a married woman has 12 percent lower odds of getting a tenure-track job.[9] The effects of marriage and children are independent of each other; each separately reduces the likelihood that women obtain tenure-track employment. Married women with children do not pay an exponentially heavier penalty when seeking an academic job.

Having a family also makes women less likely to get tenure-track jobs, according to our analysis based only on academics in the sciences (including the social sciences).[10] However, the negative effects of marriage and children function somewhat differently. Married childless women are 7 percent less likely to get tenure-track positions compared with their unmarried female colleagues. Single mothers of children under age six are 6 percent more likely than their childless unmarried same-sex colleagues to get tenure-track jobs (but 14 percent less likely to get jobs compared with men who are single parents of young children). These effects are all smaller than they are for the data that include the humanities. In the sciences, the heavy penalties accrue to only women who are both married *and* the parents of young children. Such married mothers are 35 percent less likely to get tenure-track jobs compared with married fathers of young children. The same women are 33 percent less likely to get jobs compared with unmarried women who aren't the parents of young children.[11]

These results explain the disadvantage women face on the academic job market. Recall that women in general are 7 percent less likely to get tenure-track jobs than are men. This global gender penalty disappears after accounting for the effects of marriage and children. Indeed, single women without children are 16 percent more likely to get jobs than are unmarried childless men in the analysis based on all fields; the comparable figure for analysis based only on the sciences is 4 percent. Thus women suffer at the beginning of their academic careers because they marry and have children, not because they are women.

Older children, ages six to eighteen, have no negative effect on the likelihood of obtaining a tenure-track job for either men or women. In fact, based on data that include the humanities, mothers with older children, irrespective of marital status, are 11 percent more likely to secure tenure-track employment than are childless women. Children between six and eighteen provide no such benefit for men. It's therefore unlikely that older children are signaling to employers that a candidate is more settled into adulthood and responsibility—if that were true, men would enjoy a similar boost. Instead, women with children over five are likely at a better stage in their lives to pursue tenure-track professorships; unlike women with younger children, they aren't saddled with the burden of caring for infants. It's also possible that older children indicate to a hiring committee that a female candidate is done with having children, which will mean fewer career distractions after she is hired.

Simply having kids appears to be the deciding factor here. Numbers of children—above and beyond the mere presence of younger or older kids—do not affect the likelihood that women get tenure-track jobs.

Why do marriage and children have such strong effects on women's academic careers? The next pages are devoted to this question. Although we cannot know for sure, a host of factors are probably responsible. The answer likely reflects both direct causation (marriage and young children make it more difficult to get tenure-track jobs) and selection (married women and mothers—and future mothers—feel discouraged from pursuing tenure-track employment after graduate school).

The Two-Body Problem

For academics, marriage often produces the two-body problem. Our survey of doctoral students at the University of California found that 51 percent of women and 44 percent of men are married or partnered. Nationally, 52 percent of recent doctorate recipients are married, including 49 percent of women and 54 percent of men; an additional 6 percent are living with their partners in marriage-like relationships.[12] For postdocs the numbers are even higher: 71 percent of the men and 66 percent of the women are either married or partnered.[13] Since young scholars must almost always relocate to obtain tenure-track employment, a job search typically involves finding two jobs in a new location. One body must defer, and that body is likely to be hers. Fifty-six percent of male faculty members have spouses who are employed full time, compared with 89 percent of female faculty members.[14] Sometimes the problem is even more complicated: female academics are more likely to be married to male academics (18 percent) than vice versa (13 percent).[15]

Men have traditionally been the primary wage-earners in America, including in academic couples (this male breadwinner ideal persists even though it is no longer the case for a notable minority of families.)[16] Married women may therefore forsake academic careers if pursuing them imperils their husbands' careers.[17] SDR data show that only 14 percent of unmarried and childless female science doctorates acknowledge that spousal career concerns affected their search for a permanent job (presumably these 14 percent represent women pondering marriage to nonportable partners). Thirty-eight percent of married fathers indicated such concerns, compared with about 65 percent of married women.[18] These dual-career issues often push female graduate students out of academia. For one woman in the biological sciences at the University of California, her husband's job seemed to be the final straw: "My husband has a job he loves, but it will require that we don't move; this limits my postdoc and career options so significantly. I think the chances of staying in the same city throughout the career and finding a tenure track position are almost nonexistent. However, I am not sure how much I care anymore."

Even if they are able and willing to relocate, married women may provoke resistance from academic search committees. Some committee members, particularly if older, may be skeptical of a husband's willingness to relocate for his wife's career.[19] Ms. Mentor's Impeccable Advice for Women in Academia goes so far as to advise women job candidates to tell search committee members that their husbands are employed as freelance writers.[20] More sensible is the advice that women do not volunteer information on marital status while on job talks (keeping in mind that it is illegal to ask about it).[21]

The question of spousal employment is famously difficult when both spouses are academics. Although some universities offer "split lines" (tenure-track jobs divided between spouses) and other accommodations for faculty couples, these arrangements are the exception rather than the rule.[22] Accordingly, women in these academic couples may be more likely to forsake their academic careers, or at least lower their professional aspirations.[23] If both spouses are equally qualified to be successful academics, the woman is the traditional choice to stay at home and care for children. Alternately, she may pursue lower-status employment such as an adjunct professorship, which does not require an ardu-ous "publish or perish" probationary period.[24] We will return to this topic later in the chapter.

Many female graduate students participating in our University of California survey voiced concerns related to their partners' academic careers. One such student in the physical sciences at the University of California justified her deci-sion not to pursue a tenure-track professorship by invoking her perception of the academic job market: "I am currently in a relationship with a person who does want to pursue a career in . . . academia in the same field as myself, lead-ing to the near-impossibility of finding two academic jobs in the same area." Another woman scientist appeared to acknowledge tacitly that her husband's academic career would come first: "I think it will be nearly impossible for me to get a job as a professor at a research institution due to the fact that my future spouse is also in academia and we will have to get jobs together. There are more teaching opportunities than research opportunities. I like teaching, but I also like research, and I am unhappy that it seems like I won't be given an opportu-nity to do both."

Concerns about spousal employment may dictate where academic women will choose to accept a job.[25] Sociologists Steven Kulis and Diane Sicotte found that female academics are more likely than their male counterparts to reside in large cities and other areas with clusters of colleges and universities.[26] This suggests that women take jobs in areas where it will be easier for their husbands to find a job, whether in academia or the private sector. Unmar-ried women may be perceived as loath to move to a smaller town, where dat-ing opportunities can be limited.[27] One of the coauthors of this book has an acquaintance who left a tenure-track position at an elite university in a small midwestern town because, in her own words, "I had dated everyone there that there was to date." Thus women academics are caught in a Catch-22. If they have spouses, they may be unwilling, or perceived as unwilling, to relocate; if single, they may be reluctant to move somewhere where it will be difficult to find a spouse. One woman made this point in a post on the *Chronicle of Higher Education* online forum by humorously enumerating the options women have when describing their family situations to a search committee from a small-town college or university:

> Telling them you are married to a relocate-able spouse, though, is an entirely different question. The fact is that women often get screwed in this business no matter what their status is. The way a male-dominated committee will see it, there are four possibilities:
>
> 1. You're single. How will you find a decent mate in Podunk? Surely you will leave soon.

2. You're gay. Surely you and your partner will be unhappy in Podunk
   and leave soon. And possibly Jesus doesn't like you anyway.

3. You're married to a not easily relocated spouse. Surely hubby will
   take charge and prevent you from taking the job, or will whine so
   much when you move here that you leave soon to placate him.

4. You're married to an easily relocated spouse. You still might get sick
   of Podunk and leave, but perhaps it's less likely. Probably the best
   option.[28]

Marriage to a portable spouse generally creates the fewest problems, but this is
a luxury many academics do not have.

Babies on the Academic Job Market

Sociologist Shelley Correll and her colleagues have shown that employers discriminate against mothers in numerous ways.[29] Maternal discrimination—or,
indeed, discrimination of any kind—is notoriously difficult to prove, so it is hard
to know its extent within academia, traditionally heralded as more progressive
and open-minded than the private sector. Yet there is considerable anecdotal
evidence of discrimination occurring on academic hiring committees, which
are sometimes reluctant to offer jobs to women on the "mommy track," candidates perceived to be more committed to motherhood than to scholarship.
Cognizant of discrimination toward mothers, many women go to extraordinary
lengths to conceal their maternal intentions while on academic job talks. Prejudice against mothers (and future mothers) probably helps accounts for the
lower rate at which women get tenure-track jobs, as legal scholar Joan Williams
has suggested.[30]

Mothers on the academic job market contend with the difficulties presented by children even before embarking on interviews.[31] Having children
sometimes leaves awkward gaps on their curriculum vitae. How should these
gaps be explained? As accounts from academic hiring committees make clear,
the wrong answer could spell professional doom. One search committee member simply wanted a straight answer about motherhood when screening job
applications:

> We've certainly never disapproved of applications in which the letter
> said plainly and briefly something on the order of "after being away from
> teaching for three years to finish my dissertation while looking after two
> children, I am now . . . [ellipses in original]"—but we have stewed over the
> applications with gaps that we were fairly sure said "here she followed
> her husband, here her first child was born, here they moved again, was
> there another baby?" but had no letters of any kind to cover the three

or four years with only an occasional adjunct class, always at a different school. . . . There are much darker narratives that would also explain that latter c.v., and we'd have to ask illegal questions to get answers that are not, on the other hand, illegal for you to volunteer.[32]

This account illustrates the dilemma that mothers on the academic job market often face: if they volunteer information about parenting responsibilities, they're at risk of being perceived as uncommitted or distracted; if they don't, they're suspected of covering up "darker narratives."

This question—whether to disclose a past detour onto the mommy track—appears to cause candidates a fair amount of consternation. As one mother recounted:

I too have various "gaps" of less productive periods in my past around having kids. I'm new to academia (after realizing that I would have to start all over again in my former field, and discovering that I love the academy!).

Was "search committee member" implying that it is a blanket negative to have taken a "mommy track," or reiterating that as long as you explain any gaps, nobody needs to assume the worst or ask illegal questions?

I'm freaking out here. I thought I'd be able to start over with a clean slate in a new and wonderful career . . . is it hopeless?[33]

A woman's maternal status is much more likely to come up during an on-campus interview than in a job application. These interviews typically include socializing over meals, times when questions about children can be casually, albeit illegally, asked. Presumably lying is not a viable option, since the truth would emerge when the new hire showed up for her assistant professorship with kids in tow. Her trustworthiness as a colleague would be undermined from the start, which would ultimately compromise her chances for tenure. Still, a woman need not bring up the topic of children, as one job candidate learned from her on-campus interviews:

I learned a lot from my mistakes on the job market, and based on personal experience, I decided not to talk about my child in interviews. If asked point blank, I would have answered, but no one did, I just didn't bring it up casually. I got the job. And then afterwards, I was told that the child-bearing issue was fervently discussed in regard to my hire.

I also had an experience of being in an interview, mentioning my child, and seeing the SC's [search committee head's] face fall, and that was the end of that job. Although of course there could have been a million other reasons, there is no doubt that having a child did not help my candidacy in that case.[34]

Another job candidate felt free to discuss her children to prospective employers who appeared family friendly. She later came to rue her decision:

> I had two on campus interviews. At one (a more formal, less family-oriented school), I did mention my spouse but did not mention our children. At the second (a school that seemed to, from the first contact, be very proud of its family-friendliness), I mentioned both spouse and children. Second school encouraged discussion of family throughout the interview. . . . I left the interview feeling completely comfortable with having discussed my family. In the end, however, I got an offer from the first school and not from the second. . . .
>
> My sense based on these emails is that, though many people in the department (especially the younger faculty with children of their own at home) didn't have any problem with me having a family, the more senior faculty did. It's unjustified (and, really, completely outdated), but it's been suggested that these senior faculty members subscribe to the traditional line of thinking that hiring a woman with a family is a risk, and so they voted against me as a candidate. . . . At any rate, for what it's worth, in future interviews I don't think I'll mention my kids.[35]

Of course there is no way of knowing for sure whether motherhood was an issue in this candidate's job market experiences. We do know that employers in general discriminate against mothers and that many women report that the disclosure of children creates problems during academic job interviews. In all likelihood, this is just one of several reasons why women with children get academic jobs less often than do childless women, or fathers. Marriage is the most obvious other explanation. Combined, marriage and motherhood may present a whole new Catch-22 for female job candidates. If married, women with children have to contend with spousal relocation. If single, their productivity may be called into question—how will they be able to handle the workload of an assistant professor while simultaneously caring for children all by themselves? Impressions are important, as one woman learned: "I will say that they came right out and asked me if I had children (yes), and because I don't wear a wedding ring I think they assumed I'm a single mother—and to them that spelled trouble with a capital T."[36]

The very nature of the job application process poses more problems for mothers than for childless women. Candidates generally need to fly across the country to spend one or more (and occasionally several) days with a search committee, which creates child care challenges. Keep in mind that female academics are much more likely to have employed husbands than vice versa. More promising candidates will have several interviews, compounding the child care problem. Predictably, the mothers of infants have the most trouble with job interviews. Much of the online discussion regarding interviewing as the mother of an infant concerns the difficulties of breastfeeding. One mother explained how she managed multiple job interviews while caring for an infant: "Four day campus visits all over the country, and I was expected to leave my breastfed child home? I pumped, froze [some breast milk,] and dumped some, I took him and my husband along for some, and kept them well-hidden in the hotel. Six campus visits in a two month period with a tiny baby in the house was pretty damn rough on all of us, but I managed it, and found a decent job. I knew then, though, that I cared more about having a second child than I cared about getting tenure, and if she was the cost of tenure, well, so be it."[37] Another mother recalled leaving her infant at home but nevertheless needing time during the interview to pump milk: "I interviewed while also the mother of a four month old. I had one week notice for one interview, pumped like crazy to store up milk, brought along the breast pump, pumped in airports, had two twenty minute breaks during the interview to pump, and everything was fine. Cheaper than paying for a plane ticket for husband or baby sitter . . . [ellipses in original] Just a suggestion. . . . I know some people don't want to give their babies bottles, but if you are ok with bottles I highly recommend the breast pump route!"[38]

Young children clearly present numerous difficulties for women on the academic job market. They present far fewer hardships for men. Compared with women, academic men are much more likely to have stay-at-home spouses to assist with child care. There are no bulging bellies or wet blouses to reveal incipient or new fathers. Male graduate students are surrounded by successful academic fathers who can serve as role models.[39] Indeed, married men fare better on the job market. According to the SDR, they are 9 percent more likely to secure tenure-track employment than are their unmarried counterparts. Perhaps marriage signifies to academic hiring committees, or even to the job candidates themselves, that men have assumed stable, adult roles.[40] Such men might be better bets as long-term employees; indeed, there may be advantages for husbands and fathers who represent themselves as family men. However, at least one academic hiring committee member has been put off by job candidates who sought to make a better impression by touting themselves as devoted fathers: "I am not impressed when a candidate brings up his two children within three minutes of meeting me (as one candidate did), because no matter what he intended, it looked a lot like he was trying to capitalize on the privileges of being a 'family man.' I will quickly assume that he is someone who either does not recognize the significance of what he was doing or, even worse, was making a deliberate appeal to discrimination. Either way, I would prefer to hire a colleague who will join me in trying to create a department that hires people without regard to gender, race, or family status."[41]

At the very least children present no great hindrance to men on the academic job market. For women, children cause numerous problems. They make it harder to go on job interviews. Search committees may question whether mothers are sufficiently committed to their academic careers. For these reasons, female doctorate recipients with young children may opt for career paths other than tenure-track professorships.

Academic Sharecroppers

Aside from gender equity, few issues are more frequently debated in the academy than the proliferation of contingent professorships.[42] In 1975, instructors off the tenure-track composed 43 percent of American faculty. By 2007, about 69 percent were neither tenured nor tenure-track.[43] The majority of recent full-time academic hires have been off the tenure track.[44]

Gender equity and the proliferation of adjunct faculty are inextricably linked. Instructors, lecturers, and other unranked faculty compose 22 percent of all female full-time faculty, but only 11 percent of male faculty.[45] Indeed, the proportion of contingent faculty increased over the same years as did the proportion of women in academia.[46] Although an increasing number of women now hold tenure-track professorships, they remain overrepresented among contingent faculty.[47] Social scientists speak of the "feminization of poverty," given the numbers of mother-headed families in the contemporary United States and their disproportionate likelihood of poverty.[48] The proliferation of female faculty in contingent positions can be thought of in the same way: the relegation of female scholars to second-tier positions in the academy.

In some cases contingent faculty supplement part-time teaching with a well-paying, stable outside job.[49] For these individuals, teaching provides intellectual stimulation and extra income. However, they represent a minority. For the majority of non-tenure-track faculty, teaching is a full-time profession and their primary source of income; about half work over fifty hours a week.[50] Contingent faculty are second-class citizens in almost every respect; one need only invoke the title of Wendell Fountain's 2005 book, *Academic Sharecroppers*, to make this point.[51] They are paid 26 percent less than comparable tenure-track assistant professors.[52] Contingent instructors are less likely to get the offices, computers, and other resources that ladder-rank faculty routinely receive. They are unlikely to advise students. Finally, the proliferation of adjunct professorships compromises the basic mission of American higher education. Because contingent faculty are not subject to the same scrutiny as tenure-track professors, student learning may suffer.[53] Many contingent faculty are excellent teachers, but there are rarely mechanisms in place to prevent inferior instructors from joining their ranks. The other component of higher education to suffer is academic freedom: lacking both the security of tenure and a greater stake in the academic system, contingent instructors have less protection and less incentive to defend unpopular points of view and the free exchange of ideas, both of which are central to the academic enterprise.[54] Leslie Zwillinger, a psychologist, has spent her career teaching at the same large state university as a lecturer. Her assessment of the contingent faculty life is predictably negative: "The majority of part timers are women and . . . their job is very insecure and very uncomfortable. One part timer just retired because after 20 years of teaching, the schedule came out and her name just was not there. No one talked to her or discussed anything."[55]

As Leslie's comments illustrate, we have a two-tiered system in which a large portion of the labor pool cannot be integrated, for a variety of reasons, into the tenure track as it currently exists. For many scholars, contingent professorships represent the academic graveyard, the place to go when all dreams of a tenure-track position have been extinguished.

Alternative Employment

As previously noted, about a third of Ph.D. recipients get tenure-track jobs after graduate school and, sometimes, a postdoc. How often do the rest end up in contingent teaching positions? And how do marriage and children affect the career paths of Ph.D.s who do not go straight into tenure-track employment? As with the other important professional transitions considered so far in the book, our results show noteworthy gender differences in the careers of Ph.D. recipients who don't take tenure-track jobs right out of graduate school.

Since family formation accounts for the lower rate of women in tenure-track professorships, can it also explain why they are more likely to become contingent faculty? Indeed, contingent positions may offer various benefits to female doctorates that are unavailable in tenure-track jobs. First, they provide the option of part-time employment, something very rarely found in a tenure-track position.[56] Besides the possibility of a shorter workweek and lighter teaching loads, these positions do not require burdensome work hours during a pre-tenure probationary period. Second, contingent professorships are more readily available and therefore may be sought out by married women, whose geographic mobility is frequently constrained by their husbands' careers. Relying on their husbands' incomes, married women Ph.D.s may be able to make do with the lower salary of a contingent appointment. Many of these factors apparently contributed to one woman's enthusiasm for her contingent teaching job: "I love it. This is the perfect job for me. I am full time, with benefits, but I don't have to write grants, and publishing is nice, but not a 'do or die' proposition. I don't have to supervise grad students, I get to facilitate both undergrad and grad level research, which is very satisfying. I have control over the lab course I teach. I don't travel nearly as much as my tenure track colleagues, which I like because I have 2 young kids and hate traveling. . . . I make enough to pay the bills, together with my husband's consulting money, I can occasionally leave early when kid events happen, etc."[57] For the reasons suggested by this faculty member, we anticipate that women will be more likely to be employed in contingent professorships rather than tenure-track jobs subsequent to graduate school; this should hold especially true for married women and women with young children.

Earlier in this chapter we established that women are less likely than men to get tenure-track academic appointments. Our SDR data shed light on their other career paths. Figure 2.1 shows how gender affects the likelihood of various career outcomes relative to the chances of getting a tenure-track professorship.[58] Compared with men, women who do not secure ladder-rank appointments are more likely to stay in academia, either as contingent instructors or in nonteaching positions, and are less likely to be working in nonacademic jobs. Moreover, women are more than twice as likely as men to leave the paid labor force following Ph.D. receipt.

Marriage and children have very different effects on men and women's career choices. Two employment patterns are especially common among women with families. First, women with children under six are disproportionately likely to be employed in contingent professorships. Compared with her childless counterpart, a woman with a child under six is 26 percent more likely to be employed as contingent faculty rather than a tenure-track position. Compared with a man with a young child, she is 132 percent more likely to be working in a contingent position. Conversely, a male Ph.D. with a young child is 36 percent less likely to become a contingent faculty member instead of a tenure-track professor. Children seem to have different consequences for the career paths of

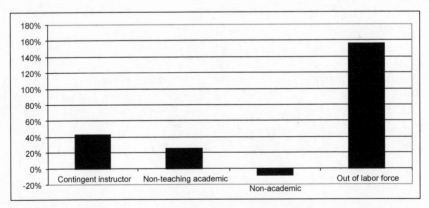

FIGURE 2.1 Chances of Women Pursuing Other Career Paths Compared to the Likelihood of a Tenure-Track Job

Source: Survey of Doctorate Recipients, National Science Foundation, 1983–1995.

N = 16,049

male and female parents after graduate school. For men, young children push them to obtain more lucrative and potentially secure employment, either via tenure-track positions or outside academia altogether. In contrast, young children lead female doctorate recipients to work in less demanding, more flexible, but lower-status and lower-income contingent professorships.

Predictably, the other common career path for female Ph.D.s with young children is to leave the paid labor force. Women with children under six are almost four times as likely to leave the labor force in lieu of a ladder-rank professorship in comparison with women without young children. Male parents with young children do not exit the paid labor force in such numbers. Marriage also leads women to leave the labor force. Compared with an unwed woman, her married counterpart is 28 percent more likely to not work. Neither marriage nor young children have any such effect for men; indeed, both increase the likelihood of taking a tenure-track job over departing the labor force. Presumably unemployment isn't an option for men with families to support. As we have suggested, marriage and fatherhood may also signify to academic search committees that men have assumed adult roles, that they are ready to become stable, productive employees.

Together, marriage and childbirth largely account for why female doctorate recipients exit the labor force. A single woman without children under six is only 10 percent less likely to be unemployed right out of graduate school than she is likely to have a tenure-stream job. The same holds true for the likelihood that she gets a contingent rather than tenure-track position. Recall that women in general are 45 percent more likely to land in contingent positions. However, a single woman without young children is only 17 percent more likely to have a second-tier job. Earlier in this chapter we established that family formation can account for the lower rate at which women become tenure-track faculty members. We now know where they go instead: contingent professorships and out of the paid labor force.

Getting Back in the Game

Academia has traditionally been conceptualized as a pipeline. The pipeline model, applied frequently to the careers of bench scientists, implies a lockstep sequence of events that can begin as early as high school.[59] At this stage, women may be underrepresented in the courses that might ultimately prepare them for scientific careers. More often, the pipeline to academic success is said to begin in graduate school. An academic job requires a doctorate; scholars cannot normally become full professors without first serving as assistants and then associates.

Some researchers have critiqued the pipeline model for failing to capture the reality of modern academic careers.[60] The pipeline model fails in at least two ways. First, it makes no allowance for life events that affect professional progress. As we have already observed, this is a serious liability. The second criticism, strongly related to the first, concerns the inability of the pipeline to account for nonstandard career trajectories. In particular, there is no mechanism for reentering the pipeline after "leaking out." This is a special problem for women who take time out of their academic careers to have children. Sociologist Phyllis Moen accordingly suggested that the linear, lockstep career model was an outdated notion.[61] Education experts Jack Schuster and Martin Finkelstein have recently claimed that time off the tenure track is a "new rung" in the academic career ladder, a common halfway point between graduate school and a tenure-track position.[62] Other scholars have called for a "revolving door" model of women's entrance into male-dominated professions and more "on-ramps," means by which women could return to the workplace after the "off-ramps" of pregnancy and childrearing.[63]

We have already seen that most Ph.D. recipients do not take tenure-track jobs immediately out of graduate school (or immediately subsequent to postdocs). In particular, married women and mothers of young children are especially likely to get out of the game, either by taking contingent positions or by leaving the paid labor force entirely. How many scholars make it back? Figure 2.2 shows how many people get tenure-track jobs after first taking a different kind of position (or leaving the paid labor force for at least two years). Overall, only one out of four people who don't take tenure-track jobs out of graduate school end up getting one later on. But this figure conceals considerable variation by type of postdoctoral employment. Over half of all Ph.D.s employed as contingent faculty right after graduate school manage to get tenure-track jobs within ten years. Reentry rates are also relatively high for people employed at colleges and universities in jobs that do not involve teaching—academic administrators, research staff, and the like. In contrast, Ph.D.s unemployed after graduate school subsequently enter the tenure track at a lower rate; the lowest, at about 10 percent, is reserved for people employed outside academia. The implication of these results is straightforward: the rigid pipeline model no longer fits academia. Many people who exit the academic pipeline will subsequently reenter it. In particular, people remaining involved with higher education are much more likely to get tenure-track jobs down the road. Taking a contingent teaching position after graduate school does not ruin one's prospects for a tenured academic career. However, as time goes by people are decreasingly likely to get tenure-track jobs.[64]

We cannot know the extent to which this association is causal. Do people who fail to get ladder-rank professorships the first time around intentionally work in contingent jobs in order to stay involved in academia? Or are these jobs the natural second choice for otherwise unemployed doctorate recipients?

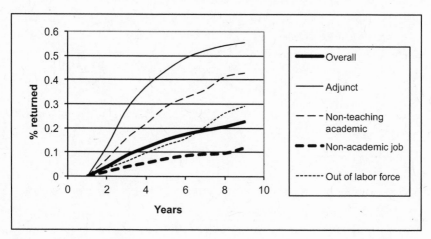

FIGURE 2.2 Reentry Rates for Ladder-Rank Employment after Time off the Tenure Track

Source: Survey of Doctorate Recipients, National Science Foundation, 1983–1995. © Nicholas H. Wolfinger, Mary Ann Mason, and Marc Goulden, "Stay in the Game: Gender, Family Formation, and Alternative Trajectories in the Academic Life Course," *Social Forces* 87, no. 3 (2009): 1607, figure 2, reprinted by permission of Oxford University Press.

N = 6,501

Either way, academic positions off the tenure track may facilitate reentry, in much the same manner that community colleges allow many students to progress to four-year schools. As we have observed, non-tenure-track academic positions can provide teaching and research experience that fill out curriculum vitae and increase one's attractiveness to academic hiring committees. Sometimes these jobs are part time, which may give scholars the opportunity to conduct research (albeit without the institutional resources available to tenure-stream faculty). They can provide professional contacts and socialization. Finally, contingent positions afford multiple years on the academic job market and therefore increase the likelihood of finding the right job: a position that's a good fit between applicant and hiring committee. For all these reasons, it may not be a professional death sentence for young doctorates to take contingent teaching positions if they cannot land the coveted tenure-track professorship (Still, we should stress that being a contingent faculty member doesn't automatically make it easy to get a permanent job.)

Recent posts to the *Chronicle of Higher Education* online forums echo these ideas. When one participant pondered taking a job in publishing, others advised him or her to keep a foot in the academic door: "Think that in competitive fields, committees will understand that candidates end up in all sorts of temporary gigs, and you might even be able to spin the publishing experience in positive ways. If the alternative is adjuncting, I don't see either one helping or hurting your chances on the job market. One option you don't mention would be to try to pick up a class on the side, giving you an academic affiliation and some additional experience in the classroom, while allowing you to have full time employment in publishing."[65] Another forum participant felt that a contingent position actually put her at an advantage when she finally secured a tenure-track job:

I got to focus on my teaching and get my courses set without having research pressure.

I got to do a lot of prep work on research, which should pay dividends in the next 2–3 years.

While I did some service, it was not the level I will be expected to perform as a TT [tenure-track] prof[essor].

All in all, these two years have given me a tremendous advantage over those who start directly into a TT position.[66]

It is worth noting that not all contingent faculty think this way. Many despair of ever finding a tenure-track position. One contingent professor at the University of California noted: "I wanted to be a tenure track professor but without having any access to research subjects or money to pursue research that goal became more and more difficult over time. I still do publish but not at the rate that is necessary to be a tenured employee. I also do not have any opportunities to collaborate with other faculty."

Aside from staying in the game, what else helps academics get back to the tenure track? We have already noted that women with children under six are disproportionately likely to take contingent positions in lieu of tenure-track jobs. Once off the tenure track, these women are 24 percent less likely to return in comparison with women without young children—and 66 percent less likely to return than are otherwise comparable fathers.[67] However, the story changes once these children reach school age. Women with children over five are 65 percent more likely to get tenure-track jobs than are their childless counterparts. Other things being equal, men and women are equally likely to return.[68]

The other major gender difference concerns people whose first postdoctoral employment lies outside academe. As we saw in figure 2.2, the people least likely to get tenure-track jobs are those who take employment outside higher education. Further analysis shows that this holds true only for men. Once ensconced in careers outside academia, they tend to stay outside. But women employed outside academia get tenure-track jobs at only 10 percent lower rates than do unemployed female doctorate recipients. Some women working in jobs outside academia may be doing so only provisionally, until their children reach school age. In contrast, men who leave academia tend to stay out. More likely to be their family's primary wage earners, these men may hesitate to forsake stable careers outside academia in order to gamble on a position that, in the long run, depends on securing tenure. Alternately they may have anticipated non-academic careers all along. It should come as little surprise that male Ph.D.s can usually get better jobs outside the academy than their female colleagues can.[69]

Taken together, these findings offer insight into how men and women who leave the tenure track go about returning. Women often do not work in ladder-rank positions when they have young children (and, perhaps, when planning to have them). They stay off the tenure track, perhaps working as contingent faculty, until their kids reach school age, at which point their rates of reentry increase. Returning is always harder than moving straight through the pipeline to ladder-rank employment after graduate school (or after postdoctoral fellowships, depending on the field). These patterns are reversed for men; they are more likely to get tenure-track positions when they have young children. Presumably their wives or partners will provide child care. Fathers may also be more open to geographical relocation when their children are young and less likely to have their school and social lives disrupted. Conversely, the fathers of older children may be loath to subject their families to the upheaval that taking an academic job may entail.

Conclusion

For many young scholars, their first postgraduate job is a life-changing moment. After many arduous and underpaid years in graduate school, and perhaps a few more in a postdoctoral fellowship, young Ph.D.s find themselves in a much better place professionally. Suddenly their salaries have increased dramatically; their professional status has also seen commensurate gains. These welcome developments often require a cross-country move. Thus the boundary between graduate school and professional employment represents a dramatic transformation—and the point at which women drop out of the academic game.[70] They drop out because an academic job seems incompatible with marriage and children. We know this is the case because unmarried women without young children obtain tenure-track jobs at higher rates than do otherwise comparable men. (Men, presumably less constrained by family considerations, continue to do better overall on the academic job market than do women.)

Traditionally, observers attempted to explain women's underrepresentation in the academy on the basis of discrimination.[71] We do not deny that women still face discrimination in the academy. However, our findings suggest that traditionally conceived gender discrimination no longer seems to account for the lower rate at which women get tenure-track jobs—indeed, if it ever did. It can also no longer be argued that female doctoral recipients eschew academic careers based on differential socialization, given that they fare better than men on the job market when unencumbered by husbands and young children. Yet prejudice against married women and mothers, as opposed to discrimination toward women in general, apparently continues. Maternal discrimination, as we shall see in the next chapter, is a primary consideration in the lawsuits that women denied tenure have brought under Title VII of the Civil Rights Act of 1964.

Marriage and younger children present many difficulties for academic women. This may become apparent as early as graduate school. Female students are unlikely to see many faculty role models who successfully combine career and family. Looking at the academic career path, these students may also see few opportunities to start a family down the road. Unfortunately there is no optimal time. Graduate students may feel too underpaid and overworked; looking ahead to their assistant professor years, they wonder how motherhood can be combined with the publish-or-perish mandate; and after tenure the fertility window may well have closed. As a result of these conflicting pressures, some graduate student women will not pursue careers as tenure-track academics (some men will of course also choose not to pursue academic careers, but their decisions are far less likely to be based on family considerations).

Other women will find that marriage and children make going on the job market more difficult. Female academics are far more likely to have spouses with careers than are men; in particular, female academics are more likely to be married to male academics than vice versa. An employed husband may make geographical relocation more difficult, and academic search committees may well come to the same conclusion. If both spouses are academics, the couple has the "two body" problem. As the traditional child care provider, the woman is more likely to subordinate her career to that of her husband. Pregnancy may signal to search committees that a woman is on the mommy track rather than the tenure track. Young children need full-time supervision, which makes academic job interviews problematic. Mothers who negotiate all these challenges then find themselves divided between demanding careers and taking care of their families.

How do academic women respond to these challenges? A common solution for mothers is to move to the second tier of contingent professorships. A fair number of these mothers will make it back to the tenure track later on. Nevertheless, they remain overrepresented in the second tier of contingent faculty, faculty at junior colleges, and other jobs that fall short of tenured professorships at four-year schools.[72] Furthermore, married women are disproportionately likely to be contingent faculty.[73] This accords with a common stereotype of young academic couples: the husband gets the high-status line appointment and his "trailing spouse" teaches part time.

Contingent teaching appointments may provide the flexibility mothers and wives need, but they represent a substantial sacrifice in terms of pay, prestige, and working conditions. Furthermore, the longer a woman (or man) remains in the second tier, the less likely she is to get a tenure-track job. Our findings suggest that many women do not intend to remain contingent faculty members for the duration of their careers, but instead use contingent professorships as an improvised solution to a male-oriented career model. Some women will enter the contingent ranks when caring for infants or toddlers, then upgrade to the tenure track once their children reach school age. Does this strategy work? We answer this question with a qualified yes, noting that over one half of people who become contingent faculty within two years of finishing graduate school manage to get tenure-track jobs down the road. However, this is a far from certain career path. In an ideal world there would be better options for female academics who want families.

What can colleges and universities do to get more wives and mothers hired into tenure-track professorships? Wives would probably be most helped by a dedicated commitment to assistance with spousal hiring. Universities often make strenuous efforts to recruit promising job candidates. These efforts need to include up-front assistance with spousal job-hunting. This is a relatively inexpensive measure that could bear great dividends for recruiting female professors. The challenge is much greater when the would-be faculty spouse is also an academic, but even then there are useful steps to be taken. Perhaps the most obvious is a formal policy on spousal hiring that is automatically communicated to all faculty job candidates. One such program, offered by the University of Rhode Island, will be discussed in greater detail in the last chapter of this book.

Making academia more welcoming to mothers requires broader action. As we suggested in the previous chapter, many graduate students are already pessimistic about the prospects of work-family balance in the academy. Were this not the case, many would feel better about going on the academic job market. However, this wouldn't in itself remedy the blatant discrimination toward mothers many women encounter as they search for jobs. Here, too, we need stronger guidelines for academic search committees. Departments conducting faculty searches need to be directly advised about the illegality of using motherhood as a hiring criterion. Academic job postings routinely advise applicants about nondiscrimination with respect to race, ethnicity, and sometimes sexual orientation. Family status should always appear on this list. Moreover, job candidates need to be informed of a university's family-friendly accommodations at the time they interview. These are no-cost interventions that would significantly assist in the recruitment of faculty mothers.

3

Capturing the Golden Ring of Tenure

On February 12, 2010, a forty-two-year-old biology professor walked into a faculty meeting at the University of Alabama at Huntsville. Amy Bishop, a Harvard-educated mother of four, had that same day been denied an appeal of her negative tenure decision. Drawing a pistol, Bishop shot three of her colleagues dead. Two other faculty members and an assistant were wounded.

In the days that followed, a strange outburst of empathy for the accused shooter emerged. Despite numerous reports that Bishop had a long history of erratic and violent behavior, many observers chose instead to blame the tenure system. Consider a typical post on the *New York Times* website: "Tenure strains institutions in ways that would never happen in industry. This tragedy is evidence of how the ivory tower is bent to breaking by the bizarre all-or-nothing prize of a job for life. . . . Tenure is costly. For it warps the behavior of those within the tower in two ways. Either they can be paid unduly while coasting, or they endure the drama of being denied that chance by peers who use tenure to enforce inflexible orthodoxy. And now murder."[1] Another *Times* reader went even further, implying that anyone denied for tenure was at risk for a shooting spree: "May we learn lessons from this event? Perhaps it will heighten our understanding of and sensitivity to the emotional states of individuals who have invested twelve or more years of their post-baccalaureate lives and have succeeded to the point of being evaluated for promotion with tenure."[2] Despite the misguided attributions of blame, these posts tap into a common sentiment in the academy: tenure is a tremendously fraught commodity. For young scholars, years of investment in an academic career hinge on a single up-or-out decision. The stakes are equally high for universities in that conferring tenure will lock the institution into a lifetime commitment of employment.

Some onlookers sought to explain Amy Bishop's shooting spree on the basis of gender; she was a woman (and a wife and a mother) in a man's world. "I can't help but observe that this was a woman in a male-dominated institution in a male-dominated field in a conservative part of the country," wrote one *New York Times* reader.[3] Compounded by a negative tenure decision, this was ostensibly enough to push her over the edge. Prominent observers also see a gender problem with tenure. Princeton University president Shirley M. Tilghman argued that the tenure system should be dropped because it makes huge demands on women at a time when they are already stressed out with young families.[4] Representative Eddie Bernice Johnson, a Texas Democrat and senior member of the House Committee on Science, Space, and Technology, introduced legislation that would, among other reforms, stop the university tenure clock for scientists with newborn children. "Federal policy makers must be more proactive in stopping the leaky pipeline that results in women departing at every major transition point while pursuing careers in engineering, physics, technology, and related fields," Johnson said.[5]

The Road to Tenure

The road to tenure can last up to ten pressure cooker years, although five to seven years is more common.[6] Job security is tenuous, and publishing peer-reviewed articles (or monographs, depending on the field) is necessary for survival. In the sciences, most assistant professors must also secure grant funding in order to subsidize their research—an increasingly difficult challenge, as federal investment in basic science research has declined in recent years.[7] Although some colleges and universities ease the process with close mentoring and regular feedback, many do not. New faculty are under daily pressure to prove that they are good teachers and are good citizens in their departments and universities and, most of all, that they have what it takes to become noted scholars. Teaching colleges, which once required only good performance in the classroom, are now more likely to require publications. One of our colleagues, now a full professor in political science, recounted his first years on the job: "The first two years I had to teach four new courses, two of which [were in subjects] I had never studied myself. One class was a large lecture, three hundred students, with six TAs. I'll bet I spent fifty hours a week just on that course and at the end the students gave me evaluations that truly stank. It got better, but at the end of two years I had only written about twenty pages—I still had a book and three articles to complete for tenure."[8]

When judgment day arrives, a candidate's credentials are carefully scrutinized both within the university and outside it. The process can be agonizingly long and the result, if negative, a crushing defeat. Assistant professors denied tenure must leave the university. Furthermore, the chances of finding another tenure-track position at a similar institution have been tarnished by a tenure denial. A recent sample of schools in the Association of American Universities suggests that just over half of assistant professors get tenure.[9] The rate is higher at schools where research is less important.[10]

The Winners and Losers in the Tenure Race

At the end of the day, women are less likely to get tenure than are men. The previous chapter told a clear story: marriage and children explain why women enter tenure-track positions at a far lower rate than do their male colleagues. We might expect a similar result for women's tenure decisions. It seems obvious that children should make it more difficult for a female assistant professor to complete the work necessary for promotion, but the Survey of Doctorate Recipients reveals that the story is more complex and appears to depend on the academic discipline. Our results raise questions about the possibility of gender discrimination not directly associated with motherhood. An ongoing series of Title VII lawsuits have pursued this theory, with, as we shall see, mixed results. And finally, there is the current debate about tenure itself. Does it inherently put women at a disadvantage? What would an academic world without tenure look like? Can tenure be reformed without being fundamentally undermined?

Looking at all academic disciplines, women are 21 percent less likely to get tenure than are their male colleagues.[11] However—and to our surprise—this result does not vary by either marital status or the presence of young children. Married women fare no better or worse than do single women. The mothers of young children are no less likely to get tenure than are childless women.[12] In all cases, women do worse than men.

The story is very different when we focus just on the sciences (including the social sciences). Having young children dramatically reduces the likelihood of tenure for female faculty members in the sciences. A female scientist with a preschool-age child (in other words, a child under six years old) is 27 percent less likely to get tenure compared with a man who has a small child. If that same woman does not have a young child, she is only 11 percent less likely to get tenure than is a male scientist.[13]

Why are the scientific disciplines particularly hard on mothers? As we have seen, the pool of women scientists who enter the tenure track is already shallow. For the women who do persist, the lack of female colleagues in some science fields may contribute to a work environment that's especially inhospitable to mothers. Angelica Stacy, a professor of chemistry at UC Berkeley, recalls bringing her newborn child and her mother (as a babysitter) to a scientific conference some twenty years ago: "There was no childcare, there were no children, and, in fact, there were very few women. They threw my mother and my baby out of the conference. They said it was unprecedented."[14] This would not occur today, but cultures change slowly.

The need to put in long hours in a lab and the requirement to secure competitive funding almost certainly put mothers at a disadvantage in the race for tenure. These are challenges that scholars in the humanities generally do not face. And federal grants, the source of funding for most scientific research, offer little accommodation for childbirth and motherhood.[15] Securing grant funding is a critical component of tenure success for faculty and researchers in the sciences. Among academics working at major research universities, professors are 65 percent more likely to achieve tenure when directly supported by federal grants.[16] Obtaining funding is so critical to success that its importance is nearly equal to making a significant scientific discovery, as Steven Cohen, director of Columbia University's Earth Institute, recently lamented: "Over the past two decades, I fear that we have reached a tipping point, where our top scientists are spending a larger and larger portion of their time raising funds and less and less time devoted to science."[17] Grants are extremely competitive, applying for them is laborious, and the revision process that follows can take an additional year or more—a long time to wait for young scholars who have only six or seven years to get tenure while simultaneously caring for young children. Unsuccessful applicants have to decide whether to revise further and submit later on, submit elsewhere, or shift the focus of their work. Regardless of the outcome, applying for funding requires a significant time investment, which necessarily means sacrificing time at the bench, working on papers, or on household and caregiving duties.

The Survey of Doctorate Recipients shows that tenure-track faculty women who are married with young children are at a distinct disadvantage when it comes to grantsmanship. They are 21 percent less likely than tenure-track men who are married with young children to have their work partially or fully supported by federal grants or contracts on a year-to-year basis in the sciences. Compared with married tenure-track women without children, these mothers are 26 percent less likely to have full or partial grant support, and compared with single women without children, mothers of young children are 19 percent less likely to have grant or contract funding.[18] Federal grants are all but necessary for tenure in many scientific fields at research universities, so these figures shed light on why young children make tenure less likely for women in the sciences.

The Benefits of Marriage and Older Children

Only young children are a liability to women's tenure decisions. In contrast, children over the age of five increase by between 14 percent and 16 percent the likelihood that men and women alike get tenure. This result holds for all academic fields. Older children may require less continuous attention than babies and toddlers, but they still take up time that could otherwise be spent doing the research, teaching, and service necessary for tenure. Clearly older children must provide some benefit that outweighs the time it takes for care for them. Virtually no respondents in our University of California survey and no posters on the online forums and blogs devoted to higher education say anything like "My children make me a more productive scholar." Still, these older offspring may exert a stabilizing effect on women that more than offsets the time lost in caring for them.

We suspect that the beneficial effect of older children on tenure decisions may reflect the efforts of women (and men) who have best figured out how to negotiate both parenthood and academia. In many cases, these children were under six when scholars were completing their doctorates or searching for academic positions. Academics, especially women, who manage to finish graduate school and obtain tenure-track employment while simultaneously caring for young children may be especially skilled in balancing the conflicting demands of work and family. They may receive more support from their partners, or have learned to be better at managing their time. They have survived the initial cut by getting tenure-track jobs while caring for younger children, so they may be well disposed to excel as assistant professors. We should also keep in mind a finding presented in the previous chapter. Some mothers take adjunct positions, in lieu of tenure-track professorships, straight out of graduate school. They had young children before they joined the tenure-track race. Some of these mothers will get tenure-track jobs after spending time off the tenure track. They are now the mothers of older children, not of labor-intensive infants, during the years they are striving for tenure.

To our surprise, marriage also offers a benefit in the sciences (but not in the humanities). Male or female, married scientists are II percent more likely to get tenure than are their unmarried colleagues. Why is this the case? For starters, married scholars seem to publish more than do their unwed colleagues.[19] This can be attributed, we suspect, to the broadly salutary effects of marriage: generally speaking, marriage makes adults happier, healthier, and more productive.[20] This higher productivity should confer an advantage when assistant professors go up for tenure. Elisabeth Rose Gruner, now a tenured professor at the University of Richmond, described the benefits of a supportive husband after becoming a mother for the second time: "That's right: in the early days of parenting (and many other times) I had a 'traditional wife,' but one who knew how to change the oil and put up drywall too. His career sacrifice enabled my success, and I am grateful for the benefits that accrued to me."[21]

Discrimination

Whether or not they are mothers, women are less likely than men to get tenure. Economist Donna Ginther and other researchers have suggested that discrimination is the primary reason why women lag behind men when it comes time for promotion.[22] Yet only one-quarter of a recent sample of American faculty believe that discrimination is responsible for the paucity of female scientists.[23] Psychologists Stephen Ceci and Wendy Williams assert that "evidence for recent sex discrimination—when it exists—is aberrant, of small magnitude, and is superseded by larger, more sophisticated analyses showing no bias, or occasionally, bias in favor of women." They acknowledge that real barriers exist, particularly for women in math-based sciences, but point instead to motherhood as the primary obstacle.[24]

Discrimination is a slippery concept that spans complex and varying prejudices, including discrimination against mothers. Sometimes this discrimination, particularly in the physical sciences, may reflect the lingering belief that women do not have the same aptitude for scientific thought that men have. In 2005, Lawrence Summers, then the president of Harvard University, speaking at an academic conference on women and underrepresented minorities in science, raised the question of whether innate gender differences might help explain why fewer women succeed in science and engineering professorships.[25] Summers's remarks, delivered to a small group of professors, were soon heard around the world.[26] They have been viewed as evidence that some highly placed academics still harbor retrograde ideas about women.

But discrimination may not concern just aptitude. The bias against caregiving in academia (and outside it) is well documented.[27] Some scientists may believe that women who have families (or may have families at some future time) cannot be serious scientists, because academic science demands exclusive attention to research. This attitude pervades other disciplines as well, where the ideal professor is still perceived to be a man whose first commitment is scholarship, and provides the origins for one notorious dismissal of female academics: "She's on the mommy track." Yet male academics are never said to be on the daddy track.

Fighting Back

Some women who believe that their tenure denial was based on discrimination fight back with lawsuits, and a few win. Since the 1980s, the American Association of University Women's Legal Advocacy Fund has supported more than sixty of these women in their long court battles.[28] Many additional contested tenure cases presumably don't come to the public's attention.

Title VII of the Civil Rights Act of 1964 prohibits employment discrimination on the basis of sex, race, national origin, or religion. The Pregnancy

Discrimination Act is an amendment to Title VII that prohibits discrimination on the basis of pregnancy, childbirth, or related medical conditions.[29] What protection those laws offer has been the subject of evolving interpretation by federal courts. In the 1980s, a forty-one-year-old English professor named Julia Prewitt Brown fought to overturn a tenure denial by Boston University, pursuing her case all the way to the federal First Circuit Court of Appeals.[30] She prevailed, obtaining tenure and winning a large settlement, in part because she had direct evidence that the university's president had commented to another woman professor who had at the time also been seeking tenure, "Your husband is a parachute, so why are you worried?" The plaintiff also supported her case by showing that her male peers with similar teaching and research records had been granted tenure.

During the past two decades, changing judicial interpretations have made it more difficult for a plaintiff in a tenure case to prove discrimination. The common reason why colleges and universities deny tenure is that the candidate's research or teaching doesn't meet departmental standards. But since the 1990s, a plaintiff has had to prove not only that the university's assessment of her work was flawed but also that the real reason for the denial was sex discrimination. If discrimination can't be proved, even if the department is found to be intentionally lying about a tenure candidate's research, other reasons for the denial, such her lack of collegiality, can be upheld.[31]

One important tenure-denial case, *Fisher v. Vassar College*, began in federal court in 1994 and eventually was heard in the U.S. Circuit Court of Appeals in 1997. Cynthia Fisher, a biologist, alleged that Vassar had discriminated against her based on her sex, marital status, and age. Fisher prevailed in her first trial, proving to the federal district court judge that she was equally or more qualified for tenure than comparable scholars. She also cited statistics showing that Vassar had a history of denying tenure to married women. But ultimately the circuit court rejected her case. It stated: "Individual decision makers may intentionally dissemble in order to hide a reason that is nondiscriminatory but unbecoming or small-minded, such as back-scratching, logrolling, horse-trading, institutional politics, envy, nepotism, spite, or personal hostility. . . . The fact that the proffered reason was false does not necessarily mean that the true motive was the illegal one argued by the plaintiff."[32] As Fisher pointed out, most academics are too smart to publicly state that "married women should stay home and take care of their families."

In a sex-discrimination lawsuit, plaintiffs may be awarded compensatory damages, back and front pay, or even reinstatement with tenure, as well as legal fees and costs. In practice, few plaintiffs are reinstated, and most compensation packages do not financially justify the enormous time and expense of the lawsuit and the shame of replaying a failure in the public eye. Moreover, your colleagues may avoid you. You may be labeled a troublemaker, which reduces the chances that you will receive another job offer. Still, the success of a few tenure cases has changed the atmosphere at many universities where administrators seem to be realizing that, as with sexual-harassment suits, a small investment in prevention is better than an expensive lawsuit. At UC Berkeley, for instance, several sex-discrimination suits were brought in the late 1980s and early 1990s. Three were resolved out of court, with the women receiving both tenure and a settlement. In a fourth, the court awarded a large settlement. As a result of those cases, the tenure process on the campus became more transparent and candidates are now overtly informed of their rights. This was a win for both men and women.[33]

The hopeful news is that because of the discrimination suits that have been pursued over the years the tenure process is more open and fair on most campuses, reducing the chances for discrimination. And there are several studies, cited earlier in this chapter, that suggest that discrimination may no longer play the role it once did in keeping women out of the sciences.[34]

Reforming Tenure

There is much discussion about the end of tenure, and many colleges and universities are moving in that direction. This trend has presumably been motivated by the prospect of short-term economic gain. Abolishing tenure, however, is a bad move both economically and intellectually. A university without tenure would not foster a creative, challenging environment in which discovery and scholarship flourish. It would be, instead, a corporation staffed by part-time and contingent employees who could be hired or fired at the whim of the corporate administrators. That would be a loss for students, for faculty members, and for the future of knowledge and innovation. Academia would no longer attract the best and the brightest. Who would choose a career of insecurity and comparably low wages when other options were available? The reputation and value of American universities is predicated on the freethinking, creative faculty they have been able to attract and retain.

The tenure system, for all its faults, should be expanded, not dismantled as is now happening at many colleges and universities. But it must be made more flexible to level the playing field and suit the modern realities of professors' lives. Most universities now provide some relief in the form of policies that allow faculty to stop the tenure clock for childbirth.[35] Although that is a welcome measure, our research at the University of California suggests that tenure-clock stoppage is not used unless (1) it is an entitlement rather than something received by special request (with this in mind, a number of research universities now make tenure-clock stoppage opt-out rather than opt in),[36] (2) it is used by fathers as well as mothers, and (3) it is supported and enforced by campus culture and regulations. The same support and enforcement is necessary to promote paid childbirth leave and relief from teaching. In our 2002–2003 survey of faculty members at the University of California system, 51 percent of eligible mothers who did not use the teaching-relief policy gave as their reason "because it might have hurt my chances for tenure or promotion."

A major step toward reforming the tenure system is to create policies that will actively involve fathers in the critical tenure years. Our account of the difficulties of academic motherhood should not be read as an indictment of women's husbands and partners. As we have seen, fathers typically do not put in a full second shift, but they do help out at home. Let us also acknowledge the social and institutional barriers that may prevent academic men from doing more. Consider the following account, from a bench scientist at the University of California:

> For our daughter's (a special needs child) first couple of years, I took her to physical therapy three times a week, losing about seven hours of work time. I was pre-tenure at that point. Everyone assumed that my wife (also a tenure-track scientist) was the primary caregiver, including the male chair and female dean and provost, so she was offered special consideration on scheduling classes and such. She had to tell them that I was the primary caregiver with respect to physical therapy, since our daughter wanted to nurse, not work, when my wife was there. No special scheduling was then offered to me. I think their minds simply couldn't get around the idea of a man being the primary caregiver.

In 39 percent of American families women are the primary or only earners.[37] Yet universities perpetuate a culture that assumes that mothers will take on the lion's share of caregiving and that men are the breadwinners. This assertion is borne out by the findings of our survey of the Association of American Universities. We found that 58 percent guaranteed at least six weeks paid leave for faculty mothers, but just 16 percent provided one week paid parental leave.[38] This is a remarkable difference.

Over the years academics have sat at many conference tables arguing with colleagues about whether new fathers should be allowed to stop the tenure clock, or receive modified duties with respect to teaching and other work. The opposition is always the same: "Men won't use the time for parenting; they'll use it to write another book or publish more articles." Fathers, for their part, even if they are full participants in parenting, don't often use parental accommodations, because, like mothers, they fear they will be considered marginal tenure candidates—why did they need the extra time to get tenure?—or less committed to their institutions. The counterargument is that unless we engage fathers in a flexible workplace, the culture will not change.

There is disagreement among the universities that do offer fathers accommodations for caregiving—usually a semester off—on what level of caregiving is required to qualify. The University of California's most recent modified-duties policy requires the academic appointee to submit a written statement certifying that he or she is responsible for 50 percent or more of a child or newborn's care. The University of Utah has a similar policy. The terms of Harvard Law School's parental and personal leave policies are more flexible, taking into account that a week contains 168 hours: "A qualified faculty member must demonstrate, to the satisfaction of the Dean, substantial and sustained responsibility for his or her child. 'Substantial and sustained responsibility' shall be deemed to be sole full-time care-giving of at least 40 hours per week, for at least one semester during the term of the initial appointment or any previous extension thereof. Care-giving shall not be deemed 'sole full-time' when any part of the required 40 hours is performed by someone other than the faculty member."[39]

A Flexible Career Track

A bolder policy than stopping the tenure clock or offering more flexible parental leave would be a part-time tenure track that allowed faculty to switch from part time to full time, depending on their family circumstances. Our survey of University of California faculty found wide support among men and women of all ages for allowing faculty members to shift to part-time status and back again; more than 60 percent of women and a third of men were interested in a flexible, prorated tenure track that would allow them to return to work full time at some point. Women support the policy mainly as a way of balancing their work with the obligations of raising small children. Both men and women mention elder care (of parents or in-laws) and phasing into retirement as reasons for supporting a flexible tenure track. Yet despite the demand for such policies, they remain relatively uncommon in academe. According to a 2001 report sponsored by the Alfred P. Sloan Foundation, a longtime sponsor of research on work and family, only 2 percent of tenure-track faculty in the United States had half-time appointments. And just 6 percent of the colleges and universities surveyed allowed half-time faculty to obtain tenure.[40] By way of contrast, a contemporaneous study of 1,057 corporations by the Families and Work Institute in New York found that 57 percent allowed employees to shuttle between half- and full-time employment.[41]

The difficulties of half-time tenure-track positions are well understood. As one female chemist at the University of California acerbically put it, "I don't think it is possible for a professor in the sciences to work part time. You can't partly run a research group." Kathleen Christensen of the Alfred P. Sloan Foundation viewed part-time professorships as untenable, "because a culture of long work hours and [a focus on] speed to tenure meant that the part timer was seen as working in a deviant fashion."[42] Certainly a part-time tenure-track faculty member would have fewer teaching responsibilities, but this would not necessarily lower a tenure committee's expectation that the candidate demonstrate a strong research track record; committee members might assume that the smaller teaching load would free up more time for research. Half-time policies are far easier to implement for senior faculty, when there is no need to calculate what half the research necessary for tenure might be. In fact, the balance of half-time appointments described in the Sloan study were men in the twilight of their careers who were ramping down for retirement.[43] But this does nothing to help the faculty most in need of half-time positions: women early in their career struggling with both children and tenure requirements.

In 2001, when we began to explore serious reform of the University of California's policies for faculty parents, we were surprised to discover that a vague policy was already on the books for a part-time tenure track. This was news to every faculty member we interviewed, and to most of the personnel staff as well. There is a very long stretch between adopting a written policy and having it actively used and supported by university culture. Upon further investigation we were again surprised to learn that some faculty members already had part-time tenure-track appointments. Most were scientists and engineers who used the flexibility of a part-time faculty position to do consulting work or start their own companies. All those arrangements, including extended leaves, had been privately negotiated with department chairs and involved only faculty members who already had tenure.

The right to return to full-time work is the key for part-time tenure-track faculty appointments. A permanent part-time position may appeal to some faculty members, but for most people it means permanently low wages and marginalization in their departments. The vague policy already on the books at the UC system did not clearly include the right to return to full-time employment. This existing policy would of course be of dubious value to a mother, whose need of a part-time position generally wanes as her children grow up.

Given the limited utility of the existing policy, we decided to craft a new policy that would accommodate faculty members' family obligations at any point in their careers. As always, the devil was in the details. Ten University of California campuses and the systemwide academic senate all had to agree to the policy. The concerns focused mostly on how to assess the productivity of a part-time, pre-tenure career and, to a lesser extent, on evaluation at regular merit reviews throughout a career. In drafting the policy, we had to choose between two options: preserving the traditional six-year "publish or perish" period but modifying the tenure standards for part timers, or maintaining the standards and lengthening the probationary pre-tenure period. Ultimately, we obtained faculty agreement on extending the tenure clock, but not on modifying the standards for tenure. We also ran up against a firm policy instituted by the University of California Board of Regents that allowed no more than ten years to elapse before a tenure vote. Even the restricted plan we came up with took two years to pass through the many levels of faculty governance and university bureaucracy.

The jury is still out, since the policy only became available in late 2006. At that time, one mother at the University of California, a history professor, told us, "I'm so glad you are doing this, but I could never have used it. I couldn't have afforded to receive half pay." On the bright side, many of the other new reforms the University of California adopted to ameliorate the inflexible tenure clock—such as offering two semesters free from teaching for mothers and one for fathers (at full pay)—appear to have been more widely invoked.

Conclusion

It is already well known that women are less likely than men to get tenure. We add to the conventional wisdom by demonstrating the important role that family formation plays in tenure decisions. A female scientist with a child under six years old is 27 percent less likely to get tenure compared to her male colleagues, whereas a childless woman is only 11 percent less likely to get tenure. The latter figure shows that motherhood does not completely explain women's lower tenure rates in the sciences (including the social sciences). Perhaps discrimination is part of the story, but we cannot know for certain.

Both marriage and older children affect tenure decisions, but not in the ways we anticipated. Married professors in the sciences, both men and women, are more likely to get tenure than are their unmarried colleagues; so too are faculty with children six years of age and older. The consequences of marriage for tenure decisions make sense given the extensive benefits of marriage for personal and social well-being. The effects of older children on tenure decisions are more difficult to understand. Certainly older children take up a lot of time, although not quite so much as preschool-age kids. But the liabilities of older children are apparently outweighed by their benefits: perhaps they signify that college faculty, both men and women, have arrived at a relatively stable time in their lives. Future scholars who become parents in graduate school (or before) are the assistant professors most likely to have older children when they come up for tenure. In this respect, graduate school appears to be the best time for academics to start families.

The exceptions to these patterns are the analyses that include humanities faculty. Here we find that neither marriage nor young children have an impact on tenure decisions (although married mothers are far less likely to enter the tenure track in the first place). The obvious explanation is that academic culture is different in the humanities than it is in the sciences, although with the data at hand we are unable to know for sure. The bench sciences demand very long hours in the laboratory, a place where children are not welcome. And compared to the sciences, few scholars in the humanities depend on federal grants and the lockstep professional progress they entail.

Although fathers are more likely to get tenure than mothers, they still experience tension between work and family. Counting both domestic and professional responsibilities, mothers put in many more hours a week than do men, but most men do make a noteworthy contribution to housework and caregiving. Indeed, many fathers want to spend more time with their family, but feel that professional demands won't allow for it.

We advocate reforming the existing tenure system, not replacing it with an insecure fungible workforce. A part-time flexible pre- and post-tenure track with the right to return would be a major step in this direction. Other supports for young faculty, including stopping the clock before tenure, teaching relief following childbirth, and childcare assistance, will be revisited in the last chapter of this book.

4

Alone in the Ivory Tower

It's true that I don't have to consider (as much) how my career decisions will affect other people's lives, but I have to make every move alone, adjust to life in new places alone, and lack the support system that other people have. To make things worse, I'm cut off from a lot of the socializing that does occur, since married couples, in my experience, rarely include single women in their social circles. . . . What this means in practice is that, in addition to not having a family to ease various burdens, is that we're often cut off from a good bit of the life of the department.

–A forum post at the *Chronicle of Higher Education* website.

The past two chapters of this book have focused on professional life, most notably, who gets the plum tenure-track positions, and who gets tenure. We have shown that family considerations play a critical role: married women and women with young children are less likely to get tenure-track jobs. Mothers in particular are more likely to move into the second tier of contingent professorships. If they do get tenure-track positions, women in the sciences with young children are less likely to get tenure. For some women, concerns about work-family balance deter pursuit of an academic career. For others, marriage and young children make it difficult to obtain tenure-track employment and harder to get tenure.

The result is pronounced gender imbalance in higher education. This inequity initially motivated our research on academic careers; more generally, the unequal American workplace has long been a concern of scholars and women alike. Men have always held better jobs.[1] They make more money, even when employed in the same positions as women.[2] Yet it is also true that there has been ongoing and steady reduction in the economic and vocational differences between the sexes.[3] According to these and other benchmarks set down by liberal feminism, gender inequality is at an all-time low.[4]

But there is another way to measure women's progress: whether their professional gains have come at the cost of having their own families.[5] Academia falls far short of being family friendly, as Lisa Gabbert, an English professor at Utah State University, has forcefully suggested: "I absolutely believe that academia is hostile towards any interests outside of itself, but particularly . . . towards relationships and towards having children. I tell people I have two competing clocks: the tenure one and the biological one. Being in Utah, I am in a child-friendly environment, yet my university (like others) does not even offer maternity leave (though they are working on it), nor does it offer day care facilities. How can we expect to succeed if even these minimum necessities are not met?"[6]

The previous chapter considered the tenure clock. We now turn our attention to the biological clock by asking whether male and, especially, female faculty have to sacrifice marriage and children in order to achieve professional success. We explore marriage, divorce, and childbearing for male and female faculty and compare academia with other professions to determine if academic women are unique among female professionals.

Two caveats are in order. First, we make an implicit assumption about family preferences. We speak of female faculty being alone in the ivory tower because most Americans and, more specifically, most academics want children.[7] Since most Americans also want to be married, we make a similar assumption about academics.[8] Like other Americans, some academics no doubt wish they were married but are in same-sex relationships and are legally unable to wed. Our Survey of Doctorate Recipients (SDR) data do not allow us to determine whether unmarried respondents, gay or straight, are in live-in relationships. Second, we consider the effects of family on career and career on family separately, keeping in mind that the question of causality is complicated. For example, we have already observed that some young scholars are making joint decisions about career and family.[9] Economists have long suggested that as fertility increases, women's labor force participation decreases (and vice versa), although there has been little agreement on which is cause and which is effect.[10] It runs both ways, according to a study by sociologist Michelle Budig.[11] Budig found that the mothers of young children were more likely to leave the paid labor force if already working and less likely to join it if not working. Furthermore, employment reduces the chances of giving birth. Acknowledging this complexity, this chapter will explore the marriage and parenthood of men and women who have already beaten the odds by becoming professors.

Marriage and Divorce at the Start of an Academic Career

We use Survey of Doctorate Recipients (SDR) data to explore gender differences in marriage and divorce when men and women start their first Ph.D.-level jobs.[12] The results indicate that a woman in a tenure-track job is half as likely as her male colleagues to be married at the beginning of her career. This accords with our findings from chapter 2, which show that marriage sharply reduces the like-lihood of a woman's landing a tenure-track job. Furthermore, it is unsurprising that women in tenure-track positions are 52 percent less likely to be married than are women in the second tier—adjuncts, part-time employees, and women out of the labor force. Conversely, tenure-track employment increases the chances of marriage for male faculty. A man in a ladder-rank position is 84 percent more likely to be married than is a man in the second tier. For men, the potential security and higher pay of tenure-track employment produce corresponding benefits in their personal lives, whereas women can have tenure-track jobs or husbands, but not always both.[13] As one woman noted on the *Chronicle of Higher Education* forums, a husband—and his career—can easily get in the way of an academic job search: "I'm geographically unattached, single and childless. In some ways, these facts did make my job search easier. I was able to apply for jobs from Florida to Oregon with no concerns about the 'moveability' of a husband or significant other. I did not need to worry about any of the other problems that academic women have: 'Will my husband have to quit his job? Will he find another? If he's an academic, will they hire him as a trailing spouse?'"[14]

This web forum post acknowledges just one of several reasons why female faculty are more likely to be single at the start of their careers than are their male colleagues. Women faculty may have been working too hard in graduate school to have found a mate. Others may have been in marriages that did not survive graduate school and the job search process. In particular, women may have dissolved relationships in order to relocate; moving is generally a require-ment for tenure-track employment. This was the case for one *Chronicle of Higher Education* forum participant. Divorce opened up new career options, which in turn helped her get over her ex-husband:

> Separated from ex-husband in the final year of my PhD, just as I was on the job market. . . . My divorce saved my life and career, and that's all that needs to be said.
>
> I got three job offers, left town with my dignity and finances more or less intact, and finished my diss[ertation] 14 months after I'd started the job I accepted, which was 12 months after I'd hoped to be finished. Lots of good things came out of that time. . . . Having these other things to focus on helped me a lot with the emotional pain. It was a huge advantage on the job market not to have to consider a trailing partner (although I didn't have children).[15]

Although some male Ph.D. recipients experience some challenges related to spousal employment, men are more likely to have spouses that defer to the requirements of their careers.[16] The SDR data provide corroborating evidence, showing that women starting tenure-track positions are 144 percent—almost two and a half times—more likely than tenure-track men to be divorced. Also, tenure-track women are 75 percent more likely than women in second-tier positions to be divorced. A tenure-track position has the opposite effect for men: they are 39 percent less likely to be divorced than are men in the second tier.

Do women Ph.D.s get divorced or remain single because they are in tenure-track positions, or merely because they are working full time? In other words, is there something unique about an academic career, or are all full-time Ph.D.-level careers, and the associated time demands, a strain on existing relationships (or an impediment to starting new relationships)? Our results show that the gender gap in marriage and divorce at the start of Ph.D. recipients' careers is mostly the product of full-time employment in general, but a distinct proportion can be uniquely attributed to employment in a tenure-track professorship. At the start of their careers, women in tenure-track professorships are 50 percent less likely to be married than their male colleagues; female Ph.D. recipients employed elsewhere full time are only 40 percent less likely to be married.[17] The difference is a 10-percentage-point "professor penalty" paid by female faculty. Moreover, the gender difference between tenure-track employment and other full-time employment holds for divorce as well as marriage. Recall that tenure-track women are 144 percent more likely than otherwise comparable men to be divorced at the beginning of their careers. The corresponding figure for Ph.D. women in other professions is only 89 percent. All full-time employment decreases women's chances of being married and increases their odds of being divorced, but tenure-track employment adds a compounding professor penalty.

These results, based on survey data from Ph.D. recipients fresh out of graduate school, are a predictable mirror image of the findings presented in the previous chapters. Married women are less likely to become tenure-track faculty and more likely to be contingent faculty; female faculty at the beginning of their careers are less likely to be married and more likely to be divorced. This, as we will see, is merely the beginning of dramatic inequities in marriage and divorce between men and women on the tenure track, as well as between women in the first and second tiers of academia.

Marriage and Divorce in the Professoriate

Data from the SDR reveal how marital behavior unfolds over the course of faculty careers.[18] The results continue to show an ongoing marriage penalty for all female Ph.D. recipients working full time. A woman in a ladder-rank professorship is 32 percent less likely to get married than is a tenure-track man. Furthermore, tenure-track female faculty are 35 percent less likely to marry than are their female counterparts employed in the second tier.[19] These results appear to be the effect of full-time employment, not specifically a consequence of working in a tenure-track professorship.[20]

The story is different for divorce. A married woman in a tenure-track job is 35 percent more likely to get divorced than is a similarly employed man. More striking, female tenure-track faculty have approximately double the odds of divorce compared with women in the second tier. However, the gender gap in divorce is larger for women Ph.D.s working full time in nonteaching positions, inside or outside academia: these women are 53 percent more likely to dissolve their marriages in comparison with male Ph.D.s working in similar jobs. The disparity in divorce rates is even greater between women working full time but not in tenure-track faculty positions and second-tier women: the former have 125 percent higher odds of divorce than do the latter.

What do these results say about the gender gaps in marriage and divorce for U.S. higher education faculty? Most important, there are substantial differences between men and women in tenure-track positions, and between women in tenure-track jobs and their counterparts in the second tier. In both cases, tenure-track women are less likely to be married and more likely to be divorced. These disparities in family status are not exclusively associated with the job title of "professor." Instead, we point to two factors. First, female faculty have high divorce rates and low marriage rates because they are working full time in demanding jobs, not merely because they are college and university professors. Women working full time generally have higher divorce rates than do men because of work-family conflict.[21] Second, whatever makes the marital behavior of female faculty unique appears to begin in graduate school, given that the gender gap in marriage and divorce is largest right when Ph.D. recipients are beginning their careers.

We cannot know for certain why women faculty so often begin their careers unmarried or divorced. Based on the evidence presented here there are at least two possibilities. First, many female graduate students perceive difficulties in combining work and family in an academic career. These perceptions may well be exaggerated, at least with respect to marriage, given that female faculty have similar marriage rates and somewhat lower divorce rates than those of Ph.D. recipients employed full time elsewhere. Nevertheless, women who anticipate marriage and children may avoid tenure-track employment out of graduate school. Second, we have presented evidence suggesting that marriage—and the children that often ensue—make it difficult for women to pursue tenure-track jobs.

Our University of California respondents had a great deal to say about the difficulties of combining children with an academic career. However, they were relatively silent about conflicts between marriage and work. We suspect this is the case because academia may not pose more challenges for women's marriages than does any other demanding full-time job. Instead, the challenge for female doctorate recipients comes right at the moment they start tenure-track jobs. Only at this professional juncture do female faculty have lower marriage rates (and higher divorce rates) than do female Ph.D.s employed elsewhere. We speculate that marriages—and romantic relationships that might otherwise culminate in marriage—sometimes do not survive when women have to relocate to take tenure-track positions (or the postdoctoral fellowships that will culminate in tenure-track positions). Jobs off the tenure track are less likely to involve a national move. Male academics have this problem less often, since their wives are less likely to be employed, especially in immobile careers. Another possibility is that relocation for a tenure-track position provides women (and some men) with an excuse to get out of bad relationships.

Why do women in tenure-track positions have lower divorce rates than do their counterparts in full-time nonteaching positions? The reasons are unclear, and this finding is particularly surprising given one well-known challenge of academic marriages—the long-distance relationship. Although fairly uncommon, they are a familiar feature of the academic landscape and a common topic for discussion on the *Chronicle of Higher Education* forums.[22] Here is a typical post: "I'm doing the together on weekends thing right now. It's a lot harder than you'd think. In some ways, it's the worst of both worlds: you get neither the regular support of living together full-time nor the space and independence of being in a truly long-distance relationship. And it makes it a lot harder when there are problems in the marriage to begin with. It's very difficult to deal with the problems, plus everything else in your life, when you see each other for only a few days each week."[23] We suspect that individuals in this sort of relationship are at considerable risk for either divorce or career change. However, these breakups seem to occur at the beginning of women's professorial careers, not later.

Baby Blues

Previous chapters offered reasons why female faculty have fewer children than their male counterparts. Many female graduate students perceive faculty careers as incompatible with parenthood. Children make it difficult to put in long hours in the lab or office or to go on academic job talks. Perhaps most important, the academic career is not structured to be conducive to childbirth. Many female faculty feel professionally secure enough to have children only once they have tenure, but by then they are already well past prime childbearing years (even the average assistant professor is in his or her early forties).[24] One female social scientist at the University of California voiced all these concerns and more:

> I am worried about having kids before getting tenure—I am worried that I would have to commute to campus and where would I put my kids in childcare, at home or near campus? I am worried about being able to

afford kids/childcare, etc when I can't even afford to live near campus. I am worried that staying single and w/o kids means that my
dept. thinks I have much more time to dedicate to the university
and they disregard that I can and do have a "family-life" outside of
my job—and they ask more of me than they would of other faculty—
thank you for this survey. . . . I am worried that by the time I decide
to have kids (after tenure) that my biological clock will say "you waited
too long!"

This women's worries are reflected in the reproductive behavior of female faculty. The basic story is straightforward: female faculty with tenure-track positions are far less likely to have young children than are comparable men. In
addition, female faculty on the tenure track have many fewer kids than do
women in the second tier. This baby gap exists both at the beginning of Ph.D.
recipients' careers and down the road.

At the University of California, female faculty most often have babies during the pre-tenure years (see figure 4.1), even though these children have a
disastrous effect on women's tenure chances in the sciences. Men continue to
experience fertility into their fifties, most likely because of the formation of a
second family following a divorce. In general, male faculty at the University of
California are much more likely than their female colleagues to have children.

The SDR data tell a similar story.[25] The baby gap is apparent when men and
women first finish graduate school. A female faculty member starting a tenure-
track job is 61 percent less likely than a comparable man to have a child under six

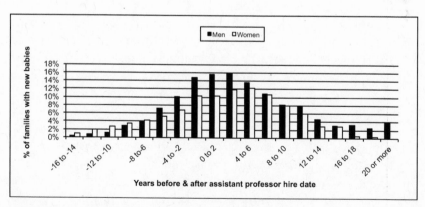

FIGURE 4.1 The Baby Gap for University of California Faculty

Source: University of California Faculty Work and Family Survey, 2002–2003. Reprinted
from Mary Ann Mason and Marc Goulden, "Marriage and Baby Blues: Redefining Gender
Equity in the Academy," *Annals of the American Academy of Political and Social Science* 596
(2004): 86–103, figure 2, by permission of Sage Publications.

N = 3,322

at home. The disparity is even greater between women on the tenure track and their counterparts in the second tier—the former have 65 percent lower odds of having a child under six. Furthermore, the baby gap for women in tenure-track faculty positions and women Ph.D.s working full time in other jobs is almost identical: both groups are far less likely to have young children in comparison with both women in the second tier and men.[26] Although many female grad students say they will seek a family-friendly alternative to a tenure-track career, in reality they may end up in full-time nonacademic jobs that are just as problematic for having children (in comparison with potentially less demanding jobs in the second tier). Obviously it is difficult to be a mother, especially of a young child, and to work full time. The results presented in chapter 3 established that mothers are less likely than male Ph.D. recipients to get tenure-track jobs and more likely to take second-tier positions, so it makes sense that women working full time after graduate school have fewer babies. Conversely, male Ph.D. holders starting tenure-track jobs are 73 percent more likely to have young children at home than are men in the second tier. Presumably the costs and other responsibilities of fatherhood impel men to take full-time teaching jobs; working part time or spending time out of the paid labor force become untenable options.

Do women in tenure-track positions eventually close the baby gap? Looking across the professional life course, we find that the gender difference in fertility is not limited to the time when young scholars start their careers. A female faculty member with a ladder-rank academic position is 35 percent less likely to have a child under six than is a male colleague. The baby gap is even larger between women on the tenure track and women in the second tier: the former are 61 percent less likely than the latter to have a young child at home.

Are women in tenure-track jobs not having kids because they are professors, or just because they are working full time? Put another way, is there something special about tenure-track professorships that discourages childbirth (or, alternately, women who aspire to have children)? The results suggest that any full-time employment for female doctorate recipients dramatically lowers their chances of having children. However, the effect is especially large for tenure-stream faculty. Female tenure-track faculty are 35 percent less likely to have babies than are tenure-track men; female Ph.D. recipients in full-time jobs off the tenure track are 24 percent less likely to have babies than are men in comparable jobs. Full-time work in general appears to reduce the chances that women have children, with female faculty incurring an extra professor penalty. As junior faculty members hustling to make tenure, women may fully realize the extent to which higher education can be hostile to family life. Some women put off having children until they are tenured, but by then it may be too late. Finally, of course, some women pursuing tenure-track careers never intended to have children in the first place.

Babies across the Professions

Over the past thirty years women have entered law and medicine in large numbers. How do faculty compare with doctors and lawyers in terms of childbearing? Overall, faculty have fewer babies than have doctors or lawyers, and this holds true for both men and women. We compare the family formation of professors with those of doctors and lawyers using data from the 2000 United States Census.[27] We chose these comparison jobs for two reasons. First, along with academia they represent coveted high-status professions that require specialized advanced degrees. Second, professors, doctors, and lawyers can all be readily identified using census data on education and occupation.

As we have seen, female faculty often put off having kids. This assessment is supported by contrasting the likelihood of a "birth event"—the presence of an infant—in the household, for doctors, lawyers, and professors. Figure 4.2 shows how birth events vary by age for members of these three fast-track professions. For comparative purposes this figure includes a trend line for all American women. We observe that women in any fast-track profession have very different fertility patterns from those of American women in general, but also that female professors have fewer birth events within each age range than do doctors or lawyers. Doctors and lawyers have the most birth events in their early thirties, but professors reach their apogee in their mid- to late thirties; in other words, after they have finished graduate school and perhaps even obtained tenure.[28]

How can this vocational disparity in childbearing be explained? Lawyers and doctors, especially if they opt for the less demanding specialties usually chosen

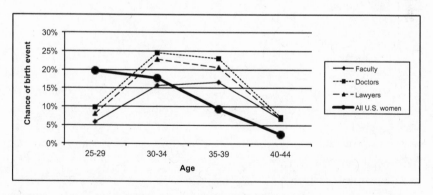

FIGURE 4.2 Female Birth Events by Age and Profession

Source: United States Census Public Use MicroSample, 2000. Reprinted from Nicholas H. Wolfinger, Marc Goulden, and Mary Ann Mason, "Alone in the Ivory Tower," *Journal of Family Issues* 31 (2010): 1652–1670, figure 1, by permission of Sage Publications.

Note: Differences by sex, age, and profession are statistically significant (p < .001).

N = 46,550

by women, generally finish their professional training at a younger age than do academics.[29] Perhaps more important, doctors and lawyers don't face "up or out" promotion decisions. Striving to make partner in an elite law firm is certainly no less stressful than trying to get tenure, but unsuccessful candidates don't lose their jobs and face relocation. This is the traumatic fate in store for failed tenure candidates, and it almost certainly weighs on the minds of assistant professors pondering parenthood. Physicians and attorneys also have higher salaries than do academics, which makes it easier for them to afford child care.[30] Sixty-one percent of female faculty and 59 percent of female lawyers are married or partnered, compared with 70 percent of physicians; fertility rates are naturally higher for married or partnered professionals.[31] This should give doctors an advantage over professors and attorneys when it comes to having children.

We conducted multivariate analysis to see if these and other differences could explain the baby gap between doctors, lawyers, and physicians. Adjusting for just age, race/ethnicity, and hours worked, female faculty are 41 percent less likely than female physicians to have a birth event. About 50 percent of this baby gap can be explained by professional differences in marital status, income, and spousal employment. If female doctors, lawyers, and professors all had the same levels of marriage, divorce, income, and spousal employment, faculty would be only 22 percent less likely than doctors to have a baby in the house. The story is somewhat different for men. Male professors are 21 percent less likely than male doctors to have birth events, but this disparity is entirely explained by differences in marital status, income, and spousal employment across the professions.

The census data do not allow us further insight into these results. We do not know if the differences in birth events can be attributed to the distinctive features of academic life described in this book. However, we suspect this is at least partially the case given the baby gap between female faculty on the tenure track and women working in other fast-track professions (doctors, lawyers, Ph.D. recipients working full time off the tenure-track). Academia has many unique job requirements. The "publish or perish" imperative isn't conducive to motherhood, as one psychiatry resident at the University of California noted in explaining the baby boom in her cohort of medical students: "I only have to put in my hours, I don't have to publish." Also, doctors and lawyers may have more options for part-time employment when caring for young children. According to a 2011 survey of 14,366 physicians conducted by the American Medical Association, 44 percent of female physicians now work part time.[32] Finally, it's possible that some academics are simply less interested in having large families, or perhaps children at all.

Fertility Intentions Thwarted

The SDR shows that 45 percent of tenured women faculty are childless, compared with 26 percent of their male colleagues.[33] Moreover, faculty have fewer kids than do doctors or lawyers. Although part of this baby gap appears to be a product of spousal employment and other measurable factors, female faculty nevertheless have especially few children. Before attempting to explain the baby gap we should pose the obvious questions, Is this what female faculty want? How many are childless by choice?

The answer, based on data from the University of California survey, is mixed. Approximately one-third of UC female faculty between the ages of forty and sixty are childless. More than a third of these childless female faculty wish they had had children. In contrast, only 22 percent of childless male faculty in the same age express comparable regrets about children. The gender difference is even greater for parents who wish they had had more children. Sixty-four percent of female faculty regretted having only one child, compared with 42 percent of men. Thirty-two percent of women with two children wanted more, compared with 13 percent of men. Even 24 percent of the mothers of large families—three or more kids—would have liked to have had more (the comparable figure for men is 8 percent). In the words of one female faculty member, "I waited to have children until I finished law school and started my career, so by the time I started, I was thirty-six and did not have enough time to reach the family size I desired—three children." But clearly, women—and indeed many men—at the University of California would like more children than their careers have allowed. This finding is corroborated by a recent study based on the top twenty Ph.D. programs in astronomy, physics, and biology in the United States.[34] The study's authors, sociologists Elaine Howard Ecklund and Anne Lincoln, find that faculty, postdocs, and graduate students alike wished they had more children, the women much more so than the men.

Not Enough Hours in the Day

It is no secret that many academics work long hours. In years gone by this was less of a barrier to parenthood, given that the bulk of academics used to be men. Thirty years ago fewer than one out of every four tenured or tenure-track faculty members was female.[35] Traditionally faculty wives provided the child care that allowed their husbands to work hard and still be fathers. Nowadays more women are professors, but these women, far more often than their male colleagues, have spouses who are working full time.[36] This means that most female academics cannot rely on their husbands for child care.

Economist and Nobel laureate Gary Becker postulates a direct conflict between the resources needed to perform both professional and home duties.[37]

Simply put, women have less time to devote to their careers when their domestic responsibilities include children. It is well established that women do much more around the house than men.[38] With dual-earner households now the norm, work-family conflict is prevalent among today's professionals, and abundant research has confirmed that this conflict extends to academics.[39] This is an intuitive finding, since we know that academics, particularly those employed at research universities, often work long hours. At the University of California system, two-thirds of faculty devote more than fifty hours a week to their jobs.[40]

Marriage by itself does not appear to pose a hardship to women's academic careers once they already have tenure-track jobs—married women academics publish more than their unmarried counterparts, and married women get tenure in the sciences at disproportionately high rates—but the story changes when children arrive.[41] Female faculty with children at the University of California devote fewer hours to their jobs than do childless women or male faculty, irrespective of children. According to data from our University of California survey, shown in figure 4.3, the average faculty mother works fifty-three hours a week. In contrast, childless women put in fifty-nine hours. Men with children work fifty-six hours; childless men, fifty-eight hours.[42] Children appear to affect women's scholarly productivity more than they do men's, given that faculty mothers put in several fewer hours a week than do other academics.[43] Other scholars offer similar findings: women with young children spend less time on research and publish less than do their childless colleagues.[44] As we have suggested, faculty mothers at the University of California devote less time to their careers because they have greater responsibilities at home. If the definition of work is expanded to include unpaid household labor, faculty mothers put in a total of ninety-four hours a week, far more than the hours worked by men or childless women. In total hours worked, childless women resemble faculty fathers more than either faculty mothers or childless male colleagues. Parenthood imposes a significant burden on already busy faculty women. With few opportunities to take a breather during the arduous early childhood years, many opt for smaller families, or no children at all.

Many faculty members who do have children report that their family responsibilities interfere with their professional activities, more so for women than for men. As table 4.1 shows, University of California mothers are far more likely than their male colleagues to report experiencing a great deal of stress in their parenting as a result of performing five different professional activities: conducting fieldwork or other research away from home, writing and publishing, attending conferences, attending seminars or meetings on campus, and teaching. This stress likely dissuades faculty mothers from having additional children. It also discourages their single colleagues from starting families. As one University of California scientist observed, "I feel as though academia (especially in the sciences) and family are somewhat incompatible. I think it can be done, but for most people it is not feasible."

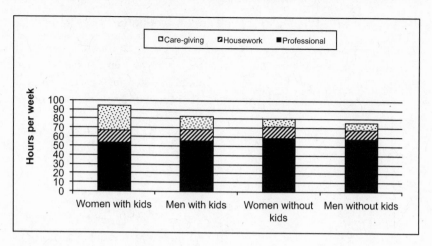

FIGURE 4.3 Professor Work Loads, Domestic and Professional, by Gender and Parental Status

Source: University of California Faculty Work and Family Survey, 2002–2003. Reprinted from Mary Ann Mason and Marc Goulden, "Marriage and Baby Blues: Redefining Gender Equity in the Academy," *Annals of the American Academy of Political and Social Science* 596 (2004): 86–103, figure 4, by permission of Sage Publications.

N = 4,239

TABLE 4.1.

University of California Faculty Parenting
Stress Resulting from Career Duties

Cause of "a great deal" of parenting stress	Women (%)	Men (%)
Doing fieldwork or other research away from home	48	27
Writing and publishing	48	29
Attending conferences or giving conference papers	46	22
Attending seminars or committee meetings	27	12
Meeting teaching obligations	22	13

N = 457–1,779

Source: University of California Faculty Work and Family Survey, 2002–2003.

What's So Special about Academia?

All full-time employment reduces the likelihood of having children. Our results have shown that women in tenure-track positions are even less likely to have kids than are female Ph.D. recipients employed in other fields. In the following pages we consider what might make academia especially discouraging to would-be mothers.

To the public, academia might seem an unusually family-friendly career choice. Aside from teaching, faculty rarely have to be at any given place at any given time, a schedule that would seem ideal for accommodating child care. Many academics, with the notable exception of bench scientists, can do the balance of their scholarly work at home or another location of their choosing. Many academics even take their children to work with them. So what's the problem?

Competition is a fundamental issue. There are finite plum positions, research grants, and opportunities for publication in top-tier scholarly journals. As a result, faculty mothers are competing with single and childless scholars, as well as fathers with stay-at-home spouses, for these limited resources and opportunities. Academics who work the longest hours will likely win the grants, publish in the top journals, and ultimately gain access to the highest-profile positions. Young children demand time and attention, and faculty parents often find that keeping up the pace and intensity of their work after a child is born is nearly impossible. Tenure can alleviate the worst pressures, but this generally occurs after the prime childbearing years. The zero-sum character of academia sets it apart from many other work environments, including some of those occupied by non-tenure-track Ph.D. employees. One woman neuroscientist at the University of California provided an eloquent statement of the problem, as well as its implications for family life:

> I think that the family unfriendly features stem largely from other aspects of the academic work environment such as emphasizing competition with others rather than emphasizing progress against the unknown. Science in particular is so macho that it favors anyone who has a secretary, long-term lab tech and someone at home to do all the family chores. Men in that position do not have much trouble raising a family and succeeding in academic science because they have a large "support staff" at home and work. Women are simply less likely to have this and so for them, combining academic science and family life [is more challenging].
>
> Given conditions like these it is not unreasonable to suspect that academia favors women who have chosen career over family.

Many academics are employed in jobs where teaching is more important than research and the environment is less Hobbesian than described by this female scientist. Still, many academics aspire to the top tier, where competition for resources is fierce. These are the departments that receive the largest share of federal funding and where most noteworthy scholarship is produced. Such departments foster working conditions that are unlikely to be kind to professors with substantial family obligations.

Both these characteristics—competition for limited resources and the demanding nature of the profession—contribute to the paucity of flexible employment options for research faculty. While other fast-track professionals such as doctors and lawyers can sometimes scale back on their work hours, this option, as we observed in the previous chapter, is generally unavailable to tenure-track faculty. Perhaps even more difficult than going part time is taking time off altogether. New mothers may get a semester or two off, but what then? The career structure of academia makes it hard to move in and out of the labor force. Tenure-track jobs can be hard to come by and few academics are willing to give up the security of a tenured professorship. Moreover, finding a new job after time off work probably entails a national move. As we suggested in chapter 2, perhaps the only academics who can readily move in and out of the labor force are adjuncts. For everyone else, the academic career system makes it difficult to take a few years off to raise children. It is this sort of concern that has led several authors to call for a more flexible career structure in the American labor market more generally.[45]

Even little everyday hassles can add up to create a sense that parenthood and academia are incompatible. Sometimes these barriers come from unexpected quarters. One is parking, long a source of faculty frustration (former Tufts University president Nils Y. Wessell once described his job as providing sex for undergraduates, football for alumni, and parking for his faculty.)[46] The problem for many faculty parents is simple: if they move their cars during the day, perhaps to take a sick child to the doctor, it becomes impossible to find a parking spot later on. More than one University of California faculty members raised this sort of concern in our survey. One female social scientist described how parking shortages in conjunction with the lack of nearby day care created considerable hardships:

> #1 on this list is infant care. There is exactly one daycare other than the university that is nearby and takes infants—Haley East. The traffic to and from Haley East can cause up [to] 2 hours a day in commuting. Plus, you are too far away to go on your lunch hour and nurse your kid—you have to pump in your office and leave bottles at the daycare. I would have preferred to see my daughter and nurse her myself. #2 isn't on the list: parking for parents. Once you have a spot up here, you can't leave, or you will never get a spot back again. This is a major hassle given #1 above. That is, you must get childcare off campus, but then you have zero flexibility in arrival and departure and return times because of parking. Here at my

building, if you don't arrive by 8:15 a.m., and stay all day, you will not be able to park. Need to take your kid to an appointment? Oh well, I guess you can't get back to your computer/students/office today!

A physical scientist had similar concerns, suspecting that his university's parking problems were politically motivated:

> it is impossible to take care of children, shop for groceries, go to medical appointments, etc. given the lack of parking at ucsb. responsibility for parking policy should be taken away from the radical leftist faculty and given to an impartial administrator. stop trying to perform social engineering with your transportation policies and instead pay attention to the day to day needs of faculty and staff.

We do not claim that parking problems by themselves dissuade female faculty members from having children, but mention them as an example of the unexpected challenges of being a faculty parent—we never anticipated that they would figure in respondents' open-ended survey responses.

Academia is a unique workplace. It offers tenure-track faculty members unparalleled freedoms, but its demanding nature, rigid career structure, and variegated professional responsibilities, and even the geographic isolation of its work sites, can challenge parents. Fathers have traditionally coped with these challenges with stay-at-home partners, or at the very least spouses who worked part time. Female faculty generally do not have these luxuries. As a result, many remain childless. Those who are parents frequently find themselves stretched to the breaking point. Perhaps this is why one female faculty member at the University of California offered this poignant advice for balancing work and family: "Only cry in private."

Peer Pressure

As we suggested in chapter 1, the difficulties would-be mothers face in academia often first become apparent in graduate school. They are even more obvious to new faculty. New Ph.D. recipients are in their early thirties, so childbirth quickly becomes problematic in purely biological terms.[47] Furthermore, assistant professors are often admonished by their peers to avoid children, or at least delay them until after tenure. One female social scientist at the University of California described her department's intense animosity toward faculty mothers:

> You will encounter hostility from your senior colleagues. When I requested maternity leave to have my second daughter, my department chair advised me to have an abortion. A subsequent chair tells female assistant professors that they have a choice between a second book and a child. When I cannot attend departmental events, I'm blamed and

ridiculed for spending too much time with my children or for using them as "an excuse." Because I commute over a[n] hour to work, I sometimes have to miss social events in the evening. My department is extremely critical and blames me for "not being around" even though I'm much more assiduous than my senior, above Step VI, male colleagues. I have tenure so they cannot fire me. But my colleagues do harass graduate students with children and make it clear to female Assistant Professors that they should not have children. The result is that few of my female colleagues have children, indeed, most are not even married. My advice to a first time faculty parent is to find a job at another university.

Another female faculty member in the arts described some of the many ways that motherhood interfered with her professional life on campus:

Children will most certainly curtail faculty presence and credibility within their department and their campus. As one of the only faculty in a department of fourteen faculty colleagues to have a child, I have found my situation as a single mother to have marginalized me from my colleagues and the community of research and scholarship. With a child under five, I have not been able to fully participate in the rigorous academic circle I was once in. In my promotion review, colleagues could not understand my drop in research, given that they have never had children and do not comprehend the degree of sacrifice made to scholarship when one chooses to be a parent.

Far more often than their colleagues of the opposite sex, faculty mothers will find themselves isolated. This creates an environment where faculty mothers feel uncomfortable and unaccepted, which doubtless further discourages childbearing.

What academic population is even more marginalized than faculty mothers? Faculty single mothers. These women, 20 percent of all tenured faculty mothers, face the same difficulties as their married colleagues, but without a partner to help with the time demands of childrearing, and only a single income to defray child care costs.[48] While single fathers may be admired for their devotion to their children, single mothers rarely receive similar praise. There is a double standard, as one female psychologist at the University of California described: "Be prepared to see single fathers being treated better than you are (as a mother). They are admired for putting their kids first, granted course reduction when they are making the transition to single parenting due to divorce. I've never seen a woman given this kind of accommodation." This raises an interesting point: criticism of faculty mothers may come from unexpected quarters. In particular, a faculty mother's potential critics are not necessarily men. Her childless female colleagues may be equally disapproving for several reasons. One is jealousy. If their own academic careers required childlessness, why should newer generations of female scholars have it any different? Accommodations for mothers may make their own sacrifice seem unwarranted, and childless faculty women may feel cheated or resentful. Other female faculty may be concerned that their unproductive female colleagues impugn the credibility of all women in academia.[49]

Many female respondents to the University of California survey recommended that faculty mothers maintain a low parenting profile. One woman in the social sciences suggested it was important not to convey the impression that parenting was affecting work in any way: "Don't ever let colleagues who are not staunch feminists know that you're on your way to pick up a child at day care, etc. Just say you're on the way to an appointment." Academia is obviously stressful for young mothers if they feel compelled to keep even their mundane daily activities secret from their colleagues. Another female social scientist acknowledged similar pressures: "I was afraid to ask for 'favors' because it would appear that I was being unprofessional. I hope things are better now. When I started my family, the staff had never dealt with a tenured woman, let alone a woman faculty member with family responsibilities." This quote illustrates another difficulty faculty mothers face: in many cases their universities simply are not used to dealing with them. As we will see shortly, this problem often extends to the very programs intended to make life easier for faculty parents.

Problems with Programs

We strongly believe that family-friendly accommodations can make life easier for faculty parents and thereby increase the representation of women in U.S. colleges and universities. These policies will be discussed in greater detail in chapter 6. For the moment, we will chronicle some of the difficulties surrounding their implementation, as well as new problems they can create when female academics ponder motherhood.

Our University of California team's 2007 tool kit contained a nonobvious suggestion: department chairs have to be aware of family-friendly programs offered by their universities.[50] Why? As the day-to-day managers of the faculty, chairs are generally in the best position to supervise the implementation of programs. If chairs do not know about programs or how they work, there is a good chance that rank-and-file faculty members won't know either. In the words of a male historian at the University of California: "One striking feature about work life programs/policies at this campus is the difficulty of obtaining regular and accurate information, from recruitment to retirement. Departments are the principal unit for most faculty here, but on the whole departments (as well as schools) are inadequately staffed to update and educate faculty. As it is, much of the information is passed on by way of an 'oral tradition.'" It works if you're in the loop, and tends to benefit those faculty (especially those with tenure) who have been around longer." This is of little consolation to graduate students, postdocs, and assistant professors, the academic populations most in need of family-friendly programs.

One of the authors of this book, Nick Wolfinger, had a similar experience at his university a number of years ago. Curious about the availability of family-friendly accommodations, he set about learning what was available. First he contacted his human resources office, but received no answers. Next he spoke to the benefits office staff, who also had no information about the university's family-friendly policies. Finally he contacted the women's resource center. They too had no idea about available accommodations for faculty parents. At this point the author stopped making calls—he had his answer. No one knew about the programs at his university. Fortunately things have changed for the better in the past few years.

Colleagues can be a useful source of advice regarding family-friendly programs. This works well in departments whose members are already using the programs, but can be problematic in heavily male departments or when new policies are introduced. Certainly would-be mothers in math, the physical sciences, and other traditionally male fields may have trouble learning about family accommodations, as one woman faculty member in a professional school observed: "I am still a new parent (2 weeks old first child) so I am new to all this. I found out that there was absolutely no knowledge about these issues (childbearing leave, tenure clock stop[age], etc . . .) in my school as I am the first woman with a newborn. I had to get the information myself." But the problem isn't limited to traditionally male fields, as one woman faculty member in art history noted: "It's also difficult to work in a dept. in which all of one's colleagues are childless. I'd offer as advice to seek out your colleagues that have families—they are a very important source of emotional and professional support." Similar sentiments were voiced by a woman in engineering: "This topic isn't easy to talk about with others in the Department b/c I am in a male-dominated field and I feel a pressure to not express my thoughts about balancing job and family."

Even when faculty and department chairs are aware of family-friendly policies, faculty parents may still avoid them if they perceive a stigma associated with their use. Some male professors at the University of California worried that accommodations for faculty parents would create more work for everyone else. These concerns were not directed specifically at faculty mothers, but they seem to be the obvious targets given that faculty fathers are more likely to have stay-at-home partners to provide child care. One man felt that faculty members should not receive special treatment for what he felt was a lifestyle choice:

> [I] have not been able to have children in my attempts to do so, and have not been terribly interested in the project since then. Having children

is both a lifestyle choice and biologically/medically contingent on good health. I am not enthusiastic about excessively subsidizing others' lifestyle choices no matter how noble they are. In my department, I think we too often bend over backwards for those with children, and the few of us without end up doing a lot of extra work and tasks, especially in maintaining the intellectual life of the department and being available for students, all evening activities (such as recruitment dinners), etc. We are forced into their meeting times, etc. I really do support family-friendly policies in general, but think we go too far sometimes in this direction. At other universities at which I have taught, parents on the faculty did not have such power to shape everything. The part-time stuff worries me if it goes on too long and is used too much because it puts more pressure on the singles, the childless and the empty nesters (which can be a small group sometimes) to do the teaching and research and attend colloquia and other matters that keep a department vibrant and intellectually alive. I suppose it is all about finding a balance.

Another male faculty member likened children to other excuses his colleagues employed to get out of teaching and committee responsibilities: "The problem is that when faculty with children teach less, serve on fewer committees, etc, the rest of us are expected to pick up the slack. There is no way around this. Everyone has an excuse for why they need a lighter teaching and committee load: young children, sick parents, pain in the ass spouse, heavy research, lots of travel, funding raising, etc. In the end, the only fair system is equal pay for equal work regardless of the family situation."

These examples suggest that family-friendly programs can backfire by fostering perceived inequities—and sometimes real inequities. Who is going to pick up the slack? As we suggest in the conclusion, universities have to ensure that programs are adequately funded. They also need to be used by fathers as well as mothers, so that they become part of university culture. Often this hasn't been the case: faculty parents of both sexes have proved reluctant to use family-friendly programs. Mothers may fear that they will be viewed as failing to do their fair share of the work. Even more common is the perception that faculty who use programs will be seen as weak and therefore not deserving of tenure. The following advice, from a woman in a University of California professional school, highlights this common fear: "Don't have children until after tenure. Don't use the extra one year on the clock unless absolutely required because male faculty interpret this as some combination of: She's not tough enough to do it or let's evaluate her as someone with seven years experience rather than someone with six years who has been given a year extra. I'm sure this doesn't happen in every department, but I have observed it happen[ing] in mine." Fortunately this does not seem to be the case in every department. Many faculty members at the University of California report having successfully used family-friendly policies there. In the words of a woman faculty member in the sciences: "Do not listen to (usually male) faculty members who tell you that you should not take advantage of the policies that are there. I have not noticed any discrimination/drawbacks for having stopped the clock or taking a 6-week leave for birth of a child, although at least one faculty member advised me not to stop the clock." Another female faculty member was even more emphatic about the need for family-friendly programs: "Had I been fully aware that there were no options to stop or slow the clock with several small children I would never have accepted my position. The only reason that I haven't resigned is that my research has gone well enough that I may make tenure after all, but it has been a terrible experience for my marriage and my children. I would never do it again, and I can't help feeling bitter that having two children under five counted for nothing."

It can be extremely difficult to balance a tenure-track faculty appointment with a young child, not to mention a spouse working full time. Family-friendly accommodations can make the difference between a failed tenure case and a successful career—or perhaps also between a failed relationship and a happy home life. We suspect they sometimes affect a faculty member's decision to have (more) children; this appears to have been the case at UC Berkeley, although we cannot know for certain. Many schools have only adopted family-friendly programs in the past few years. Not all faculty members know about them, and they can sometimes have unintended adverse consequences.

Conclusion

We have already shown that families keep women out of the academy. This chapter has shown that the academy keeps women out of families. Female professors are far less likely than either their male colleagues or female Ph.D. recipients in the second tier to be married or have children. Twelve years subsequent to Ph.D. receipt, 70 percent of male faculty are married with children, compared with just 40 percent of their female colleagues.[51] Women are also more likely than men to be single parents. These results are summarized in figure 4.4.

Female Ph.D. recipients are far less likely than their male colleagues to have children or be married at the start of their careers, and far more likely to be divorced. To a considerable extent these gender differences are the product of Ph.D.-level employment in general, not an academic career in particular. All female Ph.D. recipients employed full time have higher divorce rates and lower rates of marriage and childbearing than those of their male colleagues, or women in the second tier. This having been said, female professors have even higher divorce rates and lower marriage rates—at the beginning of their

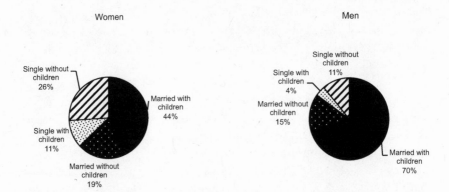

FIGURE 4.4 Family Status of Tenured Faculty Twelve Years after Ph.D. Receipt

Source: Survey of Doctorate Recipients, National Science Foundation, 1979–1995. Reprinted from Mary Ann Mason and Marc Goulden, "Marriage and Baby Blues: Redefining Gender Equity in the Academy," *Annals of the American Academy of Political and Social Science* 596 (2004): 86–103, figure 1, by permission of Sage Publications.

N = 37,142

careers, but not later—than those of their peers employed full time in nonteaching positions. In contrast, the "professor penalty" for having children comes later: female professors are less likely to have children than are female Ph.D.s employed elsewhere.

It is no surprise that employed women have fewer husbands or kids. Many of these women probably made choices while in graduate school about whether to first pursue families or careers.[52] The professor penalty to marriage comes as a greater surprise. We suspect that the cross-national relocation required by an academic job represents an additional hardship imposed by an academic career. Women intending to take academic jobs may forego marriage to their significant others or avoid forming enduring relationships in the first place. Conversely, a tenure-track job offer might provide the impetus to leave an unfulfilling marriage or other serious relationship.

The story changes once female Ph.D. recipients start full-time jobs. Marriage becomes less likely for all women who work full time, and faculty women aren't any different. Career employment may delay marriage, obviate it altogether, or reflect an earlier decision to pursue jobs instead of husbands. At this point in their lives professors become even less likely to have children than are Ph.D.-level women employed full time elsewhere, including nonteaching academic jobs, the private sector, and the government, as well as doctors and lawyers. Perhaps this is the time in their lives when women finally realize the full extent to which academia is hostile to motherhood. Female assistant professors struggling to get tenure may also delay having children, perhaps until it is too late. Finally, female tenure-stream faculty have lower divorce rates than those of women Ph.D.s employed full time elsewhere. We have little insight into why this is the case, although it does cast doubt on the notion that the two-body problem increases the divorce rate once women have already started tenure-track professorships. The two-body problem is probably most salient at the beginning of women's academic careers, when they have higher divorce rates than those of female doctorate recipients employed elsewhere. Thereafter female professors probably have higher divorce rates than those of their male colleagues for the same reasons that all full-time female workers do, most notably work-family conflict.

Data from our survey of University of California faculty shed light on these findings. The UC data show that academia is often an extraordinarily hostile environment for faculty mothers—just keep in mind the pregnant academic bluntly told to have an abortion by her department's chairman. Tenure-track employment also doesn't offer the same opportunities for part-time work or time out of the labor force that many other working mothers rely on. These challenges come on top of the constant struggle to balance work and family that the majority of American wives and mothers now face. Even the special programs designed to benefit faculty mothers come with their own costs, sometimes failing to accomplish their intended goals.

It is difficult to know the full extent of the costs academic women end up paying. Certainly female professors have fewer children than they would have liked. We know from the broader scholarly literature that unmarried academics are denied the numerous social, emotional, economic, and even physiological benefits conferred by marriage.[53] It is also clear that single professors, and particularly single women, pay a price that is unique to academia. First, academia generally requires a transnational move, and relocation poses special challenges for single people. Second, being single can remove an academic from his or her department's professional life. In our experience, participation in departmental life is often necessary for moving up the academic ranks. Yet at the same time it is assumed that being single is a convenient excuse for being saddled with more work. Department chairs can easily make requests of unmarried faculty—for instance, teaching evening courses or entertaining job candidates—that that they might be less willing to impose on their colleagues who are married or parents. All this demonstrates that there are costs to being an unmarried or childless academic.

Much of this applies to men as well as women. Keep in mind that many male faculty members at the University of California have fewer children than they might like. Male faculty also have fewer kids than do doctors or lawyers. Even for men, far more likely than women to have stay-at-home spouses, academia does not appear to be as family friendly as we might like.

But the familial costs are far greater for women. Many are indeed alone in the ivory tower. They are less likely to be married or have children than are their male colleagues. Many express remorse about not having more children, or not having any at all. Being single can make it harder for faculty to be fully integrated into the social and professional lives of their academic departments. Certainly more women are becoming professors than ever before, but it is important to view their professional gains in the context of their familial losses. The failure to have it all, suggests the *New York Times* columnist Gail Collins, is vital to understanding the recent history of American women.[54]

5

Life after Tenure

Securing a tenure-track position represents one of the most profound moments of an academic's career. After long years as a student, one suddenly becomes a titled professional. Next looms the challenge of a lifetime: getting tenure. On completion of a demanding probationary period, the academic gets a brass ring: one of the world's most secure jobs. The perquisites of the position are renowned, just as the blood, toil, tears, and sweat it often takes to get there are notorious. Subsequent to tenure comes a measure of security, yet still more hurdles. Scholars aspiring to the rank of full professor must continue to burnish their professional credentials. And at most schools, meaningful pay raises are contingent on continued scholarly productivity.

This chapter examines gender differences in academic careers after the pressure cooker pre-tenure years. In particular, we are interested in how marriage and children affect men's and women's salaries and promotion to full professor. We have already demonstrated wide-ranging gender differences in how young Ph.D. recipients enter the professoriate and obtain tenure. Do these differences extend into the midcareer years? How do marriage and children affect promotion to full professor and faculty salaries? We also explore retirement and the role of family considerations at the end of academic careers.

These topics are of special interest, given the paucity of previous research. Most higher education scholars have focused on the early career years (studies of the income gender gap are an exception).[1] To an extent this is understandable because the most conspicuous gender difference in the professoriate is simply the glaring absence of women. But as the previous chapter has shown, simply achieving gender parity isn't enough. We need also be concerned with how women fare once they receive tenure and become ensconced in their academic careers.

Promotion to Full Professor

We would expect family considerations to matter less when men and women seek promotion to the rank of full professor. The vast majority of academicians will be in their forties or older when that promotion becomes a possibility. According to the 2006 Survey of Doctorate Recipients, only 2 percent of academics become full professors within ten years of receiving their doctorates.[2] This means that promotion to full professor becomes an issue for most women when they are beyond their childbearing years. Many academics will have children in the house around the time they seek promotion, but these children are likely to be older and in school and not requiring the same degree of care that babies and toddlers do. By now, most of the academics who will ever get married have probably already done so.[3] Dual-career concerns have likely faded, since scholars seeking promotion to full professor will have been at their jobs for a number of years; presumably their partners are equally ensconced in their careers and not looking to relocate. Although family considerations can still affect women's ability to get ahead, there should be fewer challenges at this juncture than for women seeking academic jobs or working towards tenure. This was the belief of one woman faculty member in the social sciences at the University of California: "Family obligations have slowed down my research and overall career, but they haven't ended it—I still got tenure, am still a productive researcher. And I expect that the impact of parenthood will diminish somewhat as my kids become older and more independent (my younger child is 2). I think this is a great outcome—it would be unrealistic for kids not to slow down a career, especially a mother's career. Yes, I've won fewer awards, have a somewhat lower profile, have had fewer outside offers than I would have without kids. But I haven't been forced to make the hard choice between only a career and only family."

Only 19 percent of full professors in the sciences, and just 24 percent overall, are women.[4] The Survey of Doctorate Recipients sheds light on this disparity. Adjusting for various differences between respondents, we find that female associate professors in all fields are 21 percent less likely to get promoted in comparison with their male colleagues. Marriage and children, young or old, do not affect the chances of promotion differently for men and women.[5] In fact, we find marriage increases the likelihood of promotion to full professor by 23 percent for both sexes.

The benefits of marriage for promotion prospects are easy to understand. As noted in previous chapters, marriage generally makes workers more productive. Married scholars publish more than their unmarried colleagues. Indeed, chapter 3 showed that married academics in the sciences are more likely to get tenure. Marriage does not represent a career obstacle for female midcareer scholars in the same way it does for newly minted Ph.D.s poised for a transnational move. As suggested in chapter 2, spousal employment represents a formidable obstacle to women on the academic job market but does not appear to be an issue later on in their careers.

It is also easy to understand why children, who play such a critical role in women's professional fortunes earlier on, make no difference when women come up for promotion to full professor. At this point in their careers, few women still have infants or toddlers at home. Keep in mind also that mothers who have made it this far in their careers are a select group, perhaps better equipped to negotiate the challenges of balancing families and demanding jobs. This does not mean, of course, that no women are adversely affected. Some women (and, indeed, some men) may deliberately choose not to seek promotion in order to spend more time with their families, as one woman in the arts at the University of California explained: "I decided to remain at the Associate level because of [sic] my priority of family life was higher than making an international reputation in my profession." But scholars who deliberately make this choice appear to be in the minority.

If marriage and children cannot account for why women have trouble getting promoted, than what can? Until recently, social science has not had much luck in coming up with an answer.[6] The gender gap in promotion rates cannot be explained by easily measured differences between male and female academics. For lack of a better explanation, scholars have generally concluded that discrimination was preventing women from getting promoted: maybe men are fine with having women as colleagues, but not at the upper echelons. Yet recent research has cast doubt on the prevalence of discrimination in the modern professoriate.[7]

A 2011 report by a research team headed by sociologists Joya Misra and Jennifer Hickes Lundquist points to the first compelling argument about why so many women get stuck at associate professor: the unequal allotment of university service.[8] According to Misra and Lundquist, three-fourths of female associate professors at the University of Massachusetts have held major service commitments, compared with only half the men. Thirty-five percent of the women but just 17 percent of the men had served as a director of undergraduate studies. Being undergraduate director is a time-devouring, low-status position that probably does not help associate professors get promoted. Equally noteworthy, 15 percent of the women and *none* of the men had chaired their departments as associate professors (among full professors almost three times as many men had been chairs).[9] It is hard to imagine many professors doing the research necessary for promotion when saddled with the heavy administrative burden of running an academic department. Overall, women associate professors spent much more of their time teaching and doing service than did their male colleagues. Compared with the men, women spent an average of three more hours a week with students and almost five more hours a week on service to their universities. That is almost eight hours a week that women cannot spend doing the research that might otherwise get them promoted. As a result, female associate professors end up devoting only a quarter of their working hours doing research; in contrast, the men spend 37 percent of their time on scholarship. And these inequities do indeed matter. Women who serve as undergraduate directors take more than three years longer than the average faculty member to move from Ph.D. to the rank of full professor (and recall that more than one-third of female associate professors serve in this capacity).

Misra and Lundquist make clear that women associate professors aren't assuming their heavy service loads by choice. Indeed, most of the women in their study voiced dissatisfaction with the amount of service they do. But they end up getting stuck with it anyway, as one associate professor at the University of Massachusetts related: "Because departments try to shield junior faculty from service, and full professors are usually in a better position to say 'no' when asked, associate professors often carry disproportionately heavy service loads compared to their junior and senior colleagues." Perhaps men are simply better at saying no when asked to assume heavy service responsibilities. Alternately, the allocation of service positions may reflect a self-fulfilling prophecy: academic administrators assume that tenured women won't be promoted, so they get loaded up with service positions that ensure they don't get promoted—while their male colleagues, lacking heavy service burdens, go on to become full professors.

Keep in mind that these findings are based on only one institution. Perhaps there is something unusual about the University of Massachusetts. Nevertheless, the Misra and Lundquist study provides the most compelling evidence that has been offered to date about why so many women academics stagnate at the rank of associate professor.

The Ultimate Promotion: College President

For most academics, a full professorship marks the highest rung on the academic ladder. But a small percentage will climb even higher, into the ranks of academic administrators. We would expect fewer women administrators simply on the basis of the pipeline problem: fewer women than men get academic jobs, fewer still get tenure, and even fewer become full professors, generally a requirement for holding high academic office. Yet women hold the same share of full professorships as university presidencies. We base this assessment on a 2007 report by the American Council on Education, *The American College President*, that included information on 2,148 college and university presidents (unfortunately we have no comparable source of information on lesser administrative offices, such as deanships).[10]

In recent years there have been several prominent female college presidents. Shirley M. Tilghman and Drew Gilpin Faust became the first woman presidents at, respectively, Princeton and Harvard. Judith Rodin served for many years as the

first female president at the University of Pennsylvania; she was succeeded by
another woman, Amy Guttman. Yet another female scholar, Ruth Simmons, has
been at the helm at Brown University for the past ten years. However, the Ivy
League isn't typical. In 2006, just 23 percent of college and university presidents
were women—and far more women hold presidencies than used to be the case.
In 1986 just 10 percent of college and university presidents were women. The
downside, according to *The American College President*, is that the rate of growth
has slowed: "The share of new appointees who are women has not changed
appreciably since these data were first collected in 1998."[11]

The American College President offers data on marriage and children that are
fully consistent with our results. Sixty-three percent of female college presidents
are married compared with 89 percent of the men. Twenty-four percent of the
women presidents are divorced or have never been married; this holds true
for just 7 percent of the men. Sixty-eight percent of female college presidents
have children, compared with 91 percent of their male colleagues. Finally, three
times as many women college presidents (15 percent, versus 5 percent for men)
reported that they "altered career for family."

The average college president is sixty years old, up from a mean of fifty-
two in 1986. This means that most college presidents—and in particular the
women—are done with having children. They are also unlikely to get married
if they have never been married before.[12] Assuming that a college presidency is
not causing women to remain unmarried and childless, female academics likely
become college presidents *because* they remained single and childless. Ascending to the highest academic ranks takes time and hard work; it's easier for
women to devote the necessary effort to achieve this career pinnacle when they
don't have children and don't face constraints imposed by a spouse's career. We
should also keep in mind the findings presented in previous chapters. The pool
of female academics from which college presidents are drawn already contains
disproportionately few married women and few women with children.

The findings of *The American College President* are mixed and warrant
guarded optimism. It is certainly good news that more women than ever before
are becoming college and university presidents. Yet at this level of the academic
food chain women endure the same inequities concerning marriage and children as do rank-and-file faculty members. This comes as little surprise and
provides yet more evidence that we have a long way to go toward leveling the
playing field for women academics, especially those with families.

Income

A touchstone of inequality research in the United States is the gender wage gap.
As of 2009, women full-time workers made only seventy-seven cents on the

male dollar, a figure that hasn't changed much in the past few years.[13] Although scholars disagree on the reasons for this persistent inequity, most attribute the gap mainly to differences in occupation, industry, and job experience.[14] In recent years, a growing literature has emphasized the economic consequences of having children. Several studies document that each child produces an incremental wage penalty for mothers.[15]

Academia is no different from other professions, as the gender income gap has long been part of the landscape.[16] Why is this the case? Much of the income disparity seems to be attributable to the kinds of jobs women hold. Faculty in predominantly female disciplines (for example, art and social work) earn less than those in male disciplines (for example, engineering and dentistry).[17] Women are more likely to be employed at the kinds of institutions, namely baccalaureate and junior colleges, that don't pay as well as graduate universities. Female faculty make ninety-six cents on the male dollar at community colleges, but just seventy-eight cents on the male dollar at research universities.[18] And as we have shown, men are far more likely than women to hold higher academic rank. Tenured faculty make more than assistant professors; tenure-stream faculty make more than adjuncts. This all adds up in the long run.

Do marriage and children play a role here? The Survey of Doctorate Recipients (SDR) allows us to answer this question.[19] We follow the research strategy established by Michelle Budig, Paula England, Jane Waldfogel, and others by examining the income penalty produced by each child.[20] The results are straightforward. After controlling for various differences between respondents, we find that each child incrementally decreases women's salaries by 1 percent. Children exert no effect, positive or negative, on men's salaries.

This is not a large economic penalty for women compared with the difference produced by academic rank or job type (for example, community college versus research university). Nevertheless, it represents one more way in which children adversely affect women's academic careers while having no corresponding negative effect on men's careers. Even after holding constant academic rank, differences between universities, and years of professional experience, the finding is that each child decreases female faculty's salaries. Furthermore, this salary penalty adds up over time. Women start their academic careers with lower salaries than those of their male colleagues.[21] Often raises are calculated as a percentage of a faculty member's current salary. Motherhood therefore guarantees cumulatively smaller increases over time. Women are also less likely to get promoted and enjoy the associated salary bump. In the long run, women's salaries will lag far behind men's, as one *Chronicle of Higher Education* forum participant observed:

> Having been through a major gender inequity survey on this campus
> (conducted by a faculty member who is a consultant to several states

and corporations with policies about pay equity), I have to wonder if you
realize how much money a female faculty member may have lost, when
compared to male faculty with the same length of time at a college and
similar publication records, over the fifteen or twenty years of work at
the college. I'm speaking of a cumulative loss, money lost every year:
hired at a smaller salary, promoted more slowly, fewer merit raises, and
always the same percentage increase (per year, or with promotion) but
with the much smaller base to begin with (from hire, from smaller merit
increases, from extra years before tenure and before promotion). In a
case like this, it would take a good many years earning $20,000 extra per
year to make up for the total amount lost in the 15 or more years between
hire and promotion to full professor.[22]

As this web post suggests, women faculty never catch up to men when it comes
to salary.[23] To explore this idea we calculated average salaries at retirement for
male and female faculty based on SDR data extending from 1985 to 1995.[24] In 1995
constant dollars, men retired with an average salary of $79,688 whereas women
retired with an average of only $61,847—a difference of 29 percent. This disparity
represents a lifetime of lower earnings and cumulatively smaller raises. Nor has
the situation likely to have improved much in recent years.[25]

Why are children costly to female academics? As we and others have suggested, children may decrease scholarly productivity for women.[26] One University of California social scientist indeed worried that her parenting obligations
would ultimately affect her salary: "As a new parent, I feel increased anxiety
about publications and perceived performance. Parenthood has slowed down
my academic productivity, and I worry that this shift in my ability to get work
done will negatively affect salary and tenure." More generally, children mean
time away from work. As we showed in chapter 2, even mothers who obtain
ladder-rank positions may have waited longer to get their jobs. Women who
already have tenure-track jobs may go on leave when they give birth. At the very
least, they are probably doing less of the research that might otherwise increase
their salaries. Scholars who publish more get paid more (although this might be
a product of the fact that scholars who publish are more likely to work at schools
that pay well, namely, research universities).[27] And, there is evidence that time
out of the labor force reduces the salaries of women more broadly.[28]

The most common means of getting a sizeable salary increase in academia
is to get promoted. However, this cannot account for income disparities for full
professors, which tend to be larger than at lower academic ranks.[29] At this stage
in the academic game, the best way to secure a big raise is to receive a job offer
from another university. As we noted earlier in this book, the responsibilities of
childrearing make it harder for women to go on job interviews and harder for
them to attend the academic conferences that might produce such interviews.

Spousal employment may also prevent female faculty from pursuing more lucrative opportunities. Perhaps for these reasons, women are far less likely than men to pursue job offers. Fifty-three percent of married faculty mothers at the University of California say that family considerations have prevented them from seeking new jobs outside their current region of residence, compared with just 24 percent of the men.[30] This was the case for one female academic at the University of California: "I have not realistically been able to pursue outside job offers and this has definitely hurt my salary. Even though I'm a professor Step VII, my off-scale salary is far below that of others who pursued outside offers." If children and husbands prevent women from going on the academic job market right out of graduate school, they probably make it harder to do so later on.

As observed in previous chapters, faculty with children spend much more time providing care than do their childless colleagues; mothers spend much more time engaged in caregiving than do fathers. Moreover, faculty mothers continue to spend substantial hours providing care into their late fifties, as figure 5.1 illustrates. This has two implications for our discussion of the child-income penalty for female faculty. First, even full professors in the prime of their careers may have trouble getting away from their families to conduct research or to go on the job talks that might produce lucrative counteroffers. Second, the economic costs of children extend well into women's careers.

Marriage benefits both men and women in the salary department, but the rewards are not equal. Marriage increases the salaries of men by 3 percent, but by only 1 percent for women.[31] Why do men derive three times the pecuniary

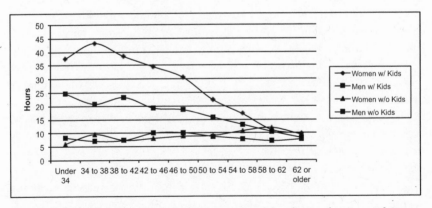

FIGURE 5.1 Average Time Spent Weekly in Care Provision, by Gender, Parental Status, and Age

Source: University of California Faculty Work and Family Survey, 2002–2003; Mary Ann Mason, Marc Goulden, and Nicholas H. Wolfinger, "Babies Matter: Pushing the Gender Equity Revolution Forward," in *The Balancing Act: Gendered Perspectives in Faculty Roles and Work Lives,* ed. S. J. Bracken et al., 9–30 (Sterling, VA: Stylus, 2006), figure 1.7.

N = 4,060

benefit from marriage that women get? The most likely reason is that the men "specialize in making money."[32] Recall that 56 percent of male faculty members have spouses that are employed full time, compared with 89 percent of female faculty members.[33] It's understood within many marriages that the man will be the primary—and perhaps exclusive—wage earner (At the same time, it should be acknowledged that modern couples share more caregiving responsibilities.)[34] So couples split their responsibilities: the man pursues professional success over almost everything else, while the woman works in paid employment but also assumes traditionally feminine duties like cooking, cleaning, arranging social activities, and "kin-keeping" (staying in touch with extended family members) and, perhaps, ramps down work to accommodate children.[35]

Retirement

Perhaps no part of the academic life course is as little understood as retirement. Scholars have examined early retirement programs, the end of mandated retirement, retirement intentions, the characteristics of retired faculty, pension preferences, and phased retirement and other incentive programs, but have said relatively little about the individual factors that affect retirement.[36] This lack of scholarly attention is puzzling, since retirement garners so much attention from both faculty and universities. The average American faculty member is fifty years old, and retirement is likely on the minds of many professors: almost half of those aged fifty-five and older say it is at least somewhat likely that they will retire within three years.[37] Academic administrators also take a keen interest in faculty retirement. Older faculty members have higher salaries, so universities can save money by replacing retiring faculty with assistant professors or adjuncts.[38] Finally, it is worth pointing out that tenure creates a retirement dynamic that is virtually unique among the professions. As one faculty member pointed out on the *New York Times* website: "One of the attractions of the professoriate is the option to choose when to retire. That and tenure are part of the total compensation package I accepted. I traded 'take-home salary' for independence and job security. If both of these are taken away from professors, 'take-home salary' will have to increase to maintain total compensation."[39] As this post suggests, faculty retirement is unique in that tenured professors are almost never forced out of their jobs.

Despite professed intentions to the contrary, most academics do not retire early. The SDR follows respondents until they turn seventy-six and therefore provides an excellent resource for studying faculty retirement. As figure 5.2 suggests, almost no faculty call it quits in the couple of years after age fifty-five, when our data start.[40] Even by age sixty-five, only 28 percent of faculty have retired. The retirement rate gradually increases but does not shoot up quickly until faculty are in their early seventies.

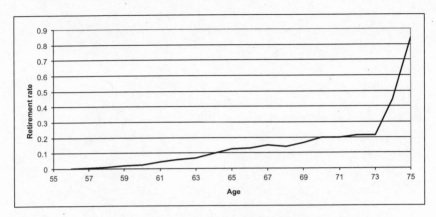

FIGURE 5.2 Retirement Rates by Age for College and University Faculty

Source: Survey of Doctorate Recipients, National Science Foundation, 1981–1995.

N = 9,426

According to the 2004 National Study of Postsecondary Faculty, 89 percent of faculty report being somewhat or very satisfied with their jobs.[41] This figure does not vary much by gender or rank and perhaps helps to explain why many faculty retire relatively late compared with other Americans.[42] As one professor put it: "Depending upon where you work, there's much to miss about employment in academia. You lose the daily chats with colleagues, the water cooler banter, the status or legitimacy of affiliation, and the sustained activity of regular work. There's the potential to 'rot' in retirement, where the complete freedom of time makes one unmotivated to achieve or thrive. I've never retired, not even close, but my most unproductive and unhappy professional periods come when I have no constraints on my free time."[43] It is telling that many academics continue to work long hours into their fifties and sixties, presumably well past the age at which they were tenured, when such long hours might have been necessary. Figure 5.3 charts weekly hours of work for tenure-track faculty in the sciences (including the social sciences). From doctoral receipt until their late fifties, science faculty work around fifty hours a week. Only in the seventh decade of life do average work hours fall to forty. These long work hours lead us to believe that a fair number of academics are decidedly ambivalent about retirement even late into their professional lives. Indeed, some are dead set against it, like this professor revealed in a post on the *New York Times* website: "We're all living longer, healthy lives, and nobody wants to walk away from their job and career, simply because they have reached what used to be 'retirement age.' These aren't creaky old antiques who are still teaching, but rather productive people who do not want to be kicked aside. I'm sixty, and still teaching

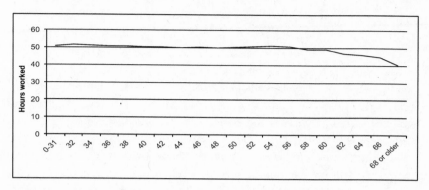

FIGURE 5.3 Average Hours Worked Weekly by Science and Social Science Tenure-Track Faculty, by Age

Source: Survey of Doctorate Recipients, National Science Foundation, 2003; Marc Goulden, Mary Ann Mason, Karie Frasch, and the Center for American Progress, "Staying Competitive: Patching America's Leaky Pipeline in the Sciences," Berkeley Center on Health, Economic, and Family Security, University of California, Berkeley, 2009, figure II, http://www.americanprogress.org/issues/2009/11/women_and_sciences.html.

N = 9,275

(albeit not tenured), and I can tell you that no one is removing me unless (1) I'm dead or (2) they've got either a court order, or a bulldozer."[44]

What factors might determine which academics retire earlier or later, and how big a role does gender play? Previous chapters have described noteworthy gender differences, so there is little reason to suspect that retirement should be any different. We know that female academics are less likely to have children than their male colleagues; in turn, academics with dependents are far less likely to have plans to retire.[45] Compared with men, female professors are more likely to hold second-tier jobs, and academics in positions in which their primary responsibility is teaching expect to retire earlier than their colleagues at research universities.[46] In addition, it is possible that salary inequities may affect gender differences in retirement timing, given that lower-paid academics are more likely to have retirement plans.[47] Finally, if work-family issues are salient before and during academic careers, they may also be consequential near the end. In particular, sociologists James Raymo and Megan Sweeney showed that workers in their fifties report a stronger preference for early retirement when perceived work-family conflict is high.[48] This could explain why women faculty members might retire earlier than do men.

Our SDR analysis examines faculty who are of retirement age, between fifty-six and seventy-five years old.[49] To our surprise, gender has no effect whatsoever on faculty retirement rates; men retire neither earlier nor later than do women. Marriage and parenthood both influence the chances of retirement and do so equally for men and women. Compared with their colleagues who have never been married, married faculty have 79 percent higher odds of retirement. The obvious interpretation is that married faculty members retire to spend more time with their spouses, but this isn't entirely clear cut: separated and divorced faculty are also more likely to be retired than are their never married colleagues, by a margin of 58 percent. One possibility is that divorced faculty members have live-in partners.[50] In general, nonmarital cohabitation has been common among the formerly married.[51] Still, we would expect separated and divorced faculty to have retirement rates closer to those of faculty who have never been married.

Children make retirement less likely. The 6 percent of retirement-age faculty who still have minor children at home are 43 percent less likely to retire in comparison with their childless colleagues. Moreover, faculty parents whose adult children have left home are 28 percent less likely to retire than are childless faculty. The interpretation is straightforward: children cost money, so faculty parents stay on in their jobs to support their families (or to build up savings that had been depleted in caring for children). Financial need is presumably greatest for the small number of retirement-age faculty who still have children at home—this is why they have lower retirement rates in comparison with faculty whose children have already left the nest. Presumably the retirement-age faculty who still have minor children at home are mostly men; recall figure 4.1, which showed continued male fertility twenty or more years after men were hired on as assistant professors at the University of California. Finally, the low retirement rates for faculty parents provide strong evidence against the notion that these faculty retire earlier in order to spend time with their grandchildren.

Retirement appears to be the only major career transition in academia in which gender makes no difference.[52] This comes as a surprise to us: women are less likely to get tenure-track jobs, are less likely to gain tenure, are less likely to be promoted, and make less money. Perhaps retirement is different because it represents the professional transition most likely to be under the total control of the faculty member herself. Dual-career constraints are unlikely to be an issue by the time retirement rolls around. Hiring or promotion committees aren't involved. There's no longer any need to care for young children. Although family does make a difference, men and women are affected equally. As we have seen, this is rarely the case in higher education.

Conclusion

Faculty members typically have long careers. Getting a foot in the academic door is a pivotal moment in the academic life course—and, we have shown, the point at which many women scholars fall by the wayside—but it is only the start of many years in the profession. Most studies of gender equity in the academy have not unreasonably focused on these early career years. Yet more challenges lie ahead for faculty members.

Midcareer is the time in an academic career when family considerations finally take a backseat to professional development. Most faculty who will ever get married have probably already done so. Subsequent to tenure, faculty have been in their jobs for a number of years, so dual-career conflict is usually less problematic than it is for recent Ph.D. recipients seeking their first jobs. Children are likely older, so they don't provide the same sort of challenge that they do for new mothers struggling simultaneously to get tenure and care for infants or toddlers.

Yet female faculty continue to lag behind their male colleagues in various ways. They are less likely to get promoted to the rank of full professor, an inequity that cannot be explained by family formation. Instead, recent research suggests that women sometimes languish in the associate ranks because they take on far more university service than do their male colleagues. Women, especially married women and mothers, are less likely than men to rise to the top of the heap to become college presidents. Female professors make far less money than do their male colleagues, and this inequity is exacerbated by children. Each child in the family incrementally decreases female wages but has no effect on male faculty's salaries.

One bit of good news is the salutary effects of marriage in the midcareer years. Marriage substantially increases the chances of promotion to full professor for both men and women. Both sexes also enjoy higher salaries when married, although men predictably receive much greater financial benefits from marriage than do women. These results are fully consistent with the broader scholarly literature on marriage. Marriage has benefits for men and women in all careers, and academics do not seem to be any different in their midcareer years.

Academic retirement is the only major transition or outcome explored in this book that doesn't seem to be gendered. Male and female faculty retire later than most Americans and at equal rates. Family considerations affect all retirement-age faculty in predictable ways. Married faculty retire sooner, presumably to spend time with their spouses, while faculty parents retire later, presumably because children are expensive.

6

Toward a Better Model

When Ezra Max Brilliant was born in August 2008, I discovered that the house of myself that I thought I knew so well after so many years had another room, and in that room there was a closet, and in that closet there was a shoebox, and in that shoebox I could fit the house that I knew before Ezra. He is the joy of the world, and I look forward to enjoying him all the more now that this book is done. That I was able to enjoy him as much as I did during his first year without risking my career owes in good measure to the architects of the UC Faculty Family Friendly Edge program. They designed enlightened policies that children of all working parents should receive, as Ezra did and for which I am forever grateful.

This acknowledgment appears in UC Berkeley assistant professor Mark Brilliant's 2010 book, *The Color of America Has Changed: How Racial Diversity Shaped Civil Rights Reform in California, 1941–1978*.[1] Rarely, we suspect, do such public tributes to university policies occur. But until recently, it was almost as rare for faculty fathers (and, indeed, most mothers) to take advantage of family-friendly policies. At many universities such policies didn't even exist. This single accolade does not signal the moment to declare victory in the campaign for family-friendly policies in higher education, but it does indicate progress.

Higher education needs these policies. The rigid career structure of academia often clashes with the caregiving responsibilities of faculty, particularly women. The graduate student and postdoc years are important, but have received comparably little attention from scholars of higher education. These are the years when many women, and some men, turn away from an academic career after evaluating the academic workplace and reaching the conclusion that they cannot achieve a successful balance of work and family. Others marry fellow academics and defer to their partner's career. And still others have babies in graduate school and postpone their careers indefinitely. These critical years represent a substantial leak in the academic pipeline. Ironically, these are the years receiving the least attention in recent campaigns to make family life more compatible with work life for academics.

Those scholars who do persist confront the pressure cooker years leading up to the tenure decision. These are also the years when family responsibilities are likely to be the greatest. Many women, and some men, defer children and marriage to focus on their careers. After tenure, family responsibilities weigh less heavily on career advancement. Still, mothers never catch up in salary or in the competition for positions of authority. Only in the decision to retire do men and women attain parity. Even then, academics with children at home will continue to work longer.

The current career structure of the university is not well adapted to the demographics of today's young scholars—women and men who have different priorities and responsibilities than previous generations of professors. The new academic workplace must create flexibility for family needs. Without this change academia will lose some of its most talented young stars. It is not just the right thing to do; it is the economically prudent strategy. Hundreds of thousands of dollars are spent by universities and the federal government to train the best and brightest through graduate school, postdoctoral fellowships, and the early tenure-track years to become the new creators of knowledge and innovation. Our sizable investment is lost when our most promising minds abandon academia after this prolonged training period.

The good news is that there is increasing awareness of the structural problems in the academy, and there are many new initiatives to transform the academic workplace into an environment in which work-family balance is a central value, not just a marginal add-on. These initiatives are not just occurring at universities; the Obama administration has taken a positive step by inaugurating new family-friendly policies for researchers funded by the National Science Foundation.[2]

This final chapter reviews existing family-friendly programs and suggests new directions. Gender equity in higher education requires sustained effort and commitment at all levels. This includes tenure reform, promoting the inclusion of fathers, offering special consideration for graduate students and postdocs, encouraging federal granting agencies to adopt family-friendly policies, and adopting strategies that promote change in institutional cultures. This cultural change is essential; new policies alone will not create a family-friendly workplace.

Some of these policies, particularly those pertaining to graduate students and postdocs, may seem more relevant to research universities than to liberal arts schools and junior colleges, but all institutions of higher education must recruit new faculty, and understanding what they want in terms of career and family balance offers schools a competitive advantage in hiring and retention. Moreover, faculty at all kinds of institutions of higher education, not just research universities, want a family-friendly workplace.

First Steps

Many colleges and universities have taken serious steps to achieve a more fair and equitable workplace for both faculty mothers and fathers. Family-friendly policies are usually first developed for faculty, but gradually they may be extended to graduate students and postdoctoral fellows. These policies are generally well known to higher education scholars. The following is a check list of reforms more or less in descending order of prevalence.[3]

- Six weeks of paid maternity leave
- Maternal and dependent health insurance
- "Stop the clock" policies for tenure and promotion decisions for mothers (usually one year)
- Modified duties for mothers after childbirth (usually relief from teaching for one semester)
- College tuition remission for dependents
- Adoption expenses
- Lactation rooms
- "Stop the clock" policies for fathers
- Dual hires
- Subsidized child care
- Paid parental leave for fathers
- Modified duties for fathers
- Child care grants for mothers to attend conferences
- Emergency child care
- Part-time tenure-track appointments, both pre- and post-tenure

The introduction of these reforms has been slow and uneven across the academic world. Research universities generally offer more accommodations, but even there the coverage is spotty. One of the most common policies, six weeks of paid maternity leave, is offered to faculty without restrictions (for example, not dependent on vacation and sick leave accruals) by only 58 percent of Association of American Universities schools. Only 16 percent of these universities provide unrestricted parental leave of at least one week.[4] A few model institutions provide nearly the whole array of possible supports, while many institutions offer just a few.

The efficacy of these policies is not yet well understood, and we need a concerted research effort to assess the effectiveness of family-friendly policies in the universities where they are in place, along with more conduits for sharing best practices among universities and coordinating efforts with federal agencies.[5] To date, there has not been much research along these lines. However, one recent study found that faculty at schools with more family-friendly policies do view their institutions as more child friendly. This is encouraging preliminary evidence that these policies do make a difference.[6]

More matters than the mere availability of family-friendly policies. At some universities they are automatic entitlements ("opt out"); in others, the faculty member must request them and they are not guaranteed.[7] And family-friendly policies don't always cover nontraditional families. If an institution's definition of family does not include domestic partners, gay and lesbian faculty may not be eligible to use family-friendly programs to care for ailing partners or to share parenting responsibilities. Among others, both the University of California and Harvard University include domestic partners in their policies, thus ensuring that a faculty or staff member can, for instance, take time off to care for the child of his or her partner.

Other popular reforms are targeted specifically at alleviating gender discrimination. A report prepared for the Standing Committee for the Status of Women at Harvard suggests many universities are adopting a number of promising policies. These include making evaluation and promotion criteria more objective and explicit; increasing the number of women in academic administration and on recruitment and promotion committees; fostering mentorship and collaboration; equalizing the distribution of teaching, research, and service tasks; and being alert for instances of gender discrimination.[8] Gender bias exists on many levels, including bias against mothers and motherhood.[9]

The Child Care Dilemma

At or near the top of the list of desired reforms for almost all faculty parents, as well as for graduate student and postdoc parents, is better access to high-quality, affordable child care. There is no simple solution to this universal problem. We have not heard from a single university that claims to have resolved the child care problem. There are no standard rules, like tenure-clock stoppage, that will work for every institution. Some universities have great private child care available in their community; most do not. A few own land and have donors to fund high-quality on-campus facilities. Other universities have subsidized day care facilities that also provide field training experience for students in human development and education. Overall, the key to the most successful child care programs is some form of support from the university, usually a contribution of land, assistance in building new facilities or renovating an existing building, and funding for staff salaries. These contributions can lower costs for all parents in the university community, most notably graduate students who might otherwise not be able to afford quality child care. Indeed, some universities offer child care on a sliding scale to accommodate graduate students, postdocs, and sometimes junior faculty.

Child care grants to attend conferences make a meaningful difference to faculty, graduate students, and postdocs. Parents, usually mothers, who don't attend conferences lose the ability to make valuable contacts and to have their work noticed. The inability to attend conferences is a major concern for faculty mothers and some fathers. Conference child care grants allow faculty members to either bring their child to a conference or pay for child care at home. Similar grants should be made available to graduate students and postdocs.

Emergency child care is a fairly recent idea. What does a faculty member do if he or she is teaching a large lecture class or her lab is receiving a one-day site visit from the National Institutes of Health and her child is running a temperature—perhaps not seriously ill but still unacceptable for child care? In our 2002–2003 survey of University of California faculty, 89 percent of mothers and 69 percent of fathers said emergency child care would be useful to them. One mother said, "For me, the absolute top priority should be the emergency back-up child care program for children who can't go to daycare for a few days (because of daycare holidays, or mild colds, etc.) This would relieve almost all the acute stress of balancing child rearing and work. Lack of backup child care is the glaring gap in our childcare system, and one that UC could fill. The co-pay could be fairly high, and it would still work because parents would use it only for the time slots they absolutely need (both parents have a key meeting, or have to teach a class). I would do almost anything to help set up such a system at [my campus]."

Many cities have professional agencies that can send an experienced baby-sitter to a faculty member's home if the agency has been placed on retainer. The university can hire an agency for the entire faculty population at reasonable cost. Following a successful two-year trial, UC Berkeley recently announced such a service, the "Back-Up Care Advantage Program," which provides faculty with heavily subsidized temporary day care or in-home care services on short notice. The program provides services for both children and adults in need of care-giving, and all faculty are eligible to use forty hours of care each year.[10] Similar programs are now in place at Princeton, the University of Virginia, and other schools.

It is too early to report usage rates—and it is difficult to measure the psychological benefits to the faculty who now have the peace of mind of knowing they have emergency child care if they need it—but the initial response has been very enthusiastic. As an untenured faculty member in the social sciences reported, "It gives me great piece [sic] of mind to know that if my daughter is running a slight fever—she has recurrent ear infections—too sick to take to childcare, but not in any real danger, I can still meet my class of 150 students."

Supporting high-quality, affordable child care, especially near campus, may be the most important single offering a college or university can provide to promote work-family balance. It may require a concerted effort to acquire needed resources from donors or other sources. Less expensive and certainly viable for most institutions is child care support for conferences and emergency back-up child care. The University of California has recently taken another step, even less expensive, toward providing quality child care to faculty. It now pays for all eligible employees to access a registry of prescreened local caregivers.[11] Finding suitable babysitters, nannies, or senior-care providers is now much less of a headache for busy faculty members.

Dual-Career Couples and the Two-Body Problem

With women increasingly earning Ph.D.s, job candidates are typically part of a dual-career couple, and universities now face a major challenge when recruiting the best and brightest faculty: finding a job for the new hire's spouse. Deans and chairs often state that it is one of the thorniest problems they face in recruiting. The problem is especially acute when both spouses are academics, and this too affects women more than men; 18 percent of female academics have professors for spouses, compared with 13 percent of male academics.[12] As we suggested in chapter 2, spousal employment is an important consideration for academics on the job market. Women, more often than men, stay out of academia if their spouse cannot find a satisfactory position, and women faculty members are more likely than their male colleagues to perceive a loss in professional mobility.[13]

According to a Stanford University report on academic couples, the number of dual hires nationally increased from 3 percent in the 1970s to 13 percent in the 2000s.[14] Dual hires now make up about 10 percent of the faculty members surveyed. Another 17 percent of faculty spouses are hired independently; they either responded to a separate advertisement for an opening or met after they were hired. For another 9 percent of academic couples, only one partner is hired and the other does not obtain an academic position. Most of the dual hires are a first hire followed by a second hire, a trailing-spouse accommodation. Seventy-four percent of all trailing spouses are women. Thirty-seven percent of the nine thousand faculty respondents in the Stanford study report that the second hire is treated with less respect than other faculty, although as scholars they are, in fact, just as productive.[15]

Academic couples are clearly an important challenge for all universities, yet few have developed clear and publicly stated protocols to deal with them. Departments typically cut deals with the university on an ad hoc basis, following tough closed-door negotiations for additional positions and resources. Recruits arriving for a job interview are unsure of what the university is willing to offer and are usually afraid to ask.

The University of Rhode Island is an exception. Its protocols are clearly (and publicly) stated on a page on its website.[16] The published policy is to assert the university's responsiveness to academic couples in all job advertisements. For those interested in dual positions the university advises the candidate, once he or she has received a tentative offer, to request assistance in identifying academic employment for his or her spouse or partner. The chair of the department that made the initial hire then contacts the appropriate department(s), and facilitates a request for a waiver to obtain a new position for the second hire. A key step in the protocol is that the partner must be given a regular job interview by the hiring department. This ensures that the department endorses the partner as a suitable candidate. Other spousal hiring practices include temporary positions, soft-money positions, or a visiting professorship. A shared appointment with a spouse or partner, if both members of the couple are in the same discipline, can also be offered as a possibility.

A well-developed and openly advertised dual-career policy, with institutional assistance to aid in the process of relocation and employment, is a major tool for recruiting sought-after candidates. It is an economic investment well spent. Such policies are important for all faculty with working husbands or wives, not just those with faculty spouses.

The Scientific Challenge

"If we're going to out-innovate and out-educate the rest of the world, we've got to open doors for everyone," said First Lady Michelle Obama at a September 2011 press conference. "We need all hands on deck, and that means clearing hurdles for women and girls as they navigate careers in science, technology, engineering, and math."[17] With that announcement, the National Science Foundation (NSF) rolled out a new initiative with a coherent set of family-friendly policies. NSF had launched targeted workplace flexibility efforts in the past, but the new initiative was the first to be applied agency-wide to help postdoctoral fellows and early-career faculty members more easily care for dependents while continuing their careers. These new policies include provisions that do the following:

- Allow postponement of grants for child birth/adoption—grant recipients can defer their awards for up to one year to care for their newborn or newly adopted child.
- Allow grant suspension for parental leave—grant recipients who wish to suspend their grants to take parental leave can extend those grants at no cost.
- Provide supplements to cover research technicians—principal investigators [PIs] can apply for stipends to pay research technicians or equivalent staff to maintain labs while PIs are on family leave.
- Publicize the availability of family-friendly opportunities—NSF will issue announcements and revise current program solicitations to expressly promote these opportunities to eligible awardees.

- Promote family-friendliness for panel reviewers—STEM [science, technology, engineering, and mathematics] researchers who review the grant proposals of their peers will have greater opportunities to conduct virtual reviews rather than travel to a central location, [thereby] increasing flexibility and reducing dependent-care needs.
- Support research and evaluation—NSF will continue to encourage the submission of proposals for research that would assess the effectiveness of policies aimed at keeping women in the STEM pipeline.
- Leverage and expand partnerships—NSF will leverage existing relationships with academic institutions to encourage tenure-clock extensions and allow for dual hiring opportunities.[18]

Although none of these proposals is bold in and of itself, the list publicly acknowledges that family-friendly policies are critical for recruiting and retaining women, particularly in the STEM fields given the extent to which scientists rely on federal grants. Other agencies will likely follow NSF's lead. It is also an acknowledgment that the structure of scientific research presents particular challenges for women and that federal agencies are key to overcoming these challenges. The research culture is largely shaped by federal funding agencies, and their rules prevail. Without federal grants it is very difficult to pursue a scientific career in the academy. It is a competitive race to obtain grant funding, and pausing for any reason, including family needs, can derail research and a career.

In 2002, nearly half (48 percent) of tenure-track scientists aged twenty-five to forty-five had work in the previous year that was partially or fully supported by contracts or grants from the federal government, with the lion's share receiving support from NIH or NSF.[19] Federal grants play a critical role in attaining promotion and tenure; among tenure-track faculty in the sciences, support from federal grants and contracts is strongly associated with career advancement, particularly at Carnegie Research I institutions, or RIs.[20] As chapter 3 indicates, scientists supported by federal grants or contracts are 18 percent more likely to get tenure. This figure increases to 65 percent for scientists at RI universities.[21]

Family status is strongly predictive of federal grant receipt. Tenure-track faculty women who are married with young children are 21 percent less likely than tenure-track men who are married with young children to have their work supported by federal grants or contracts. Tenure-track mothers are also 26 percent less likely than tenure-track women who are married without young children to have federal grant support, and 19 percent less likely than single women without children.[22]

In our focus groups, principal investigators (PIs) observed that they are put in a difficult position when researchers paid by grants need family leave or modification of duties. These PIs want to support their employees but at the same time know that their research will likely suffer. With no existing method for receiving remuneration for family leave paid out of their grants, faculty PIs report tremendous frustration. Thirty-two percent of PIs at UC Berkeley report that providing family leave to researchers had a negative impact on their work.[23]

With its recent announcement NSF has taken the lead among the federal agencies in promoting family-friendly policies, as shown in figure 6.1. NIH and to a lesser extent the Department of Energy have also taken steps toward fostering family-friendly initiatives. These include the provision of no-cost extensions for caregiving purposes (typically allowing an additional year to complete the project with no additional funds), financial supplements to support family-friendly policies, gender-equity workshops, formalized agency policies or statements supporting women in the sciences, allowing part-time effort on fellowships or grants, and extending a fellowship period for caregiving.[24]

Yet the lack of coordination between research universities and federal agencies exacerbates the inconsistency and inadequacy of family-friendly policies at both institutions. To create an environment more attractive for families and thereby increase the number of women in science, universities and federal agencies need a shared and mutually reinforcing approach. The following

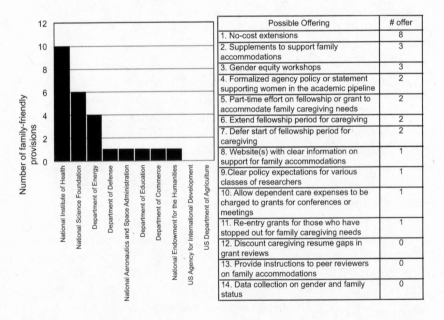

Possible Offering	# offer
1. No-cost extensions	8
2. Supplements to support family accommodations	3
3. Gender equity workshops	3
4. Formalized agency policy or statement supporting women in the academic pipeline	2
5. Part-time effort on fellowship or grant to accommodate family caregiving needs	2
6. Extend fellowship period for caregiving	2
7. Defer start of fellowship period for caregiving	2
8. Website(s) with clear information on support for family accommodations	1
9. Clear policy expectations for various classes of researchers	1
10. Allow dependent care expenses to be charged to grants for conferences or meetings	1
11. Re-entry grants for those who have stopped out for family caregiving needs	1
12. Discount caregiving resume gaps in grant reviews	0
13. Provide instructions to peer reviewers on family accommodations	0
14. Data collection on gender and family status	0

FIGURE 6.1 Family-Friendly Provisions by Federal Agencies Supporting Researchers Receiving Grants or Contracts

Source: Marc Goulden, Mary Ann Mason, Karie Frasch, and the Center for American Progress, "Staying Competitive: Patching America's Leaky Pipeline in the Sciences," Berkeley Center on Health, Economic, and Family Security, University of California, Berkeley, 2009, figure 13, http://www.americanprogress.org/issues/2009/11/women_and_sciences.html.

policies are a step towards a consistent family-friendly framework across granting agencies and academic institutions:

PROMOTE A CLEAR, WELL-COMMUNICATED, MINIMUM SET OF FAMILY-FRIENDLY BENEFITS FOR ALL CLASSES OF RESEARCHERS, FROM GRADUATE STUDENTS TO PIS, WHICH TAKE INTO ACCOUNT THE ENTIRE CAREER-FAMILY LIFE COURSE. More federal agencies could implement clearly communicated baseline family-friendly policies for their fellows and grantees, as NSF has pledged to do. At the same time, universities need to mirror this approach and adopt a minimum set of family-friendly policies for all classes of researchers, not just faculty. Graduate students and postdoctoral scholars currently receive the most limited benefits, even though their retention in the science pipeline would arguably have the largest impact on the future of U.S. science. Federal agencies can provide much more financial assistance than they currently do, by helping to offset the cost of supplying family-friendly benefits to researchers paid off grants and contracts.[25]

PROVIDE FEDERAL AGENCY OR UNIVERSITY STIPENDS TO OFFSET DECLINES IN PRODUCTIVITY ASSOCIATED WITH FAMILY NEEDS, MOST NOTABLY PARENTAL LEAVE. Without additional financial support in conjunction with family-friendly policies, faculty PIs—those with primary responsibility for the design, execution, and management of research projects—will continue to bear the financial burden of supporting family-related absences. This is unfair to PIs and sometimes creates a situation in which they have an incentive to avoid hiring researchers who might eventually start families. This ultimately becomes a de facto form of discrimination against women. Consequently, supplementary funding needs to be provided to underwrite federally funded researchers who take family-related leaves of absence.

Tenure Reform

Chapter 3 made the case for reforming the tenure system rather than abolishing it. Many of the family-friendly initiatives described in this book focus on creating a more flexible timetable for the tenure track. Adopting a tenure-clock stoppage policy for both mothers and fathers provides an extra year (or more) on the tenure clock for childbirth. Paid maternal and parental childbirth leave also provides an economic and psychological cushion.

A bolder policy would allow faculty to temporarily switch from full-time to part-time status, depending on their family circumstances. As reported earlier in the book, many University of California faculty members of all ages, both men and women, support allowing faculty members to shift to part-time status and back again; more than 60 percent of women and a third of men were interested in a flexible, prorated tenure track that would allow them to return to work full time at some point. Women were in favor of the policy mainly as a way of balancing their work with the obligations of raising small children. Both men and women mentioned elder care (of parents or in-laws) and phasing into retirement as important reasons why they supported a more flexible tenure track. Yet despite the great demand for such a policy, it remains extremely uncommon in academe—but increasingly common in the private sector. As noted in chapter 3, only 2 percent of tenure-track faculty in the United States have half-time appointments. And just 6 percent of the colleges and universities surveyed allow half-time faculty to obtain tenure.[26]

Following more than a year of heated debate the University of California system instituted a part-time tenure track with the right to return in 2006. It is too early to predict its success, but it undeniably marks an increased willingness to move toward a more flexible workplace.

Future Faculty: Graduate Students and Postdocs

As noted in chapter 1, critical career decisions are often made in graduate school or during the postdoctoral fellowship years. Most graduate students and postdocs see research universities as hostile to families. More often than men, women turn away from their original ambition to become a professor at a research university because of the apparent incompatibility between work and family. They see too few role models and too much pressure on mothers. If women do have babies during graduate school, our research suggests that they may well abandon plans for an academic research position. And women who have children while completing a postdoc are twice as likely as fathers to reject the thought of a research-intensive academic career.

Graduate student employees—research assistants and teaching assistants—and postdoctoral scholars are by definition contingent, or nonpermanent, workers. Both groups are frequently prohibited from staying in their positions for more than a certain time period, to encourage career progression and prevent exploitation (for example, the University of California caps the total time allowable in a postdoctoral fellowship at five years). The expectation is that these positions typically provide individuals with hands-on research experience that provides the minimum income necessary to continue their academic training. Graduate students and postdocs are normally viewed as trainees, not employees, and therefore are usually not eligible for normal employee benefits, such as paid parental leave.

For both doctoral student employees and postdocs the need for family-friendly policies is often overlooked, both because the trainee-employee distinction is blurred and because their positions are by definition temporary.

Furthermore, if university policies for these populations follow Family and Medical Leave Act eligibility requirements, many graduate student employees and postdoctoral scholars may not qualify because of the contingent nature of their employment. Few if any graduate students satisfy the FMLA requirement of having worked for at least 1,250 hours over one full year. Newly appointed postdoctoral fellows don't meet the FMLA requirement of twelve months of job tenure. The FMLA was purposefully designed to exclude contingent and most part-time employees, which makes it a poor model for designing family-friendly policies for nonfaculty academic researchers (the FMLA doesn't work well for faculty either—how does a new parent take twelve weeks off during the middle of the semester?).

As discussed in chapter 1, an important reason for promoting family-friendly benefits for graduate students and postdoctoral fellows is to maintain compliance with federal law. Title IX of the Education Amendments of the Civil Rights Act of 1972 states that "no person in the United States shall, on the basis of sex, be excluded from participation in, be denied the benefits of, or be subjected to discrimination under any education program or activity receiving Federal financial assistance."[27] Title IX has various implications for gender equity in the academy. In 2003, Oregon senator Ron Wyden suggested that Title IX needed to be invoked with respect to gender imbalances among science and engineering faculty.[28] Furthermore, Title IX covers maternity discrimination. Every major federal granting agency has identical Title IX regulations, including for some form of family leave for employees of educational institutions.[29] Almost all colleges and universities receive federal funds and fall under the jurisdiction of these regulations. Federal granting agencies require that universities and colleges treat pregnancy as a temporary disability and provide unpaid, job-protected leave to birth mothers "for a reasonable period of time" if the institution does not maintain its own leave policy for its employees.[30]

Universities are required to comply with Title IX for all graduate students and postdocs who receive federal funding. When properly enforced, the Title IX provisions fill shortfalls in university family-family policies by providing support for graduate students and postdoctoral fellows supported by federal grants who are facing pregnancy and motherhood. Contingent employees, such as graduate students and postdocs who do not qualify for the FMLA, still have a right to job-protected unpaid leave. With no corresponding policies in place, some universities may be violating Title IX requirements.

The best new model for graduate students would be family-friendly programs across their careers, from graduate school through the professoriate, coupled with a pro-family institutional culture. This way aspiring scholars would come to expect a life of work-family balance. As observed in chapter 1, the family-friendly initiatives that some universities have undertaken for graduate students and postdoctoral scholars are mostly the same programs offered to faculty. These include paid parental leave, affordable child care that includes emergency and drop-in options, and lactation rooms. Additional initiatives for students and postdocs include stopping the normative time-to-degree clock and providing family housing, parent centers, and organized mentoring systems that promote work-family balance and provide professional advice.

No university offers all these resources and at best most universities offer only one or two, most likely family housing and parent centers. Only 13 percent of institutions in the Association of American Universities (61 top American and Canadian research schools) offer six weeks of unrestricted paid maternity leave to doctoral students, and only 5 percent provide dependent health care for a child.[31] For postdocs, only 23 percent of AAU universities provide six weeks of unrestricted paid maternity leave, and only 8 percent provide one week of unrestricted parental leave.[32] Hopefully these privations will come to the attention of students and postdocs themselves; some graduate student teaching assistants are unionized, most often at public universities. Unions can be helpful in pushing for childbirth leave and child care, although their presence often spurs the university to take the initiative rather than give the unions credit.

Many other nations are highly conscious of the growing percentage of women in the academic labor force and are taking a progressive position on providing robust family-friendly benefits to their postdoctoral scholars. In addition to offering generous government benefits, Canadian federal agencies provide four or six months—depending on the agency—paid parental leave to postdocs and students (if they are not eligible for government employment insurance benefits).[33] In the European Union, the European Molecular Biology Organization (EMBO) has provisions to extend two-year, full-time fellowships to three years part time for postdoctoral scholars with caregiving responsibilities. The EMBO also provides three months of maternity leave.[34] In China, a recent amendment to the Employment Insurance Act provides 60 percent of salary for six months of parental leave (after one year of employment). Both parents can use the leave, providing a total of twelve months per family.[35]

Reentry for Men and Women

How does a woman who completes her graduate training later in life, perhaps having taken time off to raise children, or a man in a dual-career relationship, who deferred his career in favor of his partner's, receive fair consideration for academic jobs? The training and talents of those candidates are often dismissed; they simply do not fit the model of a thirty-something, newly minted Ph.D. or postdoc. Few good models exist in the United States for dealing with reentry (rejoining the labor force after time away).[36] A small number of federal agencies and foundations offer reentry postdocs to scientists, but usually those positions are meant to encourage people to switch into "hot" fields, such as biomedical research.

Eva, a biologist who left her postdoc when the first of her three children was born, expressed her dilemma to us: "When I made my decision I was riddled with fears. How can I keep up with the new technologies in the industry? Will I ever catch up? Now I'm back in the job market and I don't know how to compete with others that have been in the field. I don't have anything to add to my resume since 2003. I have devoted myself exclusively to my young children until they got in school full time. I believe that women need more support to achieve their full potential in science or any other career they choose, and I wish there were more resources for stay at home mothers that are moving back into the job force."[37]

European countries have given reentry more thought, perhaps because their gender gap in science is even more worrisome than in the United States. According to the European Commission's She Figures 2006 report, women earn 43 percent of Europe's doctoral degrees in science but hold only 15 percent of senior academic positions.[38] Many postdoctoral fellowships in Europe include supplements for child care and domestic help, and some focus on candidates who have taken a break from academe for family reasons. For example, the Wellcome Trust in Britain provides a two- to four-year fellowship for postdoctoral scientists, both men and women, returning to a scientific research career after a family-related break of at least two years.[39]

Reentry fellowships do not directly confront the problem of age discrimination in hiring. Although age discrimination in hiring (for workers over forty) is against the law in the United States, it is a difficult law to enforce, since a candidate's age is almost never the stated reason for rejection.[40] For instance, if an applicant is never called for an interview, he or she will probably not be able to convince a jury that age discrimination has occurred. One solution might be administrative pressure on hiring committees to discount gaps in professional experience, gaps often created by motherhood or other family circumstances, when the committees consider the CVs of older candidates. Committees should be made aware of the age discrimination law, as well as the potential loss of experienced talent.

Hiring qualified older workers is a sound business strategy. Older workers are often as competent and well trained as younger workers, and they are likely more experienced. With appropriate additional training as needed, they could be an asset to an academic community for twenty to thirty years. In addition to squandering talent, universities and the nation are forfeiting a national investment. A Ph.D. degree in the sciences represents a six-figure investment by the federal government, usually in the form of graduate stipends and postdoctoral fellowship support.[41] Nearly all doctoral students receive support from their university, the federal government, large foundations, or a combination of these. To lose this experienced talent on top of a significant training investment is a very poor business strategy for the United States.

Make Room for Fathers

Our account of academic motherhood should not be read as an indictment of husbands and partners, who, as was shown in chapter 4, typically contribute a significant number of hours to child care and housework. A major step toward reforming the tenure system is to actively involve fathers. Yet many social and institutional barriers prevent academic men from doing more. Universities perpetuate a culture that assumes that mothers will take on the lion's share of caregiving, and that men are the breadwinners. This culture is reinforced by the dramatic gender difference in faculty-leave policies at the United States' premier research universities. According to our survey of Association of American Universities schools, 58 percent guaranteed at least six weeks' unrestricted paid leave for mothers but just 16 percent provided one week unrestricted paid parental leave.[42]

Over the years many academics have sat at conference tables arguing with colleagues about whether new fathers should be allowed to stop the tenure clock or should receive modified teaching and service duties. The opposition argument is always the same: Men won't use the time for parenting; they'll use it to write another book or publish more articles. Fathers, for their part, even if they are full participants in parenting, don't often use parental accommodations. Like mothers, they fear they will be viewed as marginal tenure candidates—why did they need the extra time to get tenure?—or less committed to their institutions. The counterargument is that unless we engage fathers in a flexible workplace, the culture will not change. This has been one of the important lessons we learned at the University of California.[43]

Cultures Can Change

Mark Brilliant, the assistant professor and father introduced at the beginning of this chapter, spent meaningful time with his newborn son, Ezra, in part because he took advantage of the progressive family-friendly polices at his university, stopping the tenure clock and using parental leave to obtain a semester's worth of teaching relief.

In fact, these policies had essentially been in place in the University of California system since 1988, when a forward-looking UC president, David Gardner, introduced the most progressive family leave policies at an American university at that time. More than fifteen years later, we surveyed more than forty-four hundred tenure-track faculty in the UC system and found that among eligible faculty parents the use rates for the major family-friendly policies were surprisingly low. For example, less than half of eligible assistant professor women used Active Service-Modified Duties (relief from teaching, commonly referred to as ASMD) and less than a third took tenure-clock extensions: The use rates for eligible UC men were even lower, with at most only one in ten using any of the policies.

Why weren't faculty using these family-friendly programs? One reason is that they were not well known in 2002 and 2003, the years of our survey. Only half of UC faculty parents were aware of the teaching-relief policy, arguably the most important of the existing family-friendly provisions. In fact, only just over a quarter of eligible faculty knew about all the major policies. As one mother commented in the survey: "I was shocked to learn in . . . [a survey question] that I and/or my spouse (who is also a faculty member) might have been eligible for teaching relief, and that my spouse might have been eligible for six weeks of paid leave. I was never told about either of these programs, which is a little upsetting." Department chairs, ultimately responsible for implementing family-friendly policies, were often among the ignorant. In those days it was up to the chairs to facilitate requests originating with individual faculty members. Chairs were not required to inform faculty members of their option to use family-friendly programs. In fact, chairs sometimes discouraged faculty from availing themselves of ASMD or other family-friendly programs at the University of California. A second, equally important reason why most mothers and many fathers chose not to use family-friendly programs is concern that they would not be considered serious players if they took time off for childbirth. "Prior to tenure I would never have considered using the option—I would have considered it . . . a fatal flaw," said one faculty mother at the University of California. In addition, some fathers expressed reluctance to use a policy they believed was put in place for women. Even if they were primary caregivers, they thought they would be stigmatized for taking "maternity" leave. In the words of one faculty father at the university, "In my opinion, there is a certain 'culture' surrounding asking for teaching relief that makes it difficult for male faculty to consider this as a viable option."

This is the vicious circle of culture change. Fathers are reluctant to use parental relief because they view it as potentially compromising and as contrary to the male-breadwinner ethic. Mothers are afraid to use the policies that supposedly only women use for fear that they (and their scholarship) will be taken less seriously by both men and other women. It is difficult to change a culture that has for centuries sustained a lockstep career model, a model that stipulates uninterrupted progress from graduate school to postdoc to assistant professorship in a prescribed number of years, usually culminating in tenure around age forty. There is little allowance for slowing down or taking a break. As this book has shown, academia's male career model has placed women at a profound disadvantage. Men suffer too, by losing out on time with their wives, partners, and children.

The recent experience of women science faculty at the Massachusetts Institute of Technology offers reason to hope. A small group of tenured women faculty, 15 out of 197 professors, organized and discovered that there were wide disparities in salaries and resources.[44] Even the square footage of lab space they had been allotted was significantly less than that given to men. Women faculty at MIT also believed they were marginalized when it came to university decision making. Their persuasive fact-filled report, issued in 2002, offered the university a serious challenge, a challenge that for the most part has been met. Faculty women now have an "overwhelming[ly] positive view of MIT," according to a new report that came out in 2011.[45] They report many positive changes. In the schools of science and engineering the number of women faculty has almost doubled. Women now serve in multiple senior administrative positions, most notably that of university president. As for creating a family-friendly culture, the women science faculty report that "the real biological burden that women who bear children face is clear and family-friendly policies at MIT are viewed as very positive. However there is some unease with the emphasis on issues and benefits related to childbearing and childcare, and further, with the perception that childcare issues are 'women's' issues rather than more gender–neutral 'family' issues."[46] In addressing women faculty in engineering, the report praises family policies implemented over the past ten years, "although the cost and availability of childcare remains a concern, mostly for junior women faculty."[47]

Culture does not change easily, but there are also signs of improvement at UC Berkeley. In 2006 several new family-friendly programs were introduced, while existing programs were expanded. This comprehensive package included maternity leave, teaching relief for mothers and fathers, tenure-clock stoppage for parents, parental leave without pay, deferral of personnel reviews at the associate level or higher to accommodate family needs, and part-time appointments for family needs. Later, emergency child care was added. These changes, taken together, sent a clear and unambiguous message that faculty men and women with substantial caregiving responsibilities, most notably new parents, were *entitled* to family-friendly programs, that these programs were not special privileges available only by request. In addition, centralized funding was created to offset the teaching costs of faculty who went on parental leave.

One of the most important initiatives was to ensure that all faculty were fully aware of the family-friendly programs available to them. We launched a campaign to emphasize family-friendly policies in recruitment and retention. A brochure now greets new faculty candidates, and the orientation for new faculty members includes an extensive segment on parental polices and support systems, including day care. Chairs were pulled into the initiative with a special orientation, and they were furnished with a toolkit that clearly explains their responsibilities in promoting use of family-friendly programs. The toolkit is publicly available online for academic administrators who may be interested.[48]

Four years later these new family-friendly policies and programs were common knowledge, widely supported, and widely used.[49] Just like Mark Brilliant, more men and women are taking advantage of policies that are now entitlements, not special accommodations that people have to individually request from their department chairs. Fifty-nine percent of new fathers have obtained teaching relief via ASMD, compared with 6 percent before 2003. Eighty-six percent of mothers now obtain teaching relief. As one mother said, "I am extremely grateful and feel lucky to have benefited from UC Berkeley ASMD policies." Furthermore, the proportion of faculty women increased from 24 percent to 29 percent, not a sea change but a definite step in the right direction.

And we are experiencing a most encouraging baby boom at Berkeley. Between 2003, before the new initiatives were implemented, and 2009, the percentage of female assistant professors who reported having at least one child more than doubled, from 27 percent to 64 percent, and for men it rose from 39 percent to 59 percent. Maybe "the times, they are a-changin'"?

A Short List for Universities

There are numerous family-friendly accommodations that colleges and universities could implement right now, and many are not costly. Taken together, they would make academia more amenable to families. They would boost gender equity and lead to more successful recruitment and retention of both scholars in training (graduate students and postdocs) and existing faculty. The following interventions have been discussed throughout the book. This is not a comprehensive list, but it highlights the programs that have been considered important by researchers; faculty committees; administrators; and individual wives, husbands, partners, and parents.

Family-friendly policies for faculty include tenure-clock stoppage, paid parental leave, subsidized and emergency child care, and part-time tenure-track appointments; other accommodations are described earlier in this chapter. Many are already in place at universities. Almost all focus on the early-career years of marriage, childbirth, and care for young children. Perhaps most important for faculty recruitment are child care and dual-career hiring policies. For retention and lifelong productivity, a broad suite of offerings is necessary. These policies must be opt-out entitlements, not special requests, and they must be publicly advertised on the university's website, in its personnel office, and in other key locations. Above all, the institution must commit to sustainable programs. Essential for changing the culture are both a high-level administrator responsible for enforcement and routine training for department chairs.

Family-friendly policies for graduate students and postdocs, the young scholars who often feel discouraged by the challenge of work-family balance, include paid parental leave, affordable child care that includes emergency and drop-in options, lactation rooms (unlike most faculty, many graduate students and postdocs don't have private offices), dependent-care medical insurance, family housing, parent centers, and organized mentoring systems that promote work-family balance and provide professional advice. For graduate students, it is essential that they be able to stop the normative time-to-degree clock after childbirth.

The scientific disciplines demand special attention. Family formation takes a particularly heavy toll on mothers in the sciences, who often abandon an academic career before seeking a tenure-track position or, if they obtain a tenure-track job, fail to get tenure. Since most scientific research is funded by federal agencies, a concerted effort among NSF, NIH, and other agencies to offer these same baseline family-friendly programs is essential. Also vital is cooperation with universities to ensure delivery of these programs.

For both Ph.D.s and faculty, it is critical to have the opportunity to reenter after an absence, even of just a few years, spent taking care of family responsibilities. Losing well-trained talent is a waste for everyone. In some disciplines, particularly among the sciences, a reentry training fellowship could help to bridge the transition.

Finally, a holistic view of university life requires workplace flexibility throughout an academic career. Offering a part-time tenure track to accommodate family responsibilities, with the right of return to full-time employment, would help to retain both assistant professors and productive senior faculty faced with elder care demands. Stopping the tenure clock for childbirth is also critical. The future of tenure—and therefore the future of universities as we know them—depends on a serious rethinking of a system that has proved highly successful for scholarship, but often falls short in retaining some of our best and brightest young minds.

APPENDIX

Data and Analysis

This book is based on primarily two data sources. The first is the nationally representative Survey of Doctorate Recipients. The second is a series of surveys conducted at the University of California.

The Survey of Doctorate Recipients

For more than fifty years all new Ph.D. recipients in the United States have been administered questionnaires, composing the Survey of Earned Doctorates.[1] Since 1973, slightly under 10 percent of Survey of Earned Doctorates respondents have been selected for ongoing biennial interviews that continue until age seventy-six or relocation outside the United States. Together the repeated interviews of new and former Ph.D. recipients compose the Survey of Doctorate Recipients (SDR).[2] The result is a large and continually replenished set of panel data on academic careers. Overall response rates are good; for instance, 87 percent of respondents completed the survey in 1991.[3] Moreover, we employ survey weights that adjust for response bias. To account for the effects of the weights and sample design on t-ratios, we report the results of significance tests based on robust standard errors.[4]

It should be observed that the SDR is much broader than other data sets commonly used to study higher education faculty. Traditionally the emphasis has been on bench scientists.[5] Similarly, studies most often focused on academics at major research universities. The SDR, as a large representative sample of Ph.D. recipients, allows us to overcome both these limitations. In addition, as the SDR is a sample of Ph.D. recipients rather than of faculty members, we know about Ph.D.s who do not become tenure-track professors. These individuals provide valuable comparison groups for the analyses reported in chapters 2 and 4.

Prior to 1981 the SDR did not collect information about respondents' children, so these earlier years are not used.[6] Accordingly, most of our analyses are based on SDR data starting in that year. Select analyses begin only with the 1983 data because of dependent variable coding issues. Our time series end in one of two years depending on the composition of the sample. The SDR included humanities doctorates only through the 1995 survey; thereafter they were the victims of budget cuts. Accordingly, we present results that extend through 1995 based on all academic disciplines, and results extending through 2003 based on only the sciences (including the social sciences).

One great strength of the SDR is its large sample sizes. By the 2003 survey cycle more than 160,000 doctorate recipients had participated.[7] The *smallest* SDR sample used in any of our multivariate analyses is over 5,500; the largest, over 30,000. Sample sizes for all SDR analyses are shown in table A.1. Missing data are deleted listwise, except when large numbers of missing cases (that is, sufficient to allow estimation with dummy variables for missing data) may represent substantively meaningful differences between respondents. For these items, including race, time to complete Ph.D., quality of degree-granting institution, and type of employing institution (all categorical variables), we code additional dummy variables for missing data and, for continuous variables, mean imputation with a missing-data dummy. More sophisticated means of handling missing data, such as multiple imputation, do not produce appreciably better estimates of regression coefficients and standard errors.[8]

Finally, all reported SDR results pertaining to gender, marriage, divorce, and children are statistically significant unless otherwise noted.

University of California Surveys

We use data from three separate surveys administered at nine schools of the University of California system (the tenth, UC Merced, opened in 2005 and did not participate); a fourth survey was limited to UC Berkeley. The three UC-wide surveys were administered under the auspices of Mary Ann Mason and were fielded under the imprimatur of the president of the UC system; Marc Goulden, Angelica Stacy, and Sheldon Zedeck conducted the fourth survey. Marc Goulden and others designed the surveys, which were intended to explore work-family issues at UC. The surveys, which were administered via the Internet, produced both qualitative and quantitative data.

The first survey targeted UC tenure-stream faculty and was fielded in 2002 and 2003.[9] It had a response rate of 51 percent and produced 4,460 responses.

TABLE A.I.

Survey Years and Sample Sizes for Analyses
Based on the Survey of Doctorate Recipients

	Survey years	N	Person-years
Getting a tenure-track job (all fields)	1981–1995	30,568	95,070
Getting a tenure-track job (sciences only)	1981–2003	34,851	143,815
First job after Ph.D. receipt (all fields)	1983–1995	16,049	—
Tenure-track job after time off (all fields)	1983–1995	6,501	21,435
Getting tenure (all fields)	1981–1995	10,845	37,565
Getting tenure (sciences only)	1981–2003	11,229	47,435
Marriage at Ph.D. receipt (all fields)	1981–1995	30,874	—
Marriage across career (all fields)	1981–1995	6,366	12,700
Divorce at Ph.D. receipt (all fields)	1981–1995	30,874	—
Divorce across career (all fields)	1981–1995	16,770	39,507
Children in household at Ph.D. receipt (all fields)	1981–1995	27,870	—
Children in household across career (all fields)	1981–1995	11,161	22,325
Promotion to full professor (all fields)	1981–1995	5,766	43,216
Women's income (all fields)	1981–1995	7,717	27,113
Men's income (all fields)	1981–1995	13,202	55,609
Retirement (all fields)	1981–1995	6,356	30,383

The second survey was administered to UC doctoral students in 2006 and 2007.[10] It had a response rate of 43 percent and produced 8,373 responses. The third survey was administered to UC postdoctoral fellows in 2009.[11] It also had a response rate of 43 percent, based on 2,390 responses. The fourth survey, limited to UC Berkeley, targeted contingent instructors, academic researchers, and other academic staff.[12] It was conducted in 2009 and produced 645 responses, based on a response rate of 37 percent. It should be noted that these response rates are superior to those typically produced by surveys that employ random-digit dialing.[13] All four surveys were about fourteen pages long and took fifteen to twenty minutes to complete. The UC surveys are used for descriptive statistics and qualitative data.

Other Quantitative Data

We collected data on family-friendly policies in separate surveys administered to (1) the thirteen federal agencies that provide the majority of American research dollars and (2) the sixty-one schools belonging to the Association of American Universities.[14] These public and private schools represent the top research universities in the United States (fifty-nine schools) and Canada (two schools). The fifty-nine American AAU schools award over half the Ph.D.s conferred in the United States.[15]

Chapter 4 reports the results of analysis based on the 2000 5 percent Census Public Use Microdata Sample (commonly known as the PUMS).[16] Although the PUMS offers relatively little information on participants, it provides a large comparative sample of male and female doctors, lawyers, and professors for studying fertility. Analysis is limited to individuals aged twenty-five (the approximate lowest age at which people could have finished their professional training) to forty-four (few new parents are older). This provides a twenty-year window for observing the presence of children. There are no missing data.

Other Qualitative Data

We report data from a number of informal qualitative interviews and focus groups. Some of these interviews were initially conducted for Mary Ann Mason and Eve Mason Ekman's 2007 book, *Mothers on the Fast Track*.[17]

In many chapters we report qualitative data obtained from web logs and Internet forums, chiefly sites maintained by the *Chronicle of Higher Education* and *Inside Higher Education*. These sites provide valuable accounts of men's and women's experiences in higher education, and offer trade-offs in comparison with the qualitative data obtained from our UC surveys. On the one hand, these data are quintessentially open ended. People are volunteering their experiences, not responding to survey questions. On the other hand, we acknowledge that self-selection may influence people's accounts; only academicians motivated to recount their experiences are participating. Moreover, there may be a cascade effect. As more people contribute to a forum thread, they may feel increasingly compelled to be strident in their responses. We present these qualitative accounts not as proof, but to illustrate contentions based on SDR data and other sources.

Chapter 2 Analysis

We analyze the likelihood of getting a tenure-track job using discrete-time event history analysis, estimated via complementary log-log regression.[18] The complementary log-log is a better estimator than logit or probit when discrete data approximate a continuous time process.[19] Since time-to-event is measured in years, continuous time models would be difficult to estimate. Data from each wave of the SDR between 1981 and 1995 (or 2003) are used to construct event histories of annual employment status. For each year respondents have not obtained a tenure-track job, an additional record is created; time-to-event occurs when respondents obtain tenure-track jobs. The baseline hazard function is captured by a dummy variable for each year prior to obtaining a tenure-track position. Based on preliminary analyses we top-code the hazard functions at seven for analysis of respondents out of graduate school, and six for analysis of tenure-track job procurement after time off the tenure track. Few respondents obtained tenure-track positions after, respectively, seven and six years.

Our primary independent variables are respondent sex, fertility, and marital status. Marital status is measured with a single dummy ascertaining whether a respondent is currently in a heterosexual marriage (the data predate marriage equality in Massachusetts and other states); unfortunately it is not possible to know whether unmarried respondents have live-in partners. In addition, the SDR does not indicate whether respondent spouses are employed as faculty. Children in the household are measured with a pair of dummy variables, assessing the presence of children under six and children between six and eighteen. The SDR does not indicate whether children are biological, adopted, or stepchildren. This is not a major liability: although most are presumably biological children, any child in the household reflects a conscious decision on the part of the respondent to become a parent. In preliminary analyses we experimented with variables measuring numbers of children, but this did not produce substantially different results.[20] Both marital status and children are time-varying covariates in event history analyses. These variables are interacted with gender to explore how family formation affects men and women academics differently. We observed no statistically significant three-way interactions between sex, marital status, and the presence of children in the analysis based on all fields; conversely, our findings based on only the sciences report the results of a three-way interaction.

Control variables fall into two categories, academic and demographic characteristics. Any of these may be correlated with both respondent family formation behaviors and the outcomes we consider. Academic controls include the National Research Council ranking of respondents' Ph.D. programs,[21] time to doctoral degree, doctoral field, time since Ph.D. completion, and calendar year of Ph.D. receipt. The first two are coded as sets of dummy variables, representing quartiles of the observed continuous variables; field of employment is a dichotomous or trichotomous variable measuring whether respondents received their degrees in the humanities (omitted in select analyses), social sciences, or bench sciences (including the biological and physical sciences, engineering, and mathematics).[22]

Year of Ph.D. receipt is measured with a continuous variable. Time since Ph.D. receipt, also continuous and used only in the models predicting initial employment status (see below), accounts for delays produced by postdoctoral fellowships, Fulbrights, and other temporary positions following the completion of graduate school. This variable is time-varying in event history models. It is omitted from analysis of reentry because of its high correlation with time-to-event.

Demographic controls include respondent race/ethnicity and age. Race/ethnicity is dummy-coded with variables measuring whether a respondent is black, white, Latino, Asian, or other; age is continuous and time-varying in event history analysis. In the analysis of first job type, it is measured at the same time as employment status.

First employment type subsequent to graduate school is explored with a five-category nominal variable—tenure-track job, contingent teaching position, nonteaching job at a college or university, employment in government or the private sector, or exiting the paid labor force—analyzed via multinomial logistic regression.[23] This coding scheme ignores postdoctoral fellowships ("postdocs"), because they do not fit well into any category. A postdoc is by definition temporary. Unlike with contingent teaching positions, it is not possible to string them together perpetually to provide permanent employment. Therefore they do not belong with the five employment states listed above; indeed, postdocs may be precursors to any of them. Moreover, we view postdoctoral fellowships as the last stage of respondents' education, not the first stage of their careers (indeed, as we suggested in chapter 1, many people see postdocs as glorified research assistants.)[24] Our solution is to analyze respondents' first non-postdoc employment if respondents report being in postdocs in their first SDR interviews. Since the first interview takes place two years after respondents get their degrees, yearlong stints as contingent teachers or research associates, common means of subsistence while on the academic job market, are not captured by our dependent variable. Having had a postdoctoral fellowship is included as an independent variable. It had little effect on our results. Aside from the measure of postdoctoral fellowships, this analysis includes the same independent variables used in the analysis of obtaining a tenure-track job.

Chapter 2 also reports the analysis of reentry, the likelihood of obtaining a tenure-track position after spending time as a contingent faculty member, in a nonteaching job at a college or university, employed in government or the private sector, or being out of the paid labor force. Heterogeneity between these four states is captured with a set of dummy variables measuring (un)employment type. Sample size limitations preclude analysis for each state or separate models for different academic fields.

Analysis of reentry relies on the same event history models and independent variables employed elsewhere in the chapter. Data from each wave of the

SDR between 1983 and 1995 are used to construct event histories of time to tenure-track employment. For each year in any non-tenure-track employment status following Ph.D. receipt, an additional record is created. Failure occurs when respondents obtain tenure-track jobs. The hazard function is captured by a dummy variable for each year prior to a tenure-track job. No statistically significant analyses involving marriage were observed for this analysis.

Chapter 3 Analysis

Analysis of tenure is conducted via discrete-time event history analysis similar to that employed in chapter 2.[25] The at-risk population includes only tenure-track assistant professors. The hazard function for getting tenure is top-coded at ten years rather than seven. Control variables include race/ethnicity, age, Ph.D. calendar year, discipline, and the Carnegie classification of the employing university (Research I vs. all others).[26] Age and Carnegie classification are coded as time-varying independent variables.

Chapter 3 also reports the results of two regression models intended to ascertain whether sample selection can account for women's lower tenure rate. Both are multiequation models; each makes different assumptions about the relationship between getting an academic job and getting tenure. First, we estimate a selection model using Heckman's two-step procedure.[27] These equations are estimated using probit rather than complementary log-log because of error term behavior. Using the event history framework described above, we estimate a first-stage selection equation where the dependent variable is whether a SDR respondent gets a tenure-track job. For purposes of identification the selection equation must contain at least one independent variable that does not appear in the second-stage equation. This requirement is satisfied with the variables measuring the National Research Council ranking of respondents' Ph.D. programs and time to doctoral degree; these variables have no logical direct relationship to the likelihood of getting tenure, the dependent variable in the second-stage equation. Results from the selection equation are then used to generate the inverse of the Mills ratio (λ), which is included as a regressor in the second-stage equation in order to account for the effects of sample selection.

The advantage of this procedure is the ability to provide event history estimates of the likelihood of both getting a tenure-track job and of getting tenure. The disadvantage is that the two equations are estimated independently. It is probable that the same omitted variables affect the likelihood of both employment and tenure, so a model that permits error terms to be correlated across equations is desirable. Unfortunately there is no way to estimate such a model in an event history framework.[28] As an alternative, we estimate a bivariate probit selection model.[29] The first-stage equation ascertains whether respondents obtain tenure-track jobs within three years of Ph.D. receipt; based on visual inspection of the hazard of job procurement, most respondents who ultimately secure employment have done so by then. The second-stage equation, analyzing only respondents with tenure-track jobs, uses tenure after seven and one half years as the dependent variable; this cut-point was also verified empirically. As for the two-step selection model, the National Research Council ranking of respondents' Ph.D. programs and time to doctoral degree are used to identify the first-stage equation. Other independent variables are measured at the time of Ph.D. receipt for the first-stage equation and, for the second, when respondents obtain tenure-track jobs. The sample size for this analysis (N = 1,348) is smaller than elsewhere in this chapter because the risk set has to be defined to include both job procurement and tenure.

Both these models suggest that the low rate at which women get tenure cannot be attributed to sample selection.

Chapter 4 Analysis

This chapter includes two sets of analyses based on the SDR. Both sets focus on the same three dependent variables: marriage, divorce, and the presence of children younger than six in the household. Both sets of analyses include all Ph.D. recipients, not just those in tenure-stream positions.

The first set of analyses consists of three logistic regression models examining marriage, divorce, and children at the time respondents first completed the SDR (that is, their first survey subsequent to Ph.D. receipt). The second set examines these three dependent variables prospectively across doctorate recipients' lives using the discrete-time event history models employed in chapter 2.

The primary independent variable in both sets of analyses is a measure of career type: (1) tenure-track position, (2) the second tier (contingent teaching positions, any part-time employment, respondents out of the paid labor force), or (3) any other full-time employment. This variable is interacted with gender to explore professional differences in marriage, divorce, and fertility. All chapter 4 analyses based on the SDR control for roughly the same independent variables introduced in chapter 2: doctoral discipline, rank of doctoral program, time to degree, calendar year of Ph.D. receipt, age, race/ethnicity, and duration dependence (in the event history models).

We use data from the 2000 Census PUMS to explore differences in fertility between male and female professors, doctors, and lawyers. Profession is identified using a combination of occupational codes and education. For all three occupational groups, individuals are required to be working one or more hours a week and have one of the three relevant job titles: (1) postsecondary teacher, hereafter referred to as *professor*, (2) physician (including surgeons), or (3) lawyer.

Professors must have Ph.D.s; doctors and lawyers are required to have professional degrees (accordingly, professors of law and medicine are, respectively, treated as lawyers and doctors).

The dependent variable for these analyses is a birth event, defined as the presence of a child aged zero or one in the household. Birth events may reflect initial or higher-order births. Data on fertility history and intentions would be helpful but are not available in the PUMS.

We contrast birth events in a series of logistic regression models. Dummy variables for female doctors, lawyers, and professors allow us to determine occupational differences in fertility. All models control for age, race/ethnicity, and weekly hours worked. In successive models we introduce measures of marital/cohabitation status, income, and spousal employment. This allows us to determine whether occupational differences in fertility can be explained on the basis of measured participant and spousal characteristics.

Chapter 5 Analysis

Chapter 5 reports the results of multivariate analyses of three dependent variables: (1) promotion to full professor, (2) income, and (3) retirement.

First, we conduct a discrete-time event history analysis of promotion to the rank of full professor that is almost identical to the analyses reported in chapters 2 and 3. The at-risk sample includes only tenured associate professors. The hazard function is top-coded at ten years, as few associates are promoted subsequently. The independent variables are identical to those used in our analysis of tenure receipt.

Second, we study tenure-stream faculty income using fixed-effects models based on inflation-adjusted income.[30] Fixed-effects regression exploits longitudinal data to control for time-invariant differences between individuals. Several studies have used these models to explore the incremental effects of children on women's incomes.[31] Our analytic design differs from these studies primarily with respect to the dependent variable. These studies examine wages; we analyze respondents' base annual salary (excluding summer salary, bonuses, and the like).

We run separate analyses for male and female professors, given the impossibility of including respondent gender as an independent variable in fixed-effects models. The primary independent variables are a dummy measuring marital status (married vs. not married) and a continuous variable indicating the number of minor children in the household. Controls include a continuous variable measuring years since Ph.D. receipt, a dummy indicating whether respondents are employed at Carnegie Research I schools (with an additional dummy for missing data), dummies for academic rank (assistant, associate, full professor), a set of dummy variables for survey year, and age and age squared.[32]

All independent variables are time varying. We observed no statistically significant interactions involving gender and the control variables.

Third, we conduct a discrete-time event history analysis of retirement of Ph.D. recipients employed in higher education. This analysis includes only SDR respondents between the ages of fifty-six and seventy-five. Leaving academia before age fifty-five presumably reflects a career change, not retirement; moreover, a preliminary analysis indicated almost no earlier departures from academia. Our study ends at age seventy-five because the SDR ceases to interview respondents at this point. By this age only 8 percent of professors are still working.[33]

As in previous analyses, our primary independent variables are sex, marital status, and children. *Marital status* has four categories: married; separated/divorced; never married; and unmarried, reason unspecified. *Children* has three categories: minor children in the house during the years respondents are at risk for retirement (fifty-five and up), minor children in the house prior to age fifty-five, and no observed children. Both children and marital status are time-varying independent variables. Interactions between these variables and respondent gender were not statistically significant.

It should be observed that the SDR provides information on only coresident minor children, and only since the 1981 survey. Therefore respondents whose minor children had left the nest by 1981 are incorrectly classified as childless. This is an unavoidable flaw in the SDR for studying retirement. Nevertheless, there are no better data available. To attempt to control for censoring on the children variable we include a time-varying continuous variable that measures the number of years of SDR data for which we have information on children.

The following control variables are used in the event history analysis of retirement. Professional characteristics are Ph.D. field, job type, employer type, calendar year of Ph.D. receipt, and income. *Ph.D. field* is a set of dummy variables measuring whether respondents received their degrees in the biological sciences (the reference category), engineering or computer science, math or the physical sciences, psychology, or any other social science. *Job type* is coded as tenure-track professorship, non-tenure-track teaching position, or any other position in a college or university. A dummy variable measures whether respondents are employed at Carnegie Research I schools. *Calendar year of Ph.D. receipt* is a continuous variable. Finally, *income* reflects deciles of inflation-adjusted annual salary. Income, employer type, and job type are all time-varying independent variables.

Historical period, the years respondents are at risk of retirement, is coded as a set of dummy variables: before July 1982, July 1982 to July 1994, and July 1994 to July 1999. This coding captures the 1994 abolition of mandatory faculty retirement. A continuous variable measures the age respondents entered the population of potential retirees. Duration dependence is modeled with a set of nineteen dummy variables, one for each year that respondents are at risk of retirement.

NOTES

INTRODUCTION

1. National Center for Education Statistics, *Digest of Education Statistics: 2009* (U.S. Department of Education, Institute of Education Sciences, Washington, DC, 2009), table 275, http://nces.ed.gov/programs/digest/d09/tables/dt09_275.asp?referrer=list.
2. A recent monograph by Philipsen covers some of this territory, but without national data or a focus on family formation. Maike Ingrid Philipsen, *Challenges of the Faculty Career for Women: Success and Sacrifice*, with Timothy B. Bostic (San Francisco: Jossey-Bass, 2008).
3. National Science Foundation, Division of Science Resources Statistics, *Science and Engineering Degrees: 1966–2006* (Detailed Statistical Tables, NSF 08–321, 2008), table 2, http://www.nsf.gov/statistics/nsf08321/; National Center for Education Statistics, *Digest of Education Statistics*, table 275.
4. For Berkeley, University of California, Faculty Personnel Records, 1979–2007, Berkeley, CA; for other schools, National Science Foundation, Division of Science Resources Statistics, *Doctorate Recipients from U.S. Universities: Summary Report, 2007–08* (Special Report NSF 10–309, 2009), table 20, http://www.nsf.gov/statistics/nsf10309/; for historical figures, Lori Thurgood et al., *U.S. Doctorates in the 20th Century*, National Science Foundation, Division of Science Resources Statistics (NSF 06–319, 2006), table 3-19, http://www.nsf.gov/statistics/nsf06319/.
5. The humanities were omitted from the SDR subsequent to 1995 for budgetary reasons.
6. Mary Ann Mason and Marc Goulden, "Do Babies Matter? The Effect of Family Formation on the Lifelong Careers of Academic Men and Women," *Academe,* November–December, 2002, http://www.aaup.org/AAUP/pubsres/academe/2002/ND/Feat/Maso.htm; see also Nicholas H. Wolfinger et al., "Problems in the Pipeline: Gender, Marriage, and Fertility in the Ivory Tower," *Journal of Higher Education* 79 (2008): 388–405.
7. Mason and Goulden, "Do Babies Matter?"; Nicholas H. Wolfinger et al., "'Stay in the Game': Gender, Family Formation, and Alternative Trajectories in the Academic Life Course," *Social Forces* 87 (2009): 1591–1621.
8. Wolfinger et al., "Problems in the Pipeline."
9. Mary Ann Mason and Marc Goulden, "Do Babies Matter (Part II)? Closing the Baby Gap," *Academe* 90 (2004): 3–7, http://www.aaup.org/AAUP/pubsres/academe/2004/ND/Feat/04ndmaso.htm; Mary Ann Mason and Marc Goulden, "Marriage and Baby Blues: Redefining Gender Equity in the Academy," *Annals of the American Academy of Political and Social Science* 596 (2004): 86–103.
10. Mary Ann Mason, *The Equality Trap* (1988; Somerset, NJ: Transaction, 2002).
11. Nicholas H. Wolfinger et al., "Alone in the Ivory Tower," *Journal of Family Issues* 31 (2010): 1652–1670.

12. Karie Frasch et al., "Creating a Family Friendly Department: Chairs and Deans Toolkit," (report, University of California, Berkeley, 2007), http://ucfamilyedge.berkeley.edu/ChairsandDeansToolkitFinal7–07.pdf.

13. Mary Ann Mason et al., "Why Graduate Students Reject the Fast Track," *Academe* 95 (2009): 11–16, http://www.aaup.org/AAUP/pubsres/academe/2009/JF/Feat/maso.htm.

14. On the timing of generational overlap, Alice Rossi and Peter Rossi, *Of Human Bonding: Parent-Child Relations across the Life Course* (New York: Aldine de Gruyter, 1990).

15. Marc Goulden et al., "Staying Competitive: Patching America's Leaky Pipeline in the Sciences" (Berkeley Center on Health, Economic, and Family Security, University of California, Berkeley, 2009), http://www.americanprogress.org/issues/2009/11/women_and_sciences.html.

16. Mary Ann Mason and Eve Mason Ekman, *Mothers on the Fast Track: How a New Generation Can Balance Work and Family* (New York: Oxford University Press, 2007).

1   THE GRADUATE SCHOOL YEARS

1. Mary Ann Mason et al., "Why Graduate Students Reject the Fast Track," *Academe* 95 (2009): 11–16, http://www.aaup.org/AAUP/pubsres/academe/2009/JF/Feat/maso.htm.

2. National Science Foundation, Division of Science Resources Statistics, *Science and Engineering Degrees: 1966–2006* (Detailed Statistical Tables, NSF 08–321, 2008), table 2, http://www.nsf.gov/statistics/nsf08321/.

3. National Center for Education Statistics, Digest of Education Statistics: 2009 (Washington, DC: U.S. Department of Education, Institute of Education Sciences), table 275, http://nces.ed.gov/programs/digest/d09/tables/dt09_275.asp?referrer=list; for an explanation of this trend, Paula England et al., "Why Are Some Academic Fields Tipping toward Female? The Sex Composition of U.S. Fields of Doctoral Degree Receipt, 1971–1998" (working paper WP-03–12, Institute for Policy Research, Northwestern University, 2003), http://www.northwestern.edu/ipr/publications/papers/2003/WP-03–12.pdf.

4. National Science Foundation, Division of Science Resources Statistics, *Doctorate Recipients from U.S. Universities: Summary Report, 2007–08* (Special Report NSF 10–309, 2009), table 7, http://www.nsf.gov/statistics/nsf10309/.

5. On trends in baccalaureate and masters degrees, United States Census Bureau, *Educational Attainment in the United States: 2008*, table 2, http://www.census.gov/population/www/socdemo/education/cps2008.html.

6. National Science Foundation, *Doctorate Recipients*, table 20; for historical figures, Lori Thurgood et al., *U.S. Doctorates in the 20th Century* (National Science Foundation, Division of Science Resources Statistics, NSF 06–319, 2006), figure 3-19, http://www.nsf.gov/statistics/nsf06319/.

7. On the growth of postdocs, Nathan E. Bell, ed., "Postdocs: What We Know and What We Would Like to Know" (proceedings of a workshop sponsored by the National Science Foundation and the Commission on Professionals in Science and Technology, December 4, 2002, Washington, DC).

8. Past age thirty-five, fertility declines and the chances of birth defects are several times higher. See, for instance, American College of Obstetricians and Gynecologists (ACOG), "Age-Related Fertility Decline," ACOG Committee Opinion, no. 413 (2008), http://www.acog.org/Resources_And_Publications/Committee_Opinions/Committee_on_Gynecologic_Practice/Age-Related_Fertility_Decline; California Birth Defects Monitoring Program, "Registry Data, 1997–2001," 2005, http://www.cbdmp.org/bd_down_syn.htm.

9. Mason et al., "Graduate Students," 2009.

10. A report by the Pew Charitable Trust also noted that many graduate students turned away from the idea of a faculty career over time. Chris M. Golde and Timothy M. Dore, "At Cross Purposes: What the Experiences of Today's Doctoral Students Reveal about Doctoral Education" (Philadelphia: Pew Charitable Trust, 2001), http://www.Ph.D.completion.org/promising/Golde.pdf. Another study also finds that male graduate students voice greater preference for an academic research career, while women are more interested in teaching jobs. Mary Frank Fox and Paula E. Stephan, "Careers of Young Scientists: Preferences, Prospects, and Realities by Gender and Field," *Social Studies of Science* 31 (2001): 109–122.

11. Unless otherwise noted, qualitative data come from our University of California surveys. See the appendix for additional information.

12. Mason et al., "Graduate Students," 2009.

13. Interview conducted by the authors.

14. Universities that offer part-time degrees and a large number of master's programs are presumably more likely to attract older adults who are parents.

15. Mason et al., "Graduate Students."

16. Elga Wasserman, *The Door in the Dream: Conversations with Eminent Women in Science* (Washington, DC: Joseph Henry Press, 2000), 17.

17. "Oh the Guilt," *Academic Aspirations (blog)*, LabSpaces, October 25, 2010, http://www.labspaces.net/blog/profile/611/Dr__O.

18. Mary Ann Mason and Eve Mason Ekman, *Mothers on the Fast Track: How a New Generation Can Balance Work and Family* (New York: Oxford University Press, 2007), 9.

19. Perhaps this gender difference represents the stabilizing effect that marriage seems to have in men's lives. See Steven L. Nock, *Marriage in Men's Lives* (New York: Oxford University Press, 1998); Linda J. Waite and Maggie Gallagher, *The Case for Marriage: Why Married People Are Happier, Healthier, and Better Off Financially* (New York: Doubleday, 2000).

20. U.S. Department of Agriculture, *Expenditures on Children by Families*, 2009, http://www.cnpp.usda.gov/expendituresonchildrenbyfamilies.htm.

21. This contention is based on overall gender differences in labor force participation rates. United States Census Bureau, *Statistical Abstract of the United States: 2010*, 130th ed. (Washington, DC: U.S. Government Printing Office, 2010), http://www.census.gov/prod/www/abs/statab.html.

22. Sofia Katerina Refetoff Zahed, "Parsimony Is What We Are Taught, Not What We Live," in *Motherhood, the Elephant in the Laboratory: Women Scientists Speak Out*, ed. Emily Monosson, 187–193 (Ithaca, NY: Cornell University Press, 2008), 187.

23. Audrey Williams June, "Graduate Students' Pay and Benefits Vary Widely, Survey Shows," *Chronicle of Higher Education*, December 5, 2008.

24. Ibid.

25. Goulden et al., "Staying Competitive: Patching America's Leaky Pipeline in the Sciences" (Berkeley Center on Health, Economic, and Family Security, University of California, Berkeley, 2009), http://www.americanprogress.org/issues/2009/11/women_and_sciences.html.

26. See, for example, John A. Goldsmith et al., *The Chicago Guide to Your Academic Career: A Portable Mentor from Graduate School to Tenure* (Chicago: University of Chicago Press, 2001), 44–53.

27. Lisa Ellen Wolf-Wendel and Kelly Ward, "Academic Life and Motherhood: Variations by Institutional Type," *Higher Education* 52 (2006): 487–521.

28. Mary Ann Mason and Marc Goulden, "Do Babies Matter (Part II)? Closing the Baby Gap," *Academe*, 90 (2004) 3–7, http://www.aaup.org/AAUP/pubsres/academe/2004/ND/Feat/04ndmaso.htm; Mary Ann Mason and Marc Goulden, "Marriage and Baby

Blues: Redefining Gender Equity in the Academy," *Annals of the American Academy of Political and Social Science* 596 (2004): 86–103.

29. Mason et al., "Graduate Students."

30. It is difficult to know just how often this happens. According to one study, faculty advisors are up to a third more likely to help their male graduate students get published—and this is a study of sociologists, presumably an equity-minded group. American Sociological Association, Department of Research and Development, "The Best Time to Have a Baby: Institutional Resources and Family Strategies Among Early Career Sociologists" (research brief, July 2004), http://www.asanet.org/images/research/docs/pdf/Best%20Time%20to%20Have%20a%20Baby.pdf.

31. Mason and Ekman, *Mothers on the Fast Track*, 19.

32. National Research Council, Gender Differences at Critical Transitions in the Careers of Science, Engineering, and Mathematics Faculty (Washington, DC: National Academies Press, 2009).

33. Marc Goulden et al., "Staying Competitive"; National Science Foundation, "FY 2008 Annual Performance Report," 2008, http://www.nsf.gov/publications/pub_summ.jsp?ods_key=nsf0922; National Science Foundation, "National Science Foundation Announces Graduate Research Fellows for 2008" (press release, April 15, 2008), http://www.nsf.gov/news/news_summ.jsp?cntn_id=111452; Ruth L. Kirschstein, "Women in Research" (National Institutes of Health, Washington, DC, 2008), http://report.nih.gov/NIH_Investment/PPT_sectionwise/NIH_Extramural_Data_Book/NEDB%20SPECIAL%20TOPIC-WOMEN%20IN%20RESEARCH.ppt; Walter T. Schaffer, "Women in Biomedical Research" (National Institutes of Health, Washington, DC, 2008), www.womeninscience.nih.gov/bestpractices/docs/WalterSchaffer.pdf.

34. Comment on Mason et al., "Graduate Students," http://www.aaup.org/AAUP/pubsres/academe/2009/JF/Feat/maso.htm.

35. Wasserman, *The Door in the Dream,* 26.

36. Panel for the Study of Gender Differences in Career Outcomes of Science and Engineering Ph.D.s, Committee on Women in Science and Engineering, National Research Council, *From Scarcity to Visibility: Gender Differences in the Careers of Doctoral Scientists and Engineers*, ed. J. Scott Long (Washington DC: National Academies Press, 2001, 59). This gender difference may reflect age differences in fertility. Nicholas H. Wolfinger et al., "Alone in the Ivory Tower," *Journal of Family Issues* 31 (2010): 1652–1670.

37. Harry Etzokitz, "The 'Athena Paradox:' Bridging the Gender Gap in Science," *Journal of Technology Management & Innovation* 2 (2007): 1–3.

38. Mason and Ekman, *Mothers on the Fast Track*, 14.

39. Claudia Henrion, *Women in Mathematics: The Addition of Difference* (Indianapolis: Indiana University Press, 1997), 26.

40. "Thoughts about Women In Science," The Prodigal Academic (blog), June 1, 2010, http://theprodigalacademic.blogspot.com/.

41. Mason and Ekman, *Mothers on the Fast Track*, 2007, 14.

42. National Science Foundation, Division of Science Resources Statistics, *Science and Engineering Degrees,* table 2. The statistic cited includes the social sciences.

43. Claudia Dreifus, "The Chilling of American Science," *The New York Times*, July 6, 2004.

44. National Science Foundation, Division of Science Resources Statistics, *Science and Engineering Degrees*, table 25.

45. National Science Foundation, Division of Science Resources Statistics, *Graduate Students and Postdoctorates in Science and Engineering: Fall 2007* (Detailed Statistical Tables, NSF 10–307, 2010), table 10, http://www.nsf.gov/statistics/nsf10307.

46. National Science Foundation, "Survey of Graduate Students and Postdoctorates in Science and Engineering," webCASPAR, 2008, https://webcaspar.nsf.gov/Help/dataMap HelpDisplay.jsp?subHeader=DataSourceBySubject&type=DS&abbr=GSS&noHeader =1&JS=No; National Opinion Research Center, "Survey of Earned Doctorates," National Science Foundation, webCASPAR, 2008, https://webcaspar.nsf.gov/Help/dataMapHelp Display.jsp?subHeader=DataSourceBySubject&type=DS&abbr=DRF&noHeader =1&JS=No.

47. Curtiss L. Cobb III and Jon Krosnick, "The Effects of Postdoctoral Appointments on Career Outcomes and Job Satisfaction" (paper presented at the Using Human Resource Data from Science Resources Statistics Workshop, National Science Foundation, Arlington, Virginia, October 12, 2007).

48. Gretchen Vogel, "A Day in the Life of a Topflight Lab," *Science*, September 3, 1999, 1531–1532. A review of two issues found that 43 percent of research papers had postdocs as the first authors. We acknowledge the possibility that faculty may voluntarily relinquish first authorship to help their postdocs get jobs.

49. Geoff Davis, "Doctors without Orders," *American Scientist* 93, no. 3, supplement (2005), table YL03, http://post-doc.sigmaxi.org/results/.

50. Goulden et al., "Staying Competitive"; Marc Goulden et al., "UC Postdoctoral Scholar Career and Life Survey," University of California, Berkeley, 2008, http://ucfamilyedge .berkeley.edu/UC%20Postdoctoral%20Survey.html.

51. Davis, "Doctors without Orders," table YL17C.

52. Robin Wilson, "The Law of Physics," *Chronicle of Higher Education*, November 11, 2005, http://chronicle.com/article/The-Laws-of-Physics/35304.

53. Mason and Ekman, *Mothers on the Fast Track*, 2007, 16.

54. Mary Ann Mason and Marc Goulden, "Do Babies Matter? The Effect of Family Formation on the Lifelong Careers of Academic Men and Women," *Academe,* November–December 2002, http://www.aaup.org/AAUP/pubsres/academe/2002/ND/Feat/Maso .htm. The authors report the results of a survey of postdocs conducted at UC Berkeley and Lawrence Berkeley National Laboratory in 1999 by Maresi Nerad, Joe Cerny, and Linda McPheron.

55. Mason and Ekman, *Mothers on the Fast Track*, 2007, 21–22.

56. Mary Ann Mason, "Why So Few Doctoral-Student Parents?" *Chronicle of Higher Education*, October 21, 2009, http://chronicle.com/article/Why-So-Few-Doctoral-Student/48872/.

57. Title IX states, "A recipient shall not discriminate against any student, or exclude any student from its education program or activity, including an class or extra curricular activity, on the basis of such student's pregnancy childbirth, false pregnancy, termination of a pregnancy or recovery there from" (United States Code Section 20).

58. Ibid.

59. Mason and Goulden, "Do Babies Matter"; Nicholas H. Wolfinger et al., "Problems in the Pipeline: Gender, Marriage, and Fertility in the Ivory Tower," *Journal of Higher Education* 79 (2008): 388–405; Nicholas H. Wolfinger et al., "'Stay in the Game': Gender, Family Formation, and Alternative Trajectories in the Academic Life Course," *Social Forces* 87 (2009): 1591–1621.

60. Mason et al., "Graduate Students"; Sari M. van Anders, "Why the Academic Pipeline Leaks: Fewer Men than Women Perceive Barriers to Becoming Professors," *Sex Roles* 51 (2004): 511–521.

61. Mary Ann Mason et al., "University of California (UC) Doctoral Student Career and Life Survey Findings, 2006–2007," University of California, Berkeley, 2007, http://ucfamily edge.berkeley.edu/Rejectingthefasttrack.ppt, accessed 8/30/11.

62. Ibid.

63. Mason and Ekman, *Mothers on the Fast Track*, XX.

CHAPTER 2 GETTING INTO THE GAME

1. Thomas B. Hoffer et al., *Doctorate Recipients from United States Universities: Summary Report 2006* (Chicago: National Opinion Research Center, 2007), http://www.nsf.gov/statistics/doctorates/pdf/sed2006.pdf.

2. On the relative frequency of tenure-track job procurement, Nicholas H. Wolfinger et al., "'Stay in the Game': Gender, Family Formation, and Alternative Trajectories in the Academic Life Course," *Social Forces* 87 (2009): 1591–1621. On career expectations, Mary Ann Mason et al., "Why Graduate Students Reject the Fast Track," *Academe* 95 (2009): 11–16.

3. Mary Ann Mason and Eve Mason Ekman, *Mothers on the Fast Track: How a New Generation Can Balance Work and Family* (New York: Oxford University Press, 2007), 21–22.

4. A pseudonym is used for this individual interviewed by the authors.

5. Lisa Wolf-Wendel et al., *The Two-Body Problem: Dual-Career-Couple Hiring Practices in Higher Education* (Baltimore, MD: Johns Hopkins University Press, 2003).

6. On changing attitudes, Karin L. Brewster and Irene Padavic, "Change in Gender-Ideology, 1977–1996: The Contributions of Intracohort Change and Population Turnover," *Journal of Marriage and the Family* 62 (2000): 477–487; on relative numbers of stay-at-home mothers and fathers, United States Census Bureau, *America's Families and Living Arrangements*: 2006, 2007, table FG8, http://www.census.gov/population/www/socdemo/hh-fam/cps2006.html.

7. These results are derived from an event history analysis of first job attainment. For further details, see the appendix; see also Nicholas H. Wolfinger et al., "Problems in the Pipeline: Gender, Marriage, and Fertility in the Ivory Tower," *Journal of Higher Education* 79 (2008): 388–405.

8. National Center for Education Statistics, "The Integrated Postsecondary Education Data System (IPEDS) Salaries, Tenure, and Fringe Benefits of Full-Time Instructional Faculty Survey" (NCES, Washington, DC, 2001). This is a long-standing finding; for older research, see, *inter alia*, Michael R. Welch and Stephen Lewis, "A Mid-decade Assessment of Sex Biases in Placement of Sociology Ph.D.s: Evidence for Contextual Variation," *American Sociologist* 15 (1980): 120–127.

9. Recent work shows a corresponding marriage gap in the ranks of incoming faculty. Seventy-one percent of the men are married, compared with 61 percent of the women. Jack H. Schuster and Martin J. Finkelstein, *The American Faculty: The Restructuring of Academic Work and Careers* (Baltimore, MD: Johns Hopkins University Press, 2006), table A-3.10.

10. Humanities Ph.D.s were excluded from the SDR after 1995 because of budget cuts. The science data extend through 2003; both data sets start at 1981. We conducted an analysis of science Ph.D.s limited to the 1981–1995 period and obtained results similar to those based on data extending through 2003.

11. Observe that these effects are about equal in magnitude to the combined penalties incurred by married mothers in the analysis based on all fields. The difference is that in the sciences women have to be married *and* have young children to be at a disadvantage on the academic job market.

12. Hoffer et al., *Doctorate Recipients*, tables A3-a, A3-b, A3-c. These figures exclude doctorates in the humanities.

13. Geoff Davis. "Doctors without Orders." *American Scientist* 93, no. 3, supplement (2005), table 4, http://post-doc.sigmaxi.org/results/.

14. Jerry A. Jacobs, "The Faculty Time Divide," *Sociological Forum* 9 (2004): 3–27; see also Londa Schiebinger et al., *Dual-Career Academic Couples: What Universities Need to Know* (report, Michelle R. Clayman Institute for Gender Research, Stanford University, 2008), http://www.stanford.edu/group/gender/ResearchPrograms/DualCareer/Dual CareerFinal.pdf; Nicholas H. Wolfinger et al., "Alone in the Ivory Tower," *Journal of Family Issues* 31 (2010): 1652–1670.

15. Jacobs, "Faculty Time Divide," 3. Using a more recent, albeit smaller and nonrepresentative, sample, Schiebinger et al., *Dual-Career Academic Couples*, find that 40 percent of women and 34 percent of male academics have academic partners. See also Wolfinger et al., "Alone in the Ivory Tower."

16. On the prevalence of female breadwinners in the contemporary United States, Maria Shriver and the Center for American Progress, The Shriver Report: A Woman's Nation Changes Everything, ed. Heather Boushey and Ann O'Leary (Center for American Progress, 2009), 19; http://www.americanprogress.org/issues/2009/10/pdf/awn/a_womans_nation.pdf.

17. Emory Morrison et al., "The Differential Mobility Hypothesis and Gender Parity in Social Science Academic Careers" (paper presented at the annual meeting of the American Sociological Association, Atlanta, August 2010).

18. Mary Ann Mason et al., "Babies Matter: Pushing the Gender Equity Revolution Forward," in *The Balancing Act: Gendered Perspectives in Faculty Roles and Work Lives*, ed. S. J. Bracken et al. (Sterling, VA: Stylus, 2006), 9–30.

19. Observed anecdotally in John A. Goldsmith et al., *The Chicago Guide to Your Academic Career: A Portable Mentor from Graduate School to Tenure* (Chicago: University of Chicago Press, 2001), 80.

20. Emily Toth, *Ms. Mentor's Impeccable Advice for Women in Academia* (Philadelphia: University of Pennsylvania Press, 1997), 27.

21. On the illegality of questions about family, Lauren A. Vicker and Harriette J. Royer, *The Complete Academic Search Manual: A Systematic Approach to Successful and Inclusive Hiring* (Sterling, VA: Stylus, 2006).

22. Wolf-Wendel et al., The *Two-Body Problem*, 2003.

23. Alessandra Rusconi, "Academic Dual-Career Couples in the U.S.: Review of the North American Social Research" (working paper, Die Junge Akademie, Berlin, Germany, 2002).

24. In two-academic couples, the woman is more likely to have an adjunct position. Helen Astin and Jeffrey F. Milem, "The Status of Academic Couples in U.S. Institutions," *Academic Couples: Problems and Promises*, ed. Mary Ann Ferber and Jane W. Loeb (Urbana, Ill.: University of Illinois Press, 1997), 128–155; Schiebinger et al., *Dual-Career Academic Couples*.

25. Morrison et al., "The Differential Mobility Hypothesis."

26. Stephen Kulis and Diane Sicotte, "Women Scientists in Academia: Geographically Constrained to Big Cities, College Clusters, or the Coasts?" *Research in Higher Education* 43 (2002): 1–30; see also Gerald Marwell, Rachel Rosenfeld, and Seymour Spilerman, "Geographic Constraints on Women's Careers in Academia," *Science* 205 (1979): 1225–1231.

27. This argument appears in Goldsmith et al., *Chicago Guide*, 2001, 80.

28. *Chronicle*, http://chronicle.com/forums/index.php/topic,21594.0.html.

29. Shelley J. Correll et al., "Getting a Job: Is There a Motherhood Penalty?" *American Journal of Sociology* 112 (2007): 1297–1338.

30. Joan J. Williams. *Unbending Gender: Why Family and Work Conflict and What to Do about It* (Oxford: Oxford University Press, 2000).

31. Here we draw extensively on the online forums hosted by the *Chronicle of Higher Education*, an excellent and largely untapped source of information on women's job market experiences. They describe the hostility that academic mothers sometimes encounter on the job market, as well as the unique difficulties pregnancy and motherhood can pose for the academic job search.

32. *Chronicle*, http://chronicle.com/forums/index.php/topic,20579.0.html.

33. *Chronicle*, http://chronicle.com/forums/index.php/topic,20579.msg298129.html#msg 298129.

34. *Chronicle*, http://chronicle.com/forums/index.php/topic,36375.0.html.

35. *Chronicle*, http://chronicle.com/forums/index.php/topic,46529.0.html.

36. *Chronicle*, http://chronicle.com/forums/index.php/topic,18700.0.html.

37. Assoc. professor from a research school, "Academia Is Hostile to Children," Inside Higher Ed, http://www.insidehighered.com/news/2008/05/23/nokids.

38. *Chronicle*, http://chronicle.com/forums/index.php/topic,32149.msg438961.html#msg 438961.

39. Mary Ann Mason and Marc Goulden, "Do Babies Matter (Part II)? Closing the Baby Gap," *Academe* 90 (2004): 3.

40. On the benefits of marriage for men, Steven L. Nock, *Marriage in Men's Lives* (New York: Oxford University Press, 1998).

41. Chronicle, http://chronicle.com/forums/index.php/topic,30991.msg831220.html#msg 831220.

42. We use *contingent professors* as shorthand for instructors, adjuncts, visiting assistant professors, lecturers, and other teaching appointments off the tenure track, acknowledging that these jobs can vary with respect to pay, stability, and working conditions.

43. American Association of University Professors, "Trends in Faculty Status, 1975–2007," 2007, http://www.aaup2.org/research/TrendsinFacultyStatus2007.pdf.

44. American Association of University Professors, "Background Facts on Contingent Faculty," 2005, http://www.aaup.org/Issues/part-time/Ptfacts.htm.

45. John W. Curtis, "Faculty Salary and Faculty Distribution Fact Sheet 2003–04," American Association of University Professors, 2004.

46. *Academe*, "Inequities Persist for Women and Non-tenure-track Faculty," *Academe*, March–April (2005): 21–30, http://www.aaup.org/NR/rdonlyres/0A98969B-FA6C-40F5-8880-5E5DC3B7C36D/0/05z.pdf; John W. Curtis, "Trends in Faculty Status, 1975–2003" (unpublished manuscript, American Association of University Professors, 2005).

47. *Academe*, "Inequities Persist," 21.

48. Diane Pearce, "The Feminization of Poverty: Women, Work, and Welfare," *Urban and Social Change Review* 11 (1978): 28–36.

49. *Academe*, "Inequities Persist."

50. On full-time employment and primary income sources, *Academe*, "Inequities Persist"; on hours worked, Jacobs, "Faculty Time Divide." Levels of full-time employment by adjuncts are likely to be underreported. Sometimes faculty members are classified by their institutions as "part time," even though they teach four or five courses a term. This occurs because adjuncts split their teaching between two or more institutions of higher learning. American Association of University Professors, "Policy Statement:

Contingent Appointments and the Academic Profession," 2003, http://www.aaup.org/statements/SpchState/Statements/contingent.htm.

51. Wendell V. Fountain, *Academic Sharecroppers: Exploitation of Adjunct Faculty and the Higher Education System* (Bloomington, IN: Authorhouse, 2005).

52. James Monks, "Public versus Private University Presidents Pay Levels and Structure" (working paper 58, Cornell Higher Education Research Institute, Ithaca, New York, 2004).

53. American Association of University Professors, "Background Facts," 2005; Ernst Benjamin, "How Over-reliance on Contingent Appointments Diminishes Faculty Involvement in Student Learning," *Peer Review* 5, no, 1 (2002): 4–10. Research by Paul Umbach indeed suggests that tenure-track faculty are on average better teachers than adjuncts. Paul D. Umbach, "How Effective Are They? Exploring the Impact of Contingent Faculty on Undergraduate Education," *Review of Higher Education* 30 (2007): 91–123.

54. American Association of University Professors, "Background Facts," 2005, 1.

55. Mason and Ekman, *Mothers on the Fast Track*, 87.

56. On the scarcity of part-time tenure track positions, David W. Leslie and James T. Walke, *Out of the Ordinary: The Anomalous Academic; A Report of Research Supported by the Alfred P. Sloan Foundation* (Williamsburg, VA: College of William and Mary, 2001).

57. *Chronicle*, http://chronicle.com/forums/index.php/topic,76411.15.html.

58. These results are based on multivariate analysis of data from the 1983–1995 SDR. Additional information can be found in the appendix and in Wolfinger et al., "'Stay in the Game.'"

59. Shiela E. Widnall, "AAAS Presidential Lecture: Voices from the Pipeline," *Science* 241 (1988): 1740–1745. For examples of the pipeline in studies of gender imbalance among university faculty, Stephen Kulis et al., "More Than a Pipeline Problem: Labor Supply Constraints and Gender Stratification across Academic Science Disciplines," *Research in Higher Education* 43 (2002): 657–690; J. Scott Long, *From Scarcity to Visibility: Gender Differences in the Careers of Doctoral Scientists and Engineers* (Washington, D.C.: National Academy Press, 2001); Sari M. van Anders, "Why the Academic Pipeline Leaks: Fewer Men than Women Perceive Barriers to Becoming Professors," *Sex Roles* 51 (2004): 511–521.

60. Wolfinger et al., "'Stay in the Game'"; Yu Xie and Kimberlee A. Shauman, *Women in Science: Career Processes and Outcomes* (Cambridge, MA: Harvard University Press, 2003).

61. Phyllis Moen, *It's about Time: Couples and Careers* (Ithaca, NY: Cornell University Press, 2003), 325.

62. Schuster and Finkelstein, *American Faculty*, 221.

63. Jerry A. Jacobs, *Revolving Doors: Sex Segregation and Women's Careers* (Stanford, CA: Stanford University Press, 1989); Sylvia Ann Hewlett and Carolyn Buck Luce, "Off-Ramps and On-Ramps: Keeping Talented Women on the Road to Success," *Harvard Business Review*, March 2005, 1–11.

64. Wolfinger et al., "'Stay in the Game.'"

65. *Chronicle*, http://chronicle.com/forums/index.php/topic,51559.0.html (9/3/09).

66. *Chronicle*, http://chronicle.com/forums/index.php/topic,76411.15.html.

67. A note on terminology: we refer to movement into ladder-rank positions down the road from Ph.D. receipt as *returns* to the tenure track, reflecting the notion of a normative pathway between the completion of graduate school and the commencement of a tenure-track assistant professorship; this pathway constitutes the *track* that traditionally leads to *tenure*.

68. Schuster and Finkelstein, *American Faculty* show that men return to the tenure track more often than do women, but their finding is not based on multivariate event history analysis.

69. Xie and Shauman, *Women in Science.*
70. Wolfinger et al., "Problems in the Pipeline," 388.
71. This complicated topic is discussed at length in the next chapter.
72. Mary Ann Mason and Marc Goulden. "Do Babies Matter? The Effect of Family Forma-tion on the Lifelong Careers of Academic Men and Women," *Academe,* November–December 2002, 21–27. Higher education scholar Laura Perna finds that mothers are not overrepresented among contingent faculty. The difference between her finding and ours can probably be explained by how our dependent variable is defined. We look at all second-tier positions, while Perna considers only adjunct appointments. Also, her finding is based on a single cross-section, while ours draws on longitudinal data. Laura W. Perna, "The Relationship between Family Responsibilities and Employ-ment Status among College and University Faculty," *Journal of Higher Education* 72 (2001): 584–611.
73. Perna, "Relationship." Our research shows that marriage does not increase the like-lihood that marriage increases the likelihood of a contingent position right out of graduate school. A similar result is offered by Emory Morrison et al., "Onto, up, off the Academic Faculty Ladder: The Gendered Effects of Family on Career Transitions for a Cohort of Social Science PhDs," *Review of Higher Education* 34 (2011): 525–553. Yet Perna, "Relationship," indicates that married women are disproportionately likely to be contingent faculty. We conclude that married women take contingent positions a few years down the road, not right after graduate school. This interpretation recon-ciles our findings and Emory's with Perna's.

3   CAPTURING THE GOLDEN RING OF TENURE

1. Iris from Philadelphia (forum post), *New York Times,* http://community.nytimes.com/comments/www.nytimes.com/2010/02/13/us/13alabama.html?sort=oldest&offset=3.
2. David from St. Paul (forum post), *New York Times,* http://community.nytimes.com/comments/www.nytimes.com/2010/02/13/us/13alabama.html.
3. Tara Parker-Pope, "Genius, Madness, and Tenure," *New York Times,* February 22, 2010.
4. Elliot Marshall, "Shirley Tilghman: Princeton's Unconventional New Chief," Science Notes, *Science,* May 292 (2001): 1288–1289.
5. Committee on Science, Space, and Technology, U.S. House of Representatives, "Sub-committee Investigates Barriers to Women Seeking Science and Engineering Faculty Positions" (press release, October 17, 2007), http://archives.democrats.science.house.gov/press/PRArticle.aspx?NewsID=2000.
6. An interpretative account of the tenure process appears in William G. Tierney and Estela Mara Bensimon, *Promotion and Tenure: Community and Socialization in Academe* (Albany: State University of New York Press, 1996).
7. American Association for the Advancement of Science, "R&D Budget and Policy Pro-gram," in "Guide to R&D Funding Data—Historical Data," http://www.aaas.org/spp/rd/guihist.shtml.
8. Interview conducted by the authors.
9. Michael J. Dooris and Marianne Guidos, "Tenure Achievement Rates at Research Uni-versities" (paper presented at the annual meeting of the Association for Institutional Research, Chicago, May 2006).
10. Nicholas H. Wolfinger et al., "Problems in the Pipeline: Gender, Marriage, and Fertility in the Ivory Tower," *Journal of Higher Education* 79 (2008): 388–405.

11. See the appendix for details about this analysis; see also Wolfinger et al., "Problems in the Pipeline," 2008.

12. A similar result is offered by Emory Morrison et al., "Onto, up, off the Academic Faculty Ladder: The Gendered Effects of Family on Career Transitions for a Cohort of Social Science PhDs," *Review of Higher Education* 34 (2011): 525–553.

13. The sciences data extend through 2003, while analysis based on the humanities runs only through 1995. We explore this issue via additional analysis based on data extending through 1995 but limited to only the sciences. This enables us to determine whether the inclusion of the humanities, as opposed to the eight additional years of data, is responsible for these findings. The results of this additional analysis are virtually identical to those based on data extending through 2003. The inclusion of the humanities, rather than the eight additional years of data, are responsible for the absence of a relationship between marriage and tenure. These results also suggest that the effects of marriage and children on women's tenure decisions have not changed much over time. See the appendix for more information about this analysis.

14. Mary Ann Mason and Eve Mason Ekman, *Mothers on the Fast Track: How a New Generation Can Balance Work and Family* (New York: Oxford University Press, 2007), 37.

15. Marc Goulden et al., "Staying Competitive: Patching America's Leaky Pipeline in the Sciences," Berkeley Center on Health, Economic, and Family Security, University of California, Berkeley, 2009, http://www.americanprogress.org/issues/2009/11/women _and_sciences.html.," 2009.

16. Ibid., 19–20.

17. Steven Cohen, "The Danger of Cutting Federal Science Funding," *Huffington Post*, February 7, 2011, http://www.huffingtonpost.com/steven-cohen/the-danger-of-cutting-fed_b_819439.html.

18. Goulden et al., "Staying Competitive."

19. Helen S. Astin and Diane Davis, "Research Productivity across the Life and Career Cycles: Facilitators and Barriers for Women," in *Scholarly Writing and Publishing: Issues, Problems and Solutions*, ed. M. F. Cox (Boulder, CO: Westview Press, 1985), 147–160; Jonathan R. Cole and Harriet Zuckerman, "Marriage, Motherhood, and Research Performance in Science," *Scientific American* 255 (1987): 119–125.

20. Linda J. Waite and Maggie Gallagher, *The Case for Marriage: Why Married People Are Happier, Healthier, and Better Off Financially* (New York: Doubleday, 2000). Evidence for the benefits of marriage on professional success can also be found in a well-known study by Sanders Korenman and David Neumark. Married men are rated more highly by their supervisors, which results in more promotions. Sanders Korenman and David Neumark, "Does Marriage Really Make Men More Productive?" *Journal of Human Resources* 26 (1991): 282–307.

21. Elisabeth Rose Gruner, "I Am Not a Head on a Stick: On Being a Teacher and a Doctor and a Mommy," in *Mama, PhD: Women Write About Motherhood and Academic Life*, ed. Elrena Evans and Caroline Grant (Piscataway, NJ: Rutgers University Press, 2008), 123–128, 127.

22. Donna K. Ginther, "Does Science Discriminate against Women? Evidence from Academia, 1973–97" (working paper 2001-2, Federal Reserve Bank of Atlanta, 2001); Donna K. Ginther and Kathy J. Hayes, "Gender Differences in Salary and Promotion for Faculty in the Humanities, 1977–95" (working paper 2001-7, Federal Reserve Bank of Atlanta, 2001); Donna K. Ginther and Shulamit Kahn, "Women in Economics: Moving up or Falling off the Academic Ladder?" *Journal of Economic Perspectives* 18 (2004): 193–214.

23. Neil Gross and Solon Simmons, "The Social and Political Views of American Professors," Harvard University, 2007, table 17, http://www.wjh.harvard.edu/~ngross/lounsbery _9–25.pdf.

24. Stephen J. Ceci and Wendy M. Williams, "Understanding Current Causes of Women's Underrepresentation in Science," *Proceedings of the National Academy of Sciences of the United States*, early ed., 2011, 1–2, http://www.pnas.org/content/ early/2011/02/02/1014871108; Wendy M. Williams and Stephen J. Ceci, "When Scientists Choose Motherhood," American Scientist 100 (2012): 138–145, http://www.pnas.org/ content/early/2011/02/02/1014871108.full.pdf+html.

25. Lawrence H. Summers, "Remarks at NBER [National Bureau of Economic Research] Conference on Diversifying the Science and Engineering Workforce," Office of the President, Harvard University, 2005, http://www.harvard.edu/president/speeches/ summers_2005/nber.php.

26. Sara Rimer, "Rift Deepens as Professors at Harvard See Remarks," *New York Times*. February 19, 2005.

27. Robert Drago et al., "Bias against Care-Giving: Faculty Members Rarely Take Advantage of Family-Friendly Workplace; What Are We So Afraid Of?" *Academe* 91 (2005): 22–25; Joan Williams, *Unbending Gender. Why Family and Work Conflict and What to Do about It* (New York: Oxford University Press, 2000); Elga Wasserman, *The Door in the Dream: Conversations with Eminent Women in Science* (Washington, DC: Joseph Henry Press, 2000, 26); on bias against mothers in the workplace more generally, Shelley J. Correll et al., "Getting a Job: Is There a Motherhood Penalty?" *American Journal of Sociology* 112 (2007): 1297–1338.

28. American Association of University Women, Legal Advocacy Fund. http://www.aauw. org/act/laf/cases/casesupp.cfm.

29. American Association of University Women (AAUW), *Tenure Denied: Cases of Sex Discrimination in Academia*, American Association of University Women Educational Foundation and the American Association of University Women Legal Advocacy Fund, 2004, www.aauw.org/learn/research/upload/TenureDenied.pdf.

30. Mary Ann Mason, "Women, Tenure, and the Law," *Chronicle of Higher Education*, March 17, 2010, http://chronicle.com/article/Women-Tenurethe-Law/64646/; "Boston U. Set Back on Tenure," *New York Times*, November 8, 1989.

31. AAUW, *Tenure Denied*, 2004.

32. Fisher v. Vassar College, 70 F.3d 1420; Mason, "Women, Tenure, and the Law."

33. Mason, "Women, Tenure, and the Law."

34. Ceci and Williams, "Understanding Current Causes"; Gross and Simmons, "Social and Political Views"; Williams and Ceci, "When Scientists Choose Motherhood," 2012.

35. Karie Frasch et al., University Family Accommodations Policies and Programs for Researchers Survey (Berkeley: University of California, 2008), http://ucfamilyedge .berkeley.edu/AAU%20Family%20Friendly%20Policies%20Survey.htm; Carol S. Hollenshead et al., "Work/Family Policies in Higher Education: Survey Data and Case Studies of Policy Implementation," *New Directions for Higher Education*, Summer 2005, 41–65; Gilia C. Smith and Jean A. Waltman, "Designing and Implementing Family Friendly Policies in Higher Education," Center for the Education of Women, University of Michigan, Ann Arbor, 2006. For discussions of some of the difficulties surrounding tenure-clock stoppage, Saranna Thornton, "Implementing Flexible Tenure Clock Policies," *New Directions for Higher Education*, Summer 2005, 81–90; Kelly Ward and Lisa Ellen Wolf-Wendel, "Work and Family Perspectives from Research University Faculty," *New Directions for Higher Education*, Summer 2005, 67–80.

36. Cathy A. Trower, "Amending Higher Education's Constitution," *Academe,* September–October 2008, 16–19.

37. Maria Shriver and the Center for American Progress, *The Shriver Report: A Woman's Nation Changes Everything,* ed. Heather Boushey and Ann O'Leary (Center for American Progress, 2009), figure 2, http://www.americanprogress.org/issues/2009/10/pdf/awn/a_womans_nation.pdf.

38. Goulden et al., "Staying Competitive." The distinction between "maternal" and "parental" (as opposed to "paternal") reflects the wording of the questionnaire.

39. Harvard University Office of the Senior Vice Provost for Faculty Development and Diversity, "Guidelines for Faculty Maternity and Parental Leave," 2006, http://www.provost.harvard.edu/policies_guidelines/Maternity_and_Parental_Leave_Guidelines.pdf.

40. David W. Leslie and James T. Walke, *Out of the Ordinary: The Anomalous Academic; A Report of Research Supported by the Alfred P. Sloan Foundation* (Williamsburg, VA: College of William and Mary, 2001).

41. Robin Wilson, "Working Half Time on the Tenure Track," *Chronicle of Higher Education,* January 25, 2002, http://chronicle.com/article/Working-Half-Time-on-the/27272.

42. Mary Ann Mason, "Rethinking the Tenure Clock," *Chronicle of Higher Education,* May 28, 2009, http://chronicle.com/article/Rethinking-the-Tenure-Clock/44268/.

43. Leslie and Walke, *Out of the Ordinary,* 2001.

4 ALONE IN THE IVORY TOWER

1. See current and past editions of the U.S. Census Bureau's *Statistical Abstract of the United States.* United States Census Bureau, "Statistical Abstracts," http://www.census.gov/prod/www/statistical-abstract-us.html.

2. Daniel E. Hecker, "Earnings of College Graduates: Women Compared with Men," *Monthly Labor Review,* March 1998, 62–71, http://www.bls.gov/opub/mlr/1998/03/art5full.pdf.

3. United States Census Bureau, *Statistical Abstract of the United States,* http://www.census.gov/prod/www/abs/statab.html.

4. On the aims of liberal feminism, National Organization for Women, http://www.now.org; Benita Roth, *Separate Roads to Feminism: Black, Chicana, and White Feminist Movements in America's Second Wave* (New York: Cambridge University Press, 2003); Rosemarie Tong, *Feminist Thought* (Boulder, CO: Westview Press, 1989).

5. Mary Ann Mason, *The Equality Trap* (1988; Somerset, NJ: Transaction, 2002); see also Gail Collins, *When Everything Changed: The Amazing Journey of American Women from 1960 to the Present* (New York: Little, Brown, 2009).

6. Comment posted to online article. Scott Jaschik, "Does Academe Hinder Parenthood?" Inside Higher Ed, May 23, 2008 (date of article), http://www.insidehighered.com/news/2008/05/23/nokids.

7. For Americans, Arland Thornton and Linda Young-DeMarco, "Four Decades of Trends in Attitudes toward Family Issues in the United States: The 1960s through the 1990s," *Journal of Marriage and Family* 63 (2001): 1009–1037; for academics, Mary Ann Mason and Marc Goulden, "Marriage and Baby Blues: Redefining Gender Equity in the Academy," *Annals of the American Academy of Political and Social Science* 596 (2004): 86–103.

8. Thornton and Young-DeMarco, "Four Decades," 1009.

9. Mary Ann Mason et al., "Why Graduate Students Reject the Fast Track," *Academe* 95 (2009): 11–16, http://www.aaup.org/AAUP/pubsres/academe/2009/JF/Feat/maso.htm; Sari M. Van Anders, "Why the Academic Pipeline Leaks: Fewer Men than Women Perceive Barriers to Becoming Professors," *Sex Roles* 51 (2004): 511–521.

10. For a review, Diane J. Macunovich, "Relative Income and Price of Time: Exploring Their Effects on U.S. Fertility and Female Labor Force Participation," *Population and Development Review, Supplement: Fertility in the United States: New Patterns, New Theories* 22 (1996): 223–257.

11. Michelle J. Budig, "Are Women's Employment and Fertility Histories Interdependent? An Examination of Causal Order Using Event History Analysis," *Social Science Research* 32 (2003): 376–401.

12. For more information about these analyses, see the appendix; also, Mason and Goulden, "Marriage and Baby Blues," 2004.

13. Mary Ann Mason and Marc Goulden, "Do Babies Matter (Part II)? Closing the Baby Gap," *Academe* 90 (2004): 3–7.

14. Chronicle, http://chronicle.com/forums/index.php/topic,15281.0.html.

15. Chronicle, http://chronicle.com/forums/index.php/topic,14098.15.html.

16. Emory Morrison et al., "The Differential Mobility Hypothesis and Gender Parity in Social Science Academic Careers" (paper presented at the annual meeting of the American Sociological Association, Atlanta, August 2010). As we have noted, female faculty are much more likely than their male colleagues to have spouses working full time. Jerry A. Jacobs, "The Faculty Time Divide," *Sociological Forum* 9 (2004): 3–27; see also Nicholas H. Wolfinger et al., "Alone in the Ivory Tower," *Journal of Family Issues* 31 (2010): 1652–1670.

17. "Employment elsewhere" includes full-time jobs in research or administrative positions in academe, or employment in government or the private sector (according to the SDR, government and private sector placements outnumber nonteaching academic positions eight to one).

18. The previous set of analyses are based on Ph.D. recipients at the time they start their first jobs; the current analyses draw on longitudinal data that span careers.

19. The "second tier" includes Ph.D. recipients in contingent faculty positions, employed part time, or out of the paid labor force.

20. Women Ph.D.s working full time in other jobs have nearly identical declines in the odds of marriage compared with men (32 percent) and second-tier women (35 percent). As was the case for marriage at the time of career formation, tenure-track men are more likely to be married than are men in the second tier. One study based on a nonrandom sample finds a smaller gender gap in marriage for Ph.D.s employed outside academia. Elizabeth Rudd et al., "Finally Equal Footing for Women in Social Science Careers?" (CIRGE Spotlight on Doctoral Education 1, CIRGE, University of Washington, Seattle, 2008), http://depts.washington.edu/cirgeweb/c/wp-content/uploads/2008/07/1-finally-equal-footing-for-women1.pdf.

21. On work-family conflict and divorce in the population at large, Andrew J. Cherlin, *Marriage, Divorce, Remarriage*, rev. ed. (Cambridge, MA: Harvard University Press, 1992); Hiromi Ono, "Husbands' and Wives' Resources and Marital Disruption," *Journal of Marriage and the Family* 60 (1998): 674–689; Jay D. Teachman et al., "Demography of the Family," in *Handbook of Marriage and the Family*, ed. M. Sussman et al. (New York: Plenum, 1999), 39–76; Betsey Stephenson and Justin Wolfers, "Marriage and Divorce: Changes and their Driving Forces," *Journal of Economic Perspectives* 21 (2007): 27–52.

22. Data from the 2000 census indicate that 3 percent of male professors and 4 percent of female professors have nonresident spouses. Presumably fewer have nonresident spouses who are also academics. Wolfinger et al., "Alone in the Ivory Tower."

23. Chronicle, http://chronicle.com/forums/index.php/topic,54601.0.html.

24. Jacobs, "Faculty Time Divide," table 3.

25. A reminder: the SDR only ascertains the presence of children in the household. Presumably a small percentage are adopted or stepchildren, not a respondent's biological children. For more information about these analyses, see the appendix; also, Mason and Goulden, "Marriage and Baby Blues," 2004.

26. Women working full time at universities in research or administrative positions and those employed outside higher education are 60 percent less likely to have a child under six than are men working in similar jobs. Compared with women in the second tier, women working full time in positions other than tenure-track professorships are 65 percent less likely to have young children at home.

27. For additional information on this analysis, see the appendix; also, Wolfinger et al. "Alone in the Ivory Tower."

28. Our University of California survey data show an identical result for female faculty births. Mason and Goulden, "Do Babies Matter (Part II)."

29. Wolfinger et al., "Alone in the Ivory Tower."

30. PayScale, www.payscale.com.

31. Wolfinger et al., "Alone in the Ivory Tower."

32. Victoria Stagg Elliott, "More Doctors Work Part Time, Flexible Schedules," American Medical News (American Medical Association), March 26, 2012, http://www.ama-assn .org/amednews/2012/03/26/bil10326.htm.

33. This figure is based on SDR respondents twelve years subsequent to Ph.D. receipt, a time when most women have finished having children. It excludes the small proportion of academics who had children while relatively young. Mason and Goulden, "Do Babies Matter (Part II)." Thirty-two percent of men and 30 percent of women in our sample of University of California faculty are childless. Perhaps the University of California better accommodates its faculty mothers than do other schools. The academy may also have become more family friendly over time: the SDR data were collected between 1978 and 1994, while the UC data were gathered in 2002 and 2003.

34. Elaine Howard Ecklund and Anne E. Lincoln, "Scientists Want More Children," PLoS ONE 6 (2011): 1–4, http://www.plosone.org/article/fetchObjectAttachment.action;jses sionid=AF7AD9B03C2DE6D159361IAF3D04657D.ambrao2?uri=info%3Adoi%2F10.1371 %2Fjournal.pone.0022590&representation=PDF.

35. Ernst Benjamin, "Disparities in the Salaries and Appointments of Academic Women and Men: An Update of a 1988 Report of Committee W on the Status of Women in the Academic Profession" (American Association of University Professors, Washington, DC, 2003).

36. Jacobs, "Faculty Time Divide"; Wolfinger et al., "Alone in the Ivory Tower."

37. Gary S. Becker, A Treatise on the Family (Cambridge, MA: Harvard University Press, 1991).

38. Arlie R Hochschild, The Second Shift, with Anne Machung (New York: Avon Books, 1989); Julie E. Press and Eleanor Townsley, "Wives' and Husbands' Housework Reporting: Gender, Class, and Social Desirability," Gender and Society 12 (1998): 188–218; Beth Anne Shelton and Daphne John, "The Division of Household Labor," Annual Review of Sociology 22 (1996): 299–322; Scott J. South and Glenna Spitze, "Housework in Marital and Nonmarital Households," American Sociological Review 59 (1994): 327–347.

39. On the prevalence of dual-earner households, United States Bureau of the Census, Statistical Abstract of the United States, 2010, table 583, http://www.census.gov/prod/www/ abs/statab.html; for a review of research on work-family conflict, Tammy D. Allen et al., "Consequences Associated with Work-to-Family Conflict: A Review and Agenda for Future Research," Journal of Occupational Health Psychology 5 (2000): 278–308; for evidence of work-family conflict among academics, Carol L. Colbeck and Robert Drago,

"Accept, Avoid, Resist: How Faculty Members Respond to Bias against Caregiving . . . and How Departments Can Help," *Change: The Magazine of Higher Learning* 37 (2005): 10–17; Debra R. Comer and Susan Stites-Doe, "Antecedents and Consequences of Faculty Women's Academic-Parental Role Balancing," *Journal of Family and Economic Issues* 27 (2006): 495–512; Mary L. Gatta and Patricia A. Roos, "Balancing without a Net in Academia: Integrating Family and Work Lives" (unpublished manuscript, Rutgers University, Center for Women and Work, 2002); Jacobs, "Faculty Time Divide"; Kelly Ward and Lisa Wolf-Wendel, "Academic Motherhood: Managing Complex Roles in Research Universities," *Review of Higher Education* 27 (2004): 233–257. Other research shows that women academics do more housework than their male colleagues. J. Jill Suitor et al., "Gender, Household Labor, and Scholarly Productivity among University Professors," *Gender Issues* 19 (2001): 50–67.

40. N = 4,460; similar estimates, based on a national sample, appear in Jacobs, "Faculty Time Divide." Somewhat lower numbers can be found in Wolfinger et al., "Alone in the Ivory Tower," 2010. This discrepancy presumably reflects using census data to identify higher education faculty.

41. On marriage and scholarly productivity, Helen S. Astin and Diane Davis, "Research Productivity across the Life and Career Cycles: Facilitators and Barriers for Women," ed. M. F. Cox, *Scholarly Writing and Publishing: Issues, Problems and Solutions* (Boulder, CO: Westview Press, 1985), 147–160; Jonathan R. Cole and Harriet Zuckerman, "Marriage, Motherhood, and Research Performance in Science," *Scientific American* 255 (1987): 119–125.

42. National estimates are similar. Jerry A. Jacobs and Sarah E. Winslow, "The Academic Life Course, Time Pressures, and Gender Inequality," *Community, Work, and Family* 7 (2004): 143–161, table 6.

43. Not surprisingly, scholars who work more are more productive. Jerry A. Jacobs and Sarah E. Winslow, "Overworked Faculty: Job Stresses and Family Demands," *The Annals of the American Academy of Political and Social Science* 596 (2004): 104–129.

44. For time on research, Joya Misra et al., "Gender, Work Time, and Care Responsibilities among Faculty," *Sociological Forum* 27 (2012): 300–323; for publication, Laura A. Hunter and Erin Leahey, "Parenting and Research Productivity: New Evidence and Methods," *Social Studies of Science* 40 (2010): 433–451; J. Scott Long, "The Origins of Sex Differences in Science," *Social Forces* 68 (1990): 1297–1316; for a contrary finding, Donna K. Ginther and Shulamit Kahn, "Women in Economics: Moving up or Falling off the Academic Ladder?" *Journal of Economic Perspectives* 18 (2004): 193–214.

45. *Inter alia*, Jerry A. Jacobs, *Revolving Doors: Sex Segregation and Women's Careers* (Stanford, CA: Stanford University Press, 1989); Sylvia Ann Hewlett and Carolyn Buck Luce, "Off-Ramps and On-Ramps: Keeping Talented Women on the Road to Success," *Harvard Business Review*, March 2005, 1–11; Phyllis Moen, *It's about Time: Couples and Careers* (Ithaca, NY: Cornell University Press, 2003, 325).

46. Roger G. Smith, "Remembering Nils Wessell" (letter), *Tufts Magazine*, Summer, 2007, http://www.tufts.edu/alumni/magazine/summer2007/departments/letters.html. This job description has also been attributed to Chang-Lin Tien, former chancellor at the University of California, Berkeley.

47. National Science Foundation, Division of Science Resources Statistics, *Doctorate Recipients from U.S. Universities: Summary Report, 2007–08* (Special Report NSF 10–309, 2009), table 20, http://www.nsf.gov/statistics/nsf10309/.

48. On the number of single faculty mothers, Mason and Goulden, "Do Babies Matter (Part II)."

49. This appears to be the case at MIT, where underperforming female faculty members are sometimes held in contempt by their female peers. Nancy Hopkins, "Special Edition: A Study on the Status of Women Faculty in Science at MIT," *MIT Faculty Newsletter* 11, no. 4 (1999), http://web.mit.edu/fnl/women/women.html#The%20Study.

50. Karie Frasch et al., "Creating a Family Friendly Department: Chairs and Deans Toolkit" (report, University of California, Berkeley, 2007), http://ucfamilyedge.berkeley.edu.

51. Mason and Goulden, "Do Babies Matter (Part II)"; see also the sample qualifications discussed in note 34. The gender difference is somewhat smaller for assistant professors, who obtained their Ph.D.s more recently. Jacobs and Winslow, "Academic Life Course," table 5.

52. See chapter 2 of this book; also, Mason et al., "Graduate Students Reject"; van Anders, "Academic Pipeline," 2004.

53. Linda J. Waite and Maggie Gallagher, *The Case for Marriage: Why Married People Are Happier, Healthier, and Better Off Financially* (New York: Doubleday, 2000).

54. Collins, *When Everything Changed*, 2009.

5   LIFE AFTER TENURE

1. One of the few studies to study post-tenure academics, albeit without an emphasis on gender equity, is an interpretative monograph by Anna Neumann, *Professing to Learn: Creating Tenured Lives and Careers in the American Research University* (Baltimore, MD: Johns Hopkins University Press, 2009).

2. Calculation from National Science Foundation, Division of Science Resources Statistics, *Characteristics of Doctoral Scientists and Engineers in the United States: 2006* (Detailed Statistical Tables NSF 09–317, 2009), table 18, http://www.nsf.gov/statistics/nsf09317/.

3. First marriage at this age is unlikely but not unheard of. Joshua R. Goldstein and Catherine T. Kenney, "Marriage Delayed or Marriage Forgone? New Cohort Forecasts of First Marriage for U.S. Women," *American Sociological Review* 66 (2001): 506–519.

4. For the sciences, National Science Foundation, *Characteristics*, 2009, table 17; for all fields, Martha S. West and John W. Curtis, *AAUP Faculty Gender Equity Indicators, 2006*, American Association of University Professors, http://www.aaup.org/NR/rdonlyres/63396944–44BE-4ABA-9815–5792D93856F1/0/AAUPGenderEquityIndicators2006.pdf.

5. See the appendix for more information. Analysis based only on the sciences produces similar results, so it is omitted in the interest of brevity.

6. J. Scott Long, *From Scarcity to Visibility: Gender Differences in the Careers of Doctoral Scientists and Engineers* (Washington, D.C.: National Academy Press, 2001).

7. Stephen J. Ceci and Wendy M. Williams, "Understanding Current Causes of Women's Underrepresentation in Science," *Proceedings of the National Academy of Sciences of the United States*, early ed., 2011, 1–6, http://www.pnas.org/content/early/2011/02/02/1014871108.

8. Joya Misra et al., "The Ivory Ceiling of Service Work," *Academe* January-February, 2011; Joya Misra et al., "Associate Professors and Gendered Barriers to Advancement" (report, University of Massachusetts Amherst), http://people.umass.edu/misra/Joya_Misra/Work-Life_Research_files/Associate%20Professors%20and%20Gendered%20Barriers%20to%20Advancement%20Full%20Report.pdf.

9. We acknowledge that chairing an academic department can sometimes be a sought-after honor. However, this is not always the case, particularly when no one wants to do

it. It is in these situations, we suspect, that women associate professors, and not their male colleagues, become chairs.

10. American Council on Education, *The American College President*, 2007 ed., 20th Anniversary (Washington, DC: American Council on Education, 2007).

11. Ibid., x.

12. Goldstein and Kenney, "Marriage Delayed."

13. Institute for Women's Policy Research, "Fact Sheet IWPR #C350" (updated September 2010), http://www.iwpr.org/pdf/C350.pdf.

14. As might be suspected, this is a well-studied area. See, *inter alia*, June E. O'Neill and Dave M. O'Neill, "What Do Wage Differentials Tell Us about Labor Market Discrimination?" (working paper 11240, National Bureau of Economic Research, Cambridge, MA, 2005), http://www.nber.org/papers/w11240.pdf; United States General Accounting Office, *Women's Earnings: Work Patterns Partially Explain Difference between Men's and Women's Earnings* (GAO-04-35, 2003), http://www.gao.gov/assets/250/240547.pdf.

15. Sarah Avellar and Pamela J. Smock, "Has the Price of Motherhood Declined Over Time? A Cross-Cohort Comparison of the Motherhood Wage Penalty," *Journal of Marriage and Family* 65 (2003): 597–607; Michelle J. Budig and Paula England, "The Wage Penalty for Motherhood," *American Sociological Review* 66 (2001): 204–225; Michelle J. Budig and Melissa J. Hodges, "Differences in Disadvantage: Variation in the Motherhood Penalty across White Women's Earnings Distribution," *American Sociological Review* 75 (2010): 705–728; Jane Waldfogel, "The Effect of Children on Women's Wages," *American Sociological Review* 62 (1997): 209–217.

16. *Inter alia*, Marcia L. Bellas, "Comparable Worth in Academia: The Effects on Faculty Salaries of the Sex Composition and Labor-Market Conditions of Academic Disciplines," *American Sociological Review* 59 (1994): 807–821; Marcia L. Bellas, "Disciplinary Differences in Faculty Salaries: Does Gender Bias Play a Role?" *Journal of Higher Education* 68 (1997): 299–321; Debra Barbazet, "History of Pay Equity Studies," in *Conducting Salary-Equity Studies: Alternative Approaches to Research, ed.* R. K. Toutkoushian, *New Directions for Institutional Research* 115 (San Francisco: Jossey-Bass, 2003), 69–96; Jerry A. Jacobs, "The Faculty Time Divide," *Sociological Forum* 9 (2004): 3–27; Long, "*From Scarcity to Visibility*; Jack H. Schuster and Martin J. Finkelstein, *The American Faculty: The Restructuring of Academic Work and Careers* (Baltimore, MD: Johns Hopkins University Press, 2006); Paul D. Umbach, "Gender Equity in College Faculty Pay: A Cross-Classified Random Effects Model Examining the Impact of Human Capital, Academic Disciplines, and Institutions" (paper presented at the annual meeting of the American Educational Research Association, New York, March 2008); for recent figures, *Academe*, "It's Not over Yet: The Annual Report on the Economic Status of the Profession, 2010–11," March–April 2011, table 5, http://www.aaup.org/NR/rdonlyres/17BABE36-BA30-467D-BE2F-34C37325549A/0/zreport.pdf.

17. Bellas, "Comparable Worth"; Bellas, "Disciplinary Differences"; Umbach, "Gender Equity."

18. West and Curtis, *AAUP Faculty*.

19. Additional details about this analysis appear in the appendix.

20. Avellar and Smock, "Price of Motherhood"; Budig and England, "Wage Penalty"; Budig and Hodges, "Differences in Disadvantage"; Waldfogel, "Effect of Children."

21. *Academe*, "It's Not over Yet."

22. *Chronicle of Higher Education*, "Chronicle Forums," http://chronicle.com/forums/index.php/topic,57821.0.html.

23. Lois Haignere, *Paychecks: A Guide to Conducting Salary-Equity Studies for Higher Education Faculty*, 2nd ed. (Washington, DC: American Association of University Professors, 2002), 1, http://eric.ed.gov/ERICWebPortal/search/detailmini.jsp?_nfpb=true&_&ERICExtSearch _SearchValue_o=ED476226&ERICExtSearch_SearchType_o=no&accno=ED476226.

24. These figures are based on all disciplines. N = 832 (men) and 278 (women). Median salaries were almost identical to means.

25. Schuster and Finkelstein, *American Faculty*, 255, note that the gender gap in academic salaries did not change much between 1973 and 2000. Long, *From Scarcity to Visibility*, 211, finds that the income disparity between male and female faculty at research universities declined by 5 percentage points between 1979 and 1995.

26. Laura A. Hunter and Erin Leahey, "Parenting and Research Productivity: New Evidence and Methods," *Social Studies of Science* 40 (2010): 433–451; J. Scott Long, "The Origins of Sex Differences in Science," *Social Forces* 68 (1990): 1297–1316; for a contrary finding based on a study of economists, Donna Ginther and Shulamit Kahn, "Women in Economics: Moving up or Falling off the Academic Ladder?" *Journal of Economic Perspectives* 18 (2004): 193–214.

27. Umbach, "Gender Equity."

28. Mary C. Noonan, "The Long-Term Costs of Women's Work Interruptions" (unpublished paper, Department of Sociology, University of Iowa, 2005); see also Silke Aisenbrey et al., "Is There a Career Penalty for Mothers' Time Out? A Comparison of Germany, Sweden, and the United States," *Social Forces* 88 (2009): 573–605; Sylvia Ann Hewlett and Carolyn Buck Luce, "Off-Ramps and On-Ramps: Keeping Talented Women on the Road to Success," *Harvard Business Review*, March 2005, 1–11;

29. *Academe*, "It's Not over Yet"; West and Curtis, *AAUP Faculty*, table 6.

30. Mary Ann Mason et al., "University of California Faculty Family Friendly Edge: An Initiative for Tenure-Track Faculty at the University of California" (report, University of California, Berkeley, 2005), 18, http://ucfamilyedge.berkeley.edu/ucfamilyedge.pdf. Another study finds disproportionately low rates of professional migration for female scientists with children. Yu Xie and Kimberlee A. Shauman, *Women in Science: Career Processes and Outcomes* (Cambridge: Harvard University Press, 2003), 174–175.

31. This is net of parenthood and various other factors.

32. Linda J. Waite and Maggie Gallagher, *The Case for Marriage: Why Married People Are Happier, Healthier, and Better Off Financially* (New York: Doubleday, 2000, 102).

33. Jacobs, "Faculty Time Divide"; see also Nicholas H. Wolfinger et al., "Alone in the Ivory Tower," *Journal of Family Issues* 31 (2010): 1652–1670.

34. On shared caretaking, Suzanne M. Bianchi et al., *Changing Rhythms of American Family Life* (New York: Russell Sage, 2007).

35. On housework, Scott J. South and Glenna Spitze, "Housework in Marital and Nonmarital Households," *American Sociological Review* 59 (1994): 327–347; J. Jill Suitor, Dorothy Mecom, and Ilana S. Feld, "Gender, Household Labor, and Scholarly Productivity among University Professors," *Gender Issues* 19 (2001): 50–67; on kin-keeping, Alice Rossi and Peter Rossi, *Of Human Bonding: Parent-Child Relations across the Life Course* (New York: Aldine de Gruyter, 1990).

36. On early retirement programs: Seongsu Kim and Daniel C. Feldman, "Healthy, Wealthy, or Wise: Predicting Actual Acceptances of Early Retirement Incentives at Three Points in Time," *Personnel Psychology* 51 (1998): 623–642; Mildred M. Seltzer and Jane Karnes, "An Early Retirement Incentive Program," *Research on Aging* 10 (1988): 342–357; on the end of mandated retirement: Orley Ashenfelter and David Card, "Did the Elimination of Mandatory Retirement Affect Faculty Retirement?" *American Economic Review* 92

(2002): 957–980; Thomas B. Hoffer et al., "The End of Mandatory Retirement for Doctoral Scientists and Engineers in Postsecondary Institutions: Retirement Patterns 10 Years Later" (InfoBrief NSF 11–302, National Science Foundation, Directorate for Social, Behavioral, and Economic Sciences, December 2010); on attitudes toward retirement: Kim Anderson, "Differences in Attitudes Toward Retirement among Male and Female Faculty and Other University Professionals" (paper presented at the annual meeting of the Gerontological Society of America, Dallas, Texas, November 1978; Valerie M. Conley, "Demographics and Motives Affecting Faculty Retirement," *New Directions for Higher Education*, no. 132 (Winter 2005): 9–30; Valerie M. Conley, "Retirement and Benefits: Expectations and Realities," in *The NEA 2007 Almanac of Higher Education* (Washington, DC: National Education Association, 2007), 89–96; on characteristics of retired faculty: Lenard W. Kaye and Abraham Monk, "Sex Role Traditions and Retirement from Academe," *Gerontologist* 24 (1984): 420–426; Robert M. O'Neil, "Ending Mandatory Retirement in Two State Universities," in *To Retire or Not? Retirement Policy and Practice in Higher Education*, ed. R. L. Clark and P. B. Hammond (Philadelphia: University of Pennsylvania Press, 2001), 122–127; on pension preferences: Robert L. Clark and M. Melinda Pitts, "Faculty Choice of a Pension Plan: Defined Benefit versus Defined Contribution," *Industrial Relations* 38 (1999): 18–45; Audrey Williams June, "U. of North Carolina Lets Professor Ease Their Way into Retirement," *Chronicle of Higher Education*, June 13, 2008, http://chronicle.com/article/U-of-North-Carolina-Lets/26299; on phased retirement, John Keefe, "Survey of Early Retirement Practices in Higher Education," in *To Retire or Not? Retirement Policy and Practice in Higher Education*, ed. R. L. Clark and P. B. Hammond (Philadelphia: University of Pennsylvania Press, 2001, 65–80). To the best of our knowledge, only two studies have examined retirement using representative, longitudinal data on faculty members before and after they stopped teaching. Economists Orley Ashenfelter and David Card focused on how the abolition of mandatory retirement in 1994 affected retirement flows, not the predictors of academic retirement more generally. An NSF report by Thomas B. Hoffer, Scott Sederstrom, and Deborah Harper examined retirement using the SDR but did not report the results of multivariate analysis.

37. On average age of faculty members, Conley, "Retirement and Benefits"; on retirement intentions, Conley, "Demographics and Motives."

38. June, "U. of North Carolina"; John Pencavel, "Faculty Retirement Incentives by Colleges and Universities" (paper prepared for the TIAA-CREF Institute conference "Recruitment, Retention, and Retirement: The Three R's of Higher Education in the 21st Century," New York, April 2004), http://www.tiaa-crefinstitute.org/ucm/groups/content/@ap_ucm_p_tcp_docs/documents/document/tiaa02029363.pdf.

39. Ollie from Rochester, *New York Times*, August 16, 2010, http://www.nytimes.com/roomfordebate/2010/08/15/aging-professors-who-wont-retire/i-will-retire-as-a-professor-at-67.

40. This figure is based on data from the 1981–2003 SDR. It excludes scholars in the humanities.

41. National Center for Education Statistics, "National Study of Postsecondary Faculty," 2004, http://nces.ed.gov/surveys/nsopf/nedrc.asp.

42. By way of comparison, the average American retires at sixty-two. Murray Gendall, "Retirement Age Declines Again in 1990s," *Monthly Labor Review*, October 2001, 12–21, http://www.bls.gov/opub/mlr/2001/10/art2full.pdf.

43. *Chronicle of Higher Education,* "Chronicle Forums," http://chronicle.com/forums/index.php/topic,64432.15.html.

44. Claire Potter, "I Will Go Voluntarily at 67," *New York Times*, August 16, 2010.

45. Conley, "Demographics and Motives."

46. On second-tier jobs: chapter 2 of this book; John W. Curtis, "Faculty Salary and Faculty Distribution Fact Sheet, 2003–04," American Association of University Professors, 2004; on plans to retire, Conley, "Demographics and Motives."

47. Conley, "Demographics and Motives."

48. James M. Raymo and Megan M. Sweeney, "Work-Family Conflict and Retirement Preferences," *Journal of Gerontology: Social Sciences* 61B (2006): S161–S169.

49. We explore the predictors of academic retirement using SDR data collected between 1981 and 1995. Results excluding the humanities but extending through 2003 produced essentially similar findings. For additional information, see the appendix.

50. Keep in mind that nonmarital cohabitation cannot be measured using the SDR. Approximately 5 percent of academics have live-in partners. Wolfinger et al., "Alone in the Ivory Tower."

51. Lynne M. Casper and Philip N. Cohen, "How Does POSSLQ Measure Up? Historical Estimates of Cohabitation," *Demography* 37 (2000): 237–245. While true at the time the SDR data were collected, this may no longer be the case. Sheela Kennedy and Larry L. Bumpass, "Cohabitation and Children's Living Arrangements: New Estimates from the United States," *Demographic Research* 19 (2008): 1663–1692.

52. Hoffer et al., "End of Mandatory Retirement," do show a gender difference, but their finding is not based on multivariate event history analysis.

6   TOWARD A BETTER MODEL

1. Mark Brilliant, *The Color of America Has Changed: How Racial Diversity Shaped Civil Rights Reform in California, 1941–1978* (New York: Oxford University Press, 2010), xii.

2. "First Lady Michelle Obama: When You Make Life Easier for Working Parents, It's a Win for Everyone Involved," *The White House Blog*, September 26, 2011, http://www .whitehouse.gov/blog/2011/09/26/first-lady-michelle-obama-when-you-make-life -easier-working-parents-it-s-win-everyon.

3. Descriptions of family-friendly university policies appear in the following reports: Karie Frasch et al., "Creating a Family Friendly Department: Chairs and Deans Toolkit" (report, University of California, Berkeley, 2007), http://ucfamilyedge.berkeley .edu; Londa Schiebinger et al., "Dual-Career Academic Couples: What Universities Need to Know" (report, Michelle R. Clayman Institute for Gender Research, Stanford University, 2008), http://www.stanford.edu/group/gender/Publications/ index.html; Gilia C. Smith and Jean A. Waltman, "Designing and Implementing Family Friendly Policies in Higher Education" (report, Center for the Education of Women, University of Michigan, Ann Arbor, 2006), http://www.cew.umich .edu/sites/default/files/designing06.pdf. Useful discussions of policies, including some issues surrounding their implementation, appear in Maike Ingrid Philipsen and Timothy B. Bostic, *Helping Faculty Find Work-Life Balance: The Path Toward Family-Friendly Institutions* (San Francisco: Jossey-Bass, 2010); Saranna Thornton, "Implementing Flexible Tenure Clock Policies," *New Directions for Higher Education*, Summer 2005, 81–90; Kelly Ward and Lisa Ellen Wolf-Wendel, "Work and Family Perspectives from Research University Faculty," *New Directions for Higher Education*, Summer 2005, 67–80.

4. Marc Goulden et al., "Staying Competitive: Patching America's Leaky Pipeline in the Sciences" (Berkeley Center on Health, Economic, and Family Security, University of

California, Berkeley, 2009), 20, http://www.americanprogress.org/issues/2009/11/women_and_sciences.html.

5. For more information, American Council on Education, *An Agenda for Excellence: Creating Flexibility in Tenure-Track Faculty Careers* (Washington, DC: American Council on Education, 2005); the Women in Science and Engineering Leadership Institute at the University of Wisconsin at Madison website: http://wiseli.engr.wisc.edu/#url; The Center for Worklife [*sic*] Law: http://www.worklifelaw.org/; the Sloan Work and Family Research Network at Boston College: http://wfnetwork.bc.edu/; Karie Frasch et al., "The Devil Is in the Details: Creating Family-Friendly Departments for Faculty at the University of California," in *Establishing the Family Friendly Campus*, ed. Jamie Lester and Margaret Sallee (Sterling, VA: Stylus, 2009), 88–104.

6. Laurie M. Petty, "Department Chairs and High Chairs: The Importance of Perceived Department Chair Supportiveness on Faculty Parents' Views of Departmental and Institutional Kid-Friendliness" (unpublished masters thesis, Department of Sociology, University of Kansas, 2011).

7. Cathy A. Trower, "Amending Higher Education's Constitution," *Academe*, September–October 2008, 16–19.

8. Michèle Lamont et al., "Recruiting, Promoting, and Retaining Women Academics: Lessons from the Literature" (report for the Standing Committee for the Status of Women, Harvard University, 2004), http://www.wjh.harvard.edu/~mlamont/lessons.pdf.

9. Shelley J. Correll et al., "Getting a Job: Is There a Motherhood Penalty?" *American Journal of Sociology* 112 (2007): 1297–1338; Joan J. Williams, *Unbending Gender: Why Family and Work Conflict and What to Do about It* (Oxford: Oxford University Press, 2000).

10. http://vpaafw.chance.berkeley.edu/policies/BUCA_Announcement.pdf; the pilot program is described at http://vpaafw.chance.berkeley.edu/policies/emergency.shtml.

11. https://www.sittercity.com/register_corp_1.html?corp=universityofcalifornia&client=93.

12. Jerry A. Jacobs, "The Faculty Time Divide," *Sociological Forum* 9 (2004): 3–27; see also Londa Schiebinger et al., "*Dual-Career Academic Couples: What Universities Need to Know*" (report, Michelle R. Clayman Institute for Gender Research, Stanford University, 2008), http://www.stanford.edu/group/gender/ResearchPrograms/DualCareer/DualCareerFinal.pdf; Nicholas H. Wolfinger et al., "Alone in the Ivory Tower," *Journal of Family Issues* 31 (2010): 1652–1670.

13. Mary Ann Mason et al., "University of California Faculty Family Friendly Edge: An Initiative for Tenure-Track Faculty at the University of California" (report, University of California, Berkeley, 2005), 18, http://ucfamilyedge.berkeley.edu/ucfamilyedge.pdf; Schiebinger et al., *Dual-Career Academic Couples*, 2008.

14. Ibid.

15. Ibid.

16. University of Rhode Island, "Dual Career Guidelines," http://www.uri.edu/advance/work_life_support/dual_career_guidelines.html.

17. "First Lady Michelle Obama."

18. Ibid.

19. This includes the social sciences and is limited to scientists who acquired their Ph.D.s in the United States. Goulden et al., "Staying Competitive," 29.

20. The Carnegie Foundation now designates these schools as RU/VH "very high research activity." They are still commonly referred to as R1s. For more information, Carnegie Foundation for the Advancement of Teaching, "Summary Tables: Basic Classification," http://classifications.carnegiefoundation.org/summary/basic.php?key=805.

21. Goulden et al., "Staying Competitive," 29.

22. Ibid., 29.

23. Ibid., 31.

24. Ibid., 35.

25. Ibid., 40–42.

26. David W. Leslie and James T. Walke, *Out of the Ordinary: The Anomalous Academic; A Report of Research Supported by the Alfred P. Sloan Foundation* (Williamsburg, VA: College of William and Mary, 2001).

27. Title IX, Education Amendments of 1972, Title 20 U.S. 1681 et seq.

28. Ron Wyden, "Title IX and Women in Academics," *Computing Research News* 15 (2003): 1–8.

29. Nondiscrimination on the Basis of Sex in Education Programs or Activities Receiving Federal Financial Assistance; Final Common Rule, 65 Fed. Reg. 52,857 (August 30, 2000).

30. National Science Foundation: 45 C.F.R. 618.530; 45 CFR 86.57 (Department of Health and Human Services, including NIH); 10 CFR 1040.53 (Department of Energy).

31. On maternity leave, Goulden et al., "Staying Competitive," 19; on dependent health care, Mary Ann Mason, "Graduate Student Parents: The Underserved Minority" (paper presented at the Council of Graduate Schools, Washington DC, December 9, 2006).

32. Goulden et al., "Staying Competitive," 19–20.

33. Natural Sciences and Engineering Research Council of Canada. "Administrative Matters: Ownership of Items Purchased with Grant Funds," 2010, http://www.nserc-crsng .gc.ca/Professors-Professeurs/FinancialAdminGuide-GuideAdminFinancier/Admin Matters-QuestionAdmin_eng.asp.

34. European Molecular Biology Association, "Family-Friendly, Flexible and Far-Reaching," (press release, June 22, 2004), http://www.embo.org/documents/press04/family_flexible .pdf.

35. BNET, the CBS Interactive Business Network, "Workers on Parental Leave to Receive Subsidies for up to 6 Months," 2009, http://findarticles.com/p/articles/mi_qa5478/ is_200905/ai_n31965854/.

36. This is a common observation among social scientists. Sylvia Ann Hewlett and Carolyn Buck Luce, "Off-Ramps and On-Ramps: Keeping Talented Women on the Road to Success," *Harvard Business Review*, March 2005, 1–11; Jerry A. Jacobs, *Revolving Doors: Sex Segregation and Women's Careers* (Stanford, CA: Stanford University Press, 1989); Phyllis Moen, *It's about Time: Couples and Careers* (Ithaca, NY: Cornell University Press, 2003), 325.

37. Interview conducted by the authors.

38. European Commission Directorate-General for Research: Science and Society, "She Figures 2006: Women and Science Statistics and Indicators," 2006, http://ec.europa .eu/research/science-society/pdf/she_figures_2006_en.pdf.

39. The Wellcome Trust, "Career Re-entry Fellowships," http://www.wellcome.ac.uk/ Funding/Biomedical-science/Funding-schemes/Fellowships/Basic-biomedical-fellow ships/WTD004380.htm.

40. On the illegality of age discrimination, Age Discrimination in Employment Act of 1967, Pub. L. No. 90–202, 81 Stat. 602 (December 15, 1967), codified as Chapter 14 of Title 29 of the United States Code, 29 U.S.C. § 621 through 29 U.S.C. § 634 (ADEA),

41. Goulden et al., "Staying Competitive."

42. Ibid., 19–20.

43. This has also been one of the lessons of parental leave policies in Sweden. Katrin Bennhold, "The Female Factor; Paternity Leave Law Helps to Redefine Masculinity in Sweden," *New York Times*, June 15, 2010.

44. Nancy Hopkins et al., "The Status of Women Faculty at MIT: An Overview of Reports from the Schools of Architecture and Planning; Engineering; Humanities, Arts, and Social Sciences; and the Sloan School of Management" (report, Committee on the Status of Women Faculty, Massachusetts Institute of Technology, 2002), http://web.mit.edu/faculty/reports/overview.html.

45. Massachusetts Institute of Technology, "MIT Report on the Status of Women Faculty in Science and Engineering at MIT, 2011," http://web.mit.edu/newsoffice/images/documents/women-report-2011.pdf.

46. Ibid., 5.

47. Ibid., 6.

48. Frasch et al., "Creating a Family Friendly Department."

49. Angelica Stacy et al., "Report on the University of California, Berkeley Faculty Climate Survey" (report, University of California, Berkeley, 2011), 62, http://vpaafw.chance.berkeley.edu/Images/Faculty_Climate_Survey_Report_2011.pdf.

APPENDIX

1. National Science Foundation, "Survey of Earned Doctorates," 2011, http://www.nsf.gov/statistics/srvydoctorates/.

2. National Science Foundation, "Survey of Doctorate Recipients," 2008, http://www.nsf.gov/statistics/srvydoctoratework/.

3. National Science Foundation, "Changes to the Survey of Doctorate Recipients in 1991 and 1993: Implications for Data Users" (unpublished report, 1995).

4. Christopher Winship and Larry Radbill, "Sampling Weights and Regression Analysis," Sociological Methodology and Research 23 (1994): 230–257.

5. Examples of prominent studies limited to scientists include J. Scott Long, From Scarcity to Visibility: Gender Differences in the Careers of Doctoral Scientists and Engineers (Washington, DC: National Academy Press, 2001); Committee on Maximizing the Potential of Women in Academic Science and Engineering, National Academy of Sciences, National Academy of Engineering, and Institute of Medicine, Beyond Bias and Barriers: Fulfilling the Potential of Women in Academic Science and Engineering (Washington, DC: National Academies Press, 2007); Yu Xie and Kimberlee A. Shauman, Women in Science: Career Processes and Outcomes (Cambridge, MA: Harvard University Press, 2003).

6. On the changing SDR interview schedule, Sheldon B. Clark, "Variations in Item Content and Presentation in the Survey of Doctorate Recipients, 1973–1991" (working paper, National Science Foundation, Washington, DC, 1994).

7. Mary Ann Mason and Marc Goulden, "Marriage and Baby Blues: Redefining Gender Equity in the Academy," Annals of the American Academy of Political and Social Science 596 (2004): 86–103.

8. Christopher Paul et al., "A Cautionary Case Study of Approaches to the Treatment of Missing Data," Statistical Methods and Applications 17 (2008):351–372.

9. Mary Ann Mason et al., "The UC Faculty Work and Family Survey," 2003, http://ucfamilyedge.berkeley.edu/workfamily/htm.

10. Mary Ann Mason and Marc Goulden, "UC Doctoral Student Career Life Survey," 2008, http://ucfamilyedge.berkeley.edu/grad%20life%20survey.html.

11. Marc Goulden et al., "UC Postdoctoral Career Life Survey," 2009, http://ucfamilyedge.berkeley.edu/UC%20Postdoctoral%20Survey.html.

12. Marc Goulden et al., "UCB Non-faculty Academic Climate Survey," 2009, http://ucfamilyedge.berkeley.edu/UCB%20Academic%20Staff%20Survey.html.

13. Council on Market and Opinion Research, "Tracking Response, Cooperation, and Refusal Rates for the Industry: 2003 Results," (Wethersfield, CT: Council on Market and Opinion Research, 2003).

14. Marc Goulden et al., "Staying Competitive: Patching America's Leaky Pipeline in the Sciences" (Berkeley Center on Health, Economic, and Family Security, University of California, Berkeley, 2009), http://www.americanprogress.org/issues/2009/11/women_and_sciences.html.

15. "About AAU," Association of American Universities, http://www.aau.edu/about/default.aspx?id=58.

16. United States Census Bureau, "Public Use Microdata Sample (PUMS)," 2003, http://www.census.gov/main/www/pums.html.

17. Mary Ann Mason and Eve Mason Ekman, *Mothers on the Fast Track: How a New Generation Can Balance Work and Family* (New York: Oxford University Press, 2007).

18. It should be acknowledged that this dependent variable reflects one of several competing outcomes. Ph.D. recipients can obtain tenure-track jobs, nonladder teaching positions, or jobs outside academia, or take no jobs at all. Analyzing the likelihood of obtaining a tenure-track job without simultaneously considering the chances of other employment is not problematic, because of the likelihood that functions can be separated for competing events. Paul D. Allison, *Event History Analysis: Regression for Longitudinal Data*, Sage University Papers on Quantitative Applications in the Social Sciences, series no. 07–046 (Newbury Park, CA: Sage, 1984).

19. Paul D. Allison, *Survival Analysis Using the SAS System: A Practical Guide* (Cary, NC: SAS Institute, 1995), 216–219.

20. This is true throughout the manuscript, except in our analysis of income.

21. See Paul D. Allison and J. Scott Long, "Interuniversity Mobility of Academic Scientists," *American Sociological Review* 52 (1987): 643–652.

22. In preliminary analyses we experimented with a more elaborate twelve-category coding scheme for field of study. This did not affect our results.

23. The independence of irrelevant alternatives assumption was verified by both Hausman and Small-Hsiao tests. Daniel A. Powers and Yu Xie, *Statistical Methods for Categorical Data* (San Diego, CA: Academic Press, 2000), 245–247.

24. Curtiss L. Cobb III and Jon Krosnick, "The Effects of Postdoctoral Appointments on Career Outcomes and Job Satisfaction" (paper presented at the Using Human Resource Data from Science Resources Statistics Workshop, National Science Foundation, Arlington, VA, October 12, 2007).

25. Time-to-doctoral-degree and NRC rankings are omitted as independent variables in the analysis based on all fields. This had little effect on the results.

26. In recent years, the Carnegie Research I designation has been renamed "very high research activity"; other designations have similarly been renamed. Carnegie Foundation for the Advancement of Teaching, "Carnegie Classifications Data File," http://classifications.carnegiefoundation.org/resources/.

27. James J. Heckman, "Sample Selection Bias as a Specification Error," *Econometrica* 47 (1979): 153–161.

28. The discrete-time methods employed elsewhere in this book require the creation of different numbers of records for the first- and second-stage equations, so they cannot be estimated jointly. The aML software package permits the simultaneous estimation of two or more piecewise hazard models, but continuous time models are inappropriate for our data. On the aML package, Lee A. Lillard and Constantijn W. A. Panis, *aML Multilevel Multiprocess Statistical Software* (version 2, EconWare, Los Angeles, 2003).

29. See, for example, William H. Greene, *Econometric Analysis*, 5th ed. (Englewood Cliffs, NJ: Prentice Hall, 2002).

30. On fixed effects models, Paul D. Allison, *Fixed Effects Regression Models*, Sage University Papers on Quantitative Applications in the Social Sciences, series no. 07–160 (Thousand Oaks, CA: Sage, 2009). Income is adjusted for inflation using the consumer price index. Bureau of Labor Statistics, "Consumer Price Index," http://www.bls.gov/cpi/.

31. Sarah Avellar and Pamela J. Smock, "Has the Price of Motherhood Declined over Time? A Cross-Cohort Comparison of the Motherhood Wage Penalty," *Journal of Marriage and Family* 65 (2003): 597–607; Michelle J. Budig and Paula England, "The Wage Penalty for Motherhood," *American Sociological Review* 66 (2001): 204–225; Jane Waldfogel, "The Effect of Children on Women's Wages," *American Sociological Review* 62 (1997): 209–217.

32. On the curvilinear relationship of age to income, Lester C. Thurow, "The Optimum Lifetime Distribution of Consumption Expenditures," *American Economic Review* 59 (1969): 324–330.

33. Valerie M. Conley, "Retirement and Benefits: Expectations and Realities," *Almanac of Higher Education* (Washington, DC: National Education Association, 2007, 89–96).

BIBLIOGRAPHY

Academe. "Inequities Persist for Women and Non-tenure-track Faculty." March–April 2005, 21–30. http://www.aaup.org/NR/rdonlyres/0A98969B-FA6C-40F5-8880-5E5DC3B7C36D/0/05z.pdf.

———. "It's Not over Yet: The Annual Report on the Economic Status of the Profession, 2010–11." March–April 2011. Table 5. http://www.aaup.org/NR/rdonlyres/17BABE36-BA30-467D-BE2F-34C37325549A/0/zreport.pdf.

Aisenbrey, Silke, Marie Evertsson, and Daniela Grunow. "Is There a Career Penalty for Mothers' Time Out? A Comparison of Germany, Sweden, and the United States." *Social Forces* 88 (2009): 573–605.

Allen, Tammy D., David E. L. Herst, Carly S. Bruck, and Martha Sutton. "Consequences Associated with Work-to-Family Conflict: A Review and Agenda for Future Research." *Journal of Occupational Health Psychology* 5 (2000): 278–308.

Allison, Paul D. *Event History Analysis: Regression for Longitudinal Data*. Sage University Papers on Quantitative Applications in the Social Sciences, series no. 07-046. Newbury Park, CA: Sage, 1984.

———. *Fixed Effects Regression Models*. Sage University Papers on Quantitative Applications in the Social Sciences, series 07–160. Thousand Oaks, CA: Sage, 2009.

———. *Survival Analysis Using the SAS System: A Practical Guide*. Cary, NC: SAS Institute, 1995.

Allison, Paul D., and J. Scott Long. "Interuniversity Mobility of Academic Scientists." *American Sociological Review* 52 (1987): 643–652.

American Association for the Advancement of Science. "Trends in Federal R&D as % of GDP, FY 1976–2009." In "Guide to R&D Funding Data—Historical Data." 2008. http://www.aaas.org/spp/rd/trrdgdp09.pdf.

American Association of University Professors. "Background Facts on Contingent Faculty." 2005. http://www.aaup.org/Issues/part-time/Ptfacts.htm.

———. "Policy Statement: Contingent Appointments and the Academic Profession." 2003. http://www.aaup.org/statements/SpchState/Statements/contingent.htm.

———. "Trends in Faculty Status, 1975–2007." 2007. http://www.aaup2.org/research/TrendsinFacultyStatus2007.pdf.

American Association of University Women. "Legal Advocacy Fund Cases." http://www.aauw.org/act/laf/cases/casesupp.cfm.

———. *Tenure Denied: Cases of Sex Discrimination in Academia*. American Association of University Women Educational Foundation and the American Association of University Women Legal Advocacy Fund. 2004. www.aauw.org/learn/research/upload/TenureDenied.pdf.

American College of Obstetricians and Gynecologists (ACOG). "Age-Related Fertility Decline." *ACOG Committee Opinion* no. 413 (2008). http://www.acog.org/Resources _And_Publications/Committee_Opinions/Committee_on_Gynecologic_Practice/ Age-Related_Fertility_Decline.

American Council on Education. *An Agenda for Excellence: Creating Flexibility in Tenure-Track Faculty Careers.* Washington, DC: American Council on Education, 2005.

———. *The American College President.* 2007 ed., 20th Anniversary. Washington, DC: American Council on Education, 2007.

American Sociological Association, Department of Research and Development. "The Best Time to Have a Baby: Institutional Resources and Family Strategies among Early Career Sociologists." Research brief. July 2004. http://www.asanet.org/images/research/docs/ pdf/Best%20Time%20to%20Have%20a%20Baby.pdf.

Anderson, Kim. "Differences in Attitudes toward Retirement among Male and Female Faculty and Other University Professionals." Paper presented at the annual meeting of the Gerontological Society of America, Dallas, Texas, November 1978.

Ashenfelter, Orley, and David Card. "Did the Elimination of Mandatory Retirement Affect Faculty Retirement?" *American Economic Review* 92 (2002): 957–980.

Association of American Universities. "About AAU." 2011. http://www.aau.edu/about/ default.aspx?id=58.

Astin, Helen S., and Diane Davis. "Research Productivity across the Life and Career Cycles: Facilitators and Barriers for Women." In *Scholarly Writing and Publishing: Issues, Problems, and Solutions,* ed. M. F. Cox, 147–160. Boulder, CO: Westview Press, 1985.

Austin, Helen S., and Jeffrey P. Milem. "The Status of Academic Couples in U.S. Institutions." In *Academic Couples: Problems and Promise,* ed. Mary Ann Ferber and Jane W. Loeb, 128–155. Urbana: University of Illinois Press, 1997.

Avellar, Sarah, and Pamela J. Smock. "Has the Price of Motherhood Declined over Time? A Cross-Cohort Comparison of the Motherhood Wage Penalty." *Journal of Marriage and Family* 65 (2003): 597–607.

Barbazet, Debra. "History of Pay Equity Studies." In *Conducting Salary-Equity Studies: Alternative Approaches to Research,* ed. R. K. Toutkoushian, 69–96. *New Directions for Institutional Research* 115. San Francisco: Jossey-Bass, 2003.

Becker, Gary S. *A Treatise on the Family.* Cambridge, MA: Harvard University Press, 1991.

Bell, Nathan E., ed. "Postdocs: What We Know and What We Would Like to Know." Proceedings of a workshop sponsored by the National Science Foundation and the Commission on Professionals in Science and Technology, Washington, DC, December 2002.

Bellas, Marcia L. "Comparable Worth in Academia: The Effects on Faculty Salaries of the Sex Composition and Labor-Market Conditions of Academic Disciplines." *American Sociological Review* 59 (1994): 807–821.

———. "Disciplinary Differences in Faculty Salaries: Does Gender Bias Play a Role?" *Journal of Higher Education* 68 (1997): 299–321.

Benjamin, Ernst. "Disparities in the Salaries and Appointments of Academic Women and Men: An Update of a 1988 Report of Committee W on the Status of Women in the Academic Profession." American Association of University Professors, Washington, DC, 2003.

———. "How Over-reliance on Contingent Appointments Diminishes Faculty Involvement in Student Learning." *Peer Review* 5, no. 1 (2002): 4–10.

Bennhold, Katrin. "The Female Factor; Paternity Leave Law Helps to Redefine Masculinity in Sweden." *New York Times,* June 15, 2010.

Bianchi, Suzanne M., John P. Robinson, and Melissa A. Milkie. *Changing Rhythms of American Family Life.* New York: Russell Sage, 2007.

BNET, the CBS Interactive Business Network. "Workers on Parental Leave to Receive Subsidies for up to 6 Months." 2009. http://findarticles.com/p/articles/mi_qa5478/is _200905/ai_n31965854/.

"Boston U. Set Back on Tenure." *New York Times*, November 8, 1989.

Bramlett, Matthew D., and Williams D. Mosher. "First Marriage Dissolution, Divorce, and Remarriage: United States." *Advance Data from Vital Health Statistics*, no. 323. Hyattsville, MD: National Center for Health Statistics, 2001.

Brilliant, Mark. *The Color of America Has Changed: How Racial Diversity Shaped Civil Rights Reform in California, 1941–1978*. New York: Oxford University Press, 2010.

Brewster, Karin L., and Irene Padavic. "Change in Gender-Ideology, 1977–1996: The Contributions of Intracohort Change and Population Turnover." *Journal of Marriage and the Family* 62 (2000): 477–487.

Budig, Michelle J. "Are Women's Employment and Fertility Histories Interdependent? An Examination of Causal Order Using Event History Analysis." *Social Science Research* 32 (2003): 376–401.

Budig, Michelle J., and Paula England. "The Wage Penalty for Motherhood," *American Sociological Review* 66 (2001): 204–225.

Budig, Michelle J., and Melissa J. Hodges. "Differences in Disadvantage: Variation in the Motherhood Penalty across White Women's Earnings Distribution." *American Sociological Review* 75 (2010): 705–728.

Bureau of Labor Statistics. "Consumer Price Index." http://www.bls.gov/cpi/.

California Birth Defects Monitoring Program. "Registry Data, 1997–2001." 2005. http://www .cbdmp.org/bd_down_syn.htm.

Carnegie Foundation for the Advancement of Teaching. "Carnegie Classifications Data File." Stanford, CA. http://classifications.carnegiefoundation.org/resources/.

———. "Summary Tables: Basic Classification." http://classifications.carnegiefoundation .org/summary/basic.php?key=805.

Carr, Phyllis L., Laura Szalacha, Rosalind Barnett, Cheryl Caswell, and Thomas Inui. "A 'Ton of Feathers': Gender Disorganization in Academic Medical Careers and How to Manage It." *Journal of Women's Health* 12 (2003): 1009–1018.

Casper, Lynne M., and Philip N. Cohen. "How Does POSSLQ Measure Up? Historical Estimates of Cohabitation." *Demography* 37 (2000): 237–245.

Ceci, Stephen J., and Wendy M. Williams. "Understanding Current Causes of Women's Underrepresentation in Science." *Proceedings of the National Academy of Sciences of the United States*, early ed., 2011, 1–6. http://www.pnas.org/content/early/2011/02/02/1014871108.

Cherlin, Andrew J. *Marriage, Divorce, Remarriage*. Rev. ed. Cambridge, MA: Harvard University Press, 1992.

Chronicle of Higher Education. "Chronicle Forums." http://chronicle.com/forums/index.php/ topic.15227.15.html.

———. "Chronicle Forums." http://chronicle.com/forums.index/php/topic.18700.0.html.

———. "Chronicle Forums." http://chronicle.com/forums/index.php/topic.21594.0.html.

———. "Chronicle Forums." http://chronicle.com/forums/index.php/topic.36375.0.html.

———. "Chronicle Forums." http://chronicle.com/forums/index.php/topic.43527.0.html.

———. "Chronicle Forums." http://chronicle.com/forums/index.php/topic.53072.0.html.

———. "Chronicle Forums." http://chronicle.com/forums/index.php/topic.54079.0.html.

———. "Chronicle Forums." http://chronicle.com/forums/index.php/topic.54314.0.html.

———. "Chronicle Forums." http://chronicle.com.forums.index.php/topic.54601.0.html.

Clark, Robert L., and M. Melinda Pitts. "Faculty Choice of a Pension Plan: Defined Benefit versus Defined Contribution." *Industrial Relations* 38 (1999): 18–45.

Clark, Sheldon B. 1994. "Variations in Item Content and Presentation in the Survey of Doctorate Recipients, 1973–1991." Working paper, National Science Foundation, Washington, DC.

Cobb, Curtiss L., III, and Jon Krosnick. "The Effects of Postdoctoral Appointments on Career Outcomes and Job Satisfaction." Paper presented at the Using Human Resource Data from Science Resources Statistics Workshop, National Science Foundation, Arlington, Virginia, October 12, 2007.

Cohen, Steven. "The Danger of Cutting Federal Science Funding." *Huffington Post*, February 7, 2011. http://www.huffingtonpost.com/steven-cohen/the-danger-of-cutting-fed _b_819439.html.

Colbeck, Carol L., and Robert Drago. "Accept, Avoid, Resist: How Faculty Members Respond to Bias against Caregiving . . . and How Departments Can Help." *Change: The Magazine of Higher Learning* 37 (2005): 10–17.

Cole, Jonathan R., and Harriet Zuckerman. "Marriage, Motherhood, and Research Performance in Science." *Scientific American* 255 (1987): 119–125.

Collins, Gail. *When Everything Changed: The Amazing Journey of American Women from 1960 to the Present*. New York: Little, Brown, 2009.

Comer, Debra R., and Susan Stites-Doe. "Antecedents and Consequences of Faculty Women's Academic-Parental Role Balancing." *Journal of Family and Economic Issues* 27 (2006): 495–512.

Committee on Maximizing the Potential of Women in Academic Science and Engineering, National Academy of Sciences, National Academy of Engineering, and Institute of Medicine. *Beyond Bias and Barriers: Fulfilling the Potential of Women in Academic Science and Engineering*. Washington, DC: National Academies Press, 2007.

Committee on Science, Space, and Technology, U.S. House of Representatives. "Subcommittee Investigates Barriers to Women Seeking Science and Engineering Faculty Positions." Press release, October 17, 2007. http://sciencedems.house.gov/press/PRArticle .aspx?NewsID=2000.

Conley, Valerie M. "Demographics and Motives Affecting Faculty Retirement." *New Directions for Higher Education*, no. 132 (Winter 2005): 9–30.

———. "Retirement and Benefits: Expectations and Realities." In *The NEA 2007 Almanac of Higher Education*, 89–96. Washington, DC: National Education Association, 2007.

Correll, Shelley J., Stephen Benard, and In Paik. "Getting a Job: Is There a Motherhood Penalty?" *American Journal of Sociology* 112 (2007): 1297–1338.

Council on Market and Opinion Research. "Tracking Response, Cooperation, and Refusal Rates for the Industry: 2003 Results." Wethersfield, CT: Council on Market and Opinion Research, 2003.

Crittenden, Ann. *The Price of Motherhood: Why the Most Important Job in the World Is Still the Least Valued*. New York: Owl Books, 2002.

Curtis, John W. "Faculty Salary and Faculty Distribution Fact Sheet, 2003–04." *American Association of University Professors*, Washington, DC, 2004.

———. "Trends in Faculty Status, 1975–2003." *American Association of University Professors*, Washington, DC, 2005.

Davis, Geoff. "Doctors without Orders." *American Scientist* 93, no. 3, supplement (2005).

DeNavas-Walt, Carmen, Bernadette D. Proctor, and Cheryl Hill Lee. *Income, Poverty, and Health Insurance Coverage in the United States: 2005*. U.S. Census Bureau, Current Population Reports. Washington, DC: U.S. Government Printing Office, 2006.

Dooris, Michael J., and Marianne Guidos. "Tenure Achievement Rates at Research Universities." Paper presented at the annual forum of the Association for Institutional Research, Chicago, May 2006.

Drago, Robert, Carol Colbeck, Kai Dawn Stauffer, Amy Pirretti, Kurt Burkum, Jennifer Fazioli, Gabriela Lazarro, and Tara Habasevich. "Bias against Care-Giving: Faculty Members Rarely Take Advantage of Family-Friendly Workplace; What Are We So Afraid Of?" *Academe* 91 (2005): 22–25. http://www.aaup.org/AAUP/pubsres/academe/2005/SO/Feat/drag.htm.

Dreifus, Claudia. "The Chilling of American Science." *New York Times*, July 6, 2004.

Ecklund, Elaine Howard, and Anne E. Lincoln. "Scientists Want More Children." *PLoS ONE* 6 (2011): 1–4. http://www.plosone.org/article/fetchObjectAttachment.action;jsession id=AF7AD9B03C2DE6D159361IAF3D04657D.ambrao2?uri=info%3Adoi%2FI0.1371%2F journal.pone.0022590&representation=PDF.

Elliott, Victoria Stagg. "More Doctors Work Part Time, Flexible Schedules." *American Medical News* (American Medical Association), March 26, 2012. http://www.ama-assn.org/amednews/2012/03/26/bil10326.htm.

England, Paula, Paul Allison, Su Li, Noah Mark, Jennifer Thompson, Michelle Budig, and Han Sun. "Why Are Some Academic Fields Tipping toward Female? The Sex Composition of U.S. Fields of Doctoral Degree Receipt, 1971–1998." Working paper WP-03–12, Institute for Policy Research, Northwestern University, 2003. http://www.northwestern.edu/ipr/publications/papers/2003/WP-03–12.pdf.

Etzokitz, Harry. "The 'Athena Paradox:' Bridging the Gender Gap in Science." *Journal of Technology Management and Innovation* 2 (2007): 1–3.

European Commission Directorate-General for Research: Science and Society. "She Figures 2006: Women and Science Statistics and Indicators." 2006. http://ec.europa.eu/research/science-society/pdf/she_figures_2006_en.pdf.

Fidell, L. S. "Empirical Verification of Sex Discrimination in Hiring Practices in Psychology." *American Psychologist* 25 (1970): 1094–1098.

"First Lady Michelle Obama: When You Make Life Easier for Working Parents, It's a Win for Everyone Involved." *The White House Blog*, September 26, 2011. http://www.whitehouse.gov/blog/2011/09/26/first-lady-michelle-obama-when-you-make-life-easier-working-parents-it-s-win-everyon.

Fisher v. Vassar College, 70 F.3d 1420—Court of Appeals, 2nd Circuit 1995. http://scholar.google.com/scholar_case?case=10068614741292431392&q=Fisher+v.+Vassar+College,+70+F.3d+1420&hl=en&as_sdt=2,45&as_vis=1.

Fountain, Wendell V. *Academic Sharecroppers: Exploitation of Adjunct Faculty and the Higher Education System.* Bloomington, IN: Authorhouse, 2005.

Fox, Mary Frank, and Paula E. Stephan. "Careers of Young Scientists: Preferences, Prospects, and Realities by Gender and Field." *Social Studies of Science* 31 (2001): 109–122.

Frasch, Karie, Marc Goulden, and Mary Ann Mason. "University Family Accommodations Policies and Programs for Researchers Survey." Report, University of California, Berkeley, 2008. http://ucfamilyedge.berkeley.edu/AAU%20Family%20Friendly%20Policies%20Survey.html.

Frasch, Karie, Mary Ann Mason, Angelica Stacy, Marc Goulden, and Carol Hoffman. "Creating a Family Friendly Department: Chairs and Deans Toolkit." Report, University of California, Berkeley, 2007. http://ucfamilyedge.berkeley.edu/ChairsandDeansToolkitFinal7-07.pdf.

Frasch, Karie, Angelica Stacy, Mary Ann Mason, Sharon Page-Medrich, and Marc Goulden. "The Devil Is in the Details: Creating Family-Friendly Departments for Faculty at the University of California." In *Establishing the Family Friendly Campus,* ed. Jamie Lester and Margaret Sallee, 88–104. Sterling, VA: Stylus, 2009.

Gatta, Mary L., and Patricia A. Roos. "Balancing without a Net in Academia: Integrating Family and Work Lives." Unpublished manuscript, Rutgers University, Center for Women and Work, 2002.

Gendall, Murray. "Retirement Age Declines Again in 1990s." *Monthly Labor Review*, October 2001, 12–21. http://www.bls.gov/opub/mlr/2001/10/art2full.pdf.

Ginther, Donna K. "Does Science Discriminate against Women? Evidence from Academia, 1973–97." Working paper 2001–2, Federal Reserve Bank of Atlanta, 200l.

Ginther, Donna K., and Kathy J. Hayes. "Gender Differences in Salary and Promotion for Faculty in the Humanities, 1977–95." Working paper 2001–7, Federal Reserve Bank of Atlanta, 2001.

Ginther, Donna K., and Shulamit Kahn. "Women in Economics: Moving up or Falling off the Academic Ladder?" *Journal of Economic Perspectives* 18 (2004): 193–214.

Golde, Chris M., and Timothy M. Dore. "At Cross Purposes: What the Experiences of Today's Doctoral Students Reveal about Doctoral Education." Pew Charitable Trust, Philadelphia, 2001. http://www.phdcompletion.org/promising/Golde.pdf.

Goldsmith, John A., John Komlos, and Penny Schine Gold. *The Chicago Guide to Your Academic Career: A Portable Mentor from Graduate School to Tenure.* Chicago: University of Chicago Press, 2001.

Goldstein, Joshua R., and Catherine T. Kenney. "Marriage Delayed or Marriage Forgone? New Cohort Forecasts of First Marriage for U.S. Women." *American Sociological Review* 66 (2001): 506–519.

Goulden, Marc, Karie Frasch, and Mary Ann Mason. "UC Postdoctoral Scholar Career and Life Survey." University of California, Berkeley, 2008. http://ucfamilyedge.berkeley.edu/UC%20Postdoctoral%20Survey.html.

Goulden, Marc, Mary Ann Mason, Karie Frasch, and the Center for American Progress. "Staying Competitive: Patching America's Leaky Pipeline in the Sciences." Berkeley Center on Health, Economic, and Family Security, University of California, Berkeley, 2009. http://www.americanprogress.org/issues/2009/11/women_and_sciences.html.

Greene, William H. *Econometric Analysis*. 5th ed. Englewood Cliffs, NJ: Prentice Hall, 2002.

Gross, Neil, and Solon Simmons. "The Social and Political Views of American Professors." Harvard University, 2007. http://www.wjh.harvard.edu/~ngross/lounsbery_9-25.pdf.

Gruner, Elisabeth Rose. "I am Not a Head on a Stick: On Being a Teacher and a Doctor and a Mommy." In *Mama, PhD: Women Write about Motherhood and Academic Life*, ed. Elrena Evans and Caroline Grant, 123–128. Piscataway, NJ: Rutgers University Press, 2008.

Haignere, Lois. *Paychecks: A Guide to Conducting Salary-Equity Studies for Higher Education Faculty.* 2nd ed. Washington, DC: American Association of University Professors, 2002. http://eric.ed.gov/ERICWebPortal/search/detailmini.jsp?_nfpb=true&_&ERICExtSearch_SearchValue_0=ED476226&ERICExtSearch_SearchType_0=no&accno=ED476226.

Harvard University Office of the Senior Vice Provost for Faculty Development and Diversity. "Guidelines for Faculty Maternity and Parental Leave." 2006. http://www.provost.harvard.edu/policies_guidelines/Maternity_and_Parental_Leave_Guidelines.pdf.

Hecker, Daniel E. "Earnings of College Graduates: Women Compared with Men." *Monthly Labor Review*, March 1998, 62–71. http://www.bls.gov/opub/mlr/1998/03/art5full.pdf.

Heckman, James J. "Sample Selection Bias as a Specification Error." *Econometrica* 47 (1979): 153–161.

Henrion, Claudia. *Women in Mathematics: The Addition of Difference.* Indianapolis: Indiana University Press, 1997.

Hewlett, Sylvia Ann, and Carolyn Buck Luce. "Off-Ramps and On-Ramps: Keeping Talented Women on the Road to Success." *Harvard Business Review*, March 2005, 1–11.

Hochschild, Arlie R. *The Second Shift.* With Anne Machung. New York: Avon Books, 1989.

—. *The Time Bind: When Work Becomes Home and Home Becomes Work.* New York: Metropolitan Books, 1997.

Hoffer, Thomas B., Mary Hess, Vincent Welch, Jr., and Kimberly Williams. *Doctorate Recipients from United States Universities: Summary Report, 2006.* Chicago: National Opinion Research Center, 2007. http://www.nsf.gov/statistics/doctorates/pdf/sed2006.pdf.

Hoffer, Thomas B., Scott Sederstrom, and Deborah Harper. "The End of Mandatory Retirement for Doctoral Scientists and Engineers in Postsecondary Institutions: Retirement Patterns 10 Years Later." InfoBrief NSF 11–302, National Science Foundation, Directorate for Social, Behavioral, and Economic Sciences, Arlington, VA, December 2010. http://www.nsf.gov/statistics/infbrief/nsf11302/nsf11302.pdf.

Hoffer, Thomas B., Vincent Welch, Jr., Kristy Webber, Kimberly Williams, Brian Lisek, Mary Hess, Daniel Loew, and Isabel Guzman-Barron. *Doctorate Recipients from United States Universities: Summary Report, 2005.* Chicago: National Opinion Research Center, 2006. http://www.nsf.gov/statistics/doctorates/pdf/sed2005.pdf.

Hollenshead, Carol S., Beth Sullivan, Gilia C. Smith, Louise August, and Susan Hamilton. "Work/Family Policies in Higher Education: Survey Data and Case Studies of Policy Implementation." *New Directions for Higher Education*, Summer 2005, 41–65.

Nancy Hopkins, Lotte Bailyn, Lorna Gibson, Evelynn Hammonds, and the Council on Faculty Diversity. "The Status of Women Faculty at MIT: An Overview of Reports from the Schools of Architecture and Planning; Engineering; Humanities, Arts, and Social Sciences; and the Sloan School of Management." Report, Committee on the Status of Women Faculty, Massachusetts Institute of Technology, 2002. http://web.mit.edu/faculty/reports/overview.html.

Hunter, Laura A., and Erin Leahey. "Parenting and Research Productivity: New Evidence and Methods." *Social Studies of Science* 40 (2010): 433–451.

Inside Higher Ed. http://www.insidehighered.com/news/2008/05/23/nokids.

Institute for Women's Policy Research. "Fact Sheet IWPR #C350." Updated September 2010. http://www.iwpr.org/pdf/C350.pdf.

InterAcademy Council, Women for Science. "An Overview and Agenda for Change." http://www.interacademycouncil.net/Object.File/Master/11/039/2.%20An%20overview%20agenda%2ofor%2ochange.pdf.

Jacobs, Jerry A. "The Faculty Time Divide." *Sociological Forum* 9 (2004): 3–27.

—. *Revolving Doors: Sex Segregation and Women's Careers.* Stanford, CA: Stanford University Press, 1989.

Jacobs, Jerry A., and Sarah F. Winslow. "The Academic Life Course, Time Pressures, and Gender Inequality." *Community, Work and Family* 7 (2004): 143–161.

—. "Overworked Faculty: Jobs, Stresses, and Family Demands." *Annals of the American Academy of Political and Social Science* 596 (2004): 104–129.

Jaschik, Scott. "Does Academe Hinder Parenthood?" *Inside Higher Ed*, May 23, 2008. http://www.insidehighered.com/news/2008/05/23/nokids.

June, Audrey Williams. "Graduate Students' Pay and Benefits Vary Widely, Survey Shows." *Chronicle of Higher Education*, December 5, 2008. http://chronicle.com/article/Graduate-Students-Pay/36366/.

—. "U. of North Carolina Lets Professors Ease Their Way into Retirement." *Chronicle of Higher Education*, June 13, 2008. http://chronicle.com/article/U-of-North-Carolina-Lets/26299.

Kaye, Lenard W., and Abraham Monk. "Sex Role Traditions and Retirement from Academe." *Gerontologist* 24 (1984): 420–426.

Keefe, John. "Survey of Early Retirement Practices in Higher Education." In *To Retire or Not? Retirement Policy and Practice in Higher Education*, ed. R. L. Clark and P. B. Hammond, 65–80. Philadelphia: University of Pennsylvania Press, 2001.

Kennedy, Sheela, and Larry L. Bumpass. "Cohabitation and Children's Living Arrangements: New Estimates from the United States." *Demographic Research* 19 (2008): 1663–1692.

Kim, Seongsu, and Daniel C. Feldman. "Healthy, Wealthy, or Wise: Predicting Actual Acceptances of Early Retirement Incentives at Three Points in Time." *Personnel Psychology* 51 (1998): 623–642.

Kirschstein, Ruth L. "Women in Research." National Institutes of Health, Washington, DC, 2008. http://report.nih.gov/NIH_Investment/PPT_sectionwise/NIH_Extramural _Data_Book/NEDB%20SPECIAL%20TOPIC-WOMEN%20IN%20RESEARCH.ppt.

Korenman, Sanders, and David Neumark, "Does Marriage Really Make Men More Productive?" *Journal of Human Resources* 26 (1991): 282–307.

Kulis, Stephen, and Dianne Sicotte. "Women Scientists in Academia: Geographically Constrained to Big Cities, College Clusters, or the Coasts?" *Research in Higher Education* 43 (2002): 1–30.

Kulis, Stephen, Dianne Sicotte, and Shawn Collins. "More Than a Pipeline Problem: Labor Supply Constraints and Gender Stratification across Academic Science Disciplines." *Research in Higher Education* 43 (2002): 657–690.

Lamont, Michèle, Alexandra Kalev, Shawna Bowden, and Ethan Fosse. "Recruiting, Promoting, and Retaining Women Academics: Lessons from the Literature." Report for the Standing Committee for the Status of Women, Harvard University, 2004. http://www .wjh.harvard.edu/~mlamont/lessons.pdf.

Leslie, David W., and James T. Walke. *Out of the Ordinary: The Anomalous Academic; A Report of Research Supported by the Alfred P. Sloan Foundation.* Williamsburg, VA: College of William and Mary, 2001.

Lillard, Lee A., and Constantijn W. A. Panis. *aML Multilevel Multiprocess Statistical Software.* Version 2. EconWare, Los Angeles, 2003.

Panel for the Study of Gender Differences in Career Outcomes of Science and Engineering Ph.D.s, Committee on Women in Science and Engineering, National Research Council. *From Scarcity to Visibility: Gender Differences in the Careers of Doctoral Scientists and Engineers.* Ed. J. Scott Long. Washington, DC: National Academy Press, 2001.

———. "The Origins of Sex Differences in Science." *Social Forces* 68 (1990): 1297–1316.

Long, J. Scott, Paul D. Allison, and Robert McGinnis. "Rank Advancement in Academic Careers: Sex Differences and the Effects of Productivity." *American Sociological Review* 58 (1993): 703–722.

Macunovich, Diane J. "Relative Income and Price of Time: Exploring Their Effects on U.S. Fertility and Female Labor Force Participation." *Population and Development Review. Supplement: Fertility in the United States: New Patterns, New Theories* 22 (1996): 223–257.

Marshall, Elliot. "Shirley Tilghman: Princeton's Unconventional New Chief." Science Notes. *Science* 292 (2001): 1288–1289.

Marwell, Gerald, Rachel Rosenfeld, and Seymour Spilerman. "Geographic Constraints on Women's Careers in Academia." *Science* 205 (1979): 1225–1231.

Mason, Mary Ann. *The Equality Trap.* 1988. Somerset, NJ: Transaction, 2002.

———. "Graduate Student Parents: The Underserved Minority." Paper presented at the Council of Graduate Schools, Washington DC, December 9, 2006.

———. "Rethinking the Tenure Clock." *Chronicle of Higher Education*, May 28, 2009. http:// chronicle.com/article/Rethinking-the-Tenure-Clock/44268/.

———. "Why So Few Doctoral-Student Parents?" *Chronicle of Higher Education*, October 21, 2009. http://chronicle.com/article/Why-So-Few-Doctoral-Student/48872/.

———. "Women, Tenure, and the Law." *Chronicle of Higher Education*, March 17, 2010. http://chronicle.com/article/Women-Tenurethe-Law/64646/.

Mason, Mary Ann, and Eve Mason Ekman. *Mothers on the Fast Track: How a New Generation Can Balance Work and Family.* New York: Oxford University Press, 2007.

Mason, Mary Ann, and Marc Goulden. "Do Babies Matter? The Effect of Family Formation on the Lifelong Careers of Academic Men and Women." *Academe*, November–December 2002. http://www.aaup.org/AAUP/pubsres/academe/2002/ND/Feat/Maso.htm.

———. "Do Babies Matter (Part II)? Closing the Baby Gap." *Academe* 90 (2004): 3–7.

———. "Marriage and Baby Blues: Redefining Gender Equity in the Academy." *Annals of the American Academy of Political and Social Science* 596 (2004): 86–103.

Mason, Mary Ann, Marc Goulden, and Karie Frasch. "Why Graduate Students Reject the Fast Track," *Academe* 95 (2009): 11–16. http://www.aaup.org/AAUP/pubsres/academe/2009/JF/Feat/maso.htm.

Mason, Mary Ann, Marc Goulden, Karie Frasch, and Sharon Page-Medrich. "University of California (UC) Doctoral Student Career and Life Survey Findings, 2006–2007." University of California, Berkeley, 2007. http://ucfamilyedge.berkeley.edu/Rejectingthefasttrack.ppt.

Mason, Mary Ann, Marc Goulden, and Nicholas H. Wolfinger. "Babies Matter: Pushing the Gender Equity Revolution Forward." In *The Balancing Act: Gendered Perspectives in Faculty Roles and Work Lives*, ed. S. J. Bracken et al., 9–30. Sterling, VA: Stylus, 2006.

Mason, Mary Ann, Angelica Stacy, and Marc Goulden. "The UC Faculty Work and Family Survey." 2003. http://ucfamilyedge.berkeley.edu.

Mason, Mary Ann, Angelica Stacy, Marc Goulden, Carol Hoffman, and Karie Frasch. "University of California Faculty Family Friendly Edge: An Initiative for Tenure-Track Faculty at the University of California." Report, University of California, Berkeley, 2005. http://ucfamilyedge.berkeley.edu/ucfamilyedge.pdf.

Misra, Joya, Jennifer Hickes Lundquist, Elissa Dahlberg Holmes, and Stephanie Agiomavritis. "The Ivory Ceiling of Service Work." *Academe,* January–February 2011. http://www.aaup.org/AAUP/pubsres/academe/2011/JF/feat/misr.htm.

Misra, Joya, Jennifer Hickes Lundquist, and Abby Templer. "Gender, Work Time, and Care Responsibilities among Faculty." *Sociological Forum* 27 (2012): 300–323.

Misra, Joya, Jennifer Lundquist, Elissa Dahlberg Holmes, and Stephanie Agiomavritis. "Associate Professors and Gendered Barriers to Advancement." Report, University of Massachusetts, Amherst, 2011. http://people.umass.edu/misra/Joya_Misra/Work-Life_Research_files/Associate%20Professors%20and%20Gendered%20Barriers%20to%20Advancement%20Full%20Report.pdf.

Moen, Phyllis. *It's about Time: Couples and Careers.* Ithaca, NY: Cornell University Press, 2003.

Monks, James. "Public versus Private University Presidents Pay Levels and Structure." Working paper 58, Cornell Higher Education Research Institute, 2004.

Morrison, Emory, Elizabeth Rudd, Guangqing Chi, and Maresi Nerad. "The Differential Mobility Hypothesis and Gender Parity in Social Science Academic Careers." Paper presented at the annual meeting of the American Sociological Association, Atlanta, August 2010.

Morrison, Emory, Elizabeth Rudd, and Maresi Nerad. "Onto, up, off the Academic Faculty Ladder: The Gendered Effects of Family on Career Transitions for a Cohort of Social Science PhDs." *Review of Higher Education* 34 (2011): 525–553.

National Center for Education Statistics. *Digest of Education Statistics: 2009.* Washington, DC: U.S. Department of Education, Institute of Education Sciences, 2009. Table 275. http://nces.ed.gov/programs/digest/d09/tables/dt09_275.asp?referrer=list.

———. "The Integrated Postsecondary Education Data System (IPSEDS) Salaries, Tenure, and Fringe Benefits of Full-Time Instructional Faculty Survey." NCES, Washington, DC, 2001.

———. "National Study of Postsecondary Faculty." 2004. http://nces.ed.gov/surveys/nsopf/nedrc.asp.

National Institutes of Health. "NIH Data Book." http://report.nih.gov/ndb/index.aspx.

National Opinion Research Center. "Survey of Earned Doctorates." National Science Foundation, webCASPAR, 2008. https://webcaspar.nsf.gov/Help/dataMapHelpDisplay.jsp?subHeader=DataSourceBySubject&type=DS&abbr=DRF&noHeader=1&JS=No.

National Organization for Women. 2008. http://www.now.org.

National Research Council. *Gender Differences at Critical Transitions in the Careers of Science, Engineering, and Mathematics Faculty*. Washington, DC: National Academies Press, 2009.

National Science Foundation. "Changes to the Survey of Doctorate Recipients in 1991 and 1993: Implications for Data Users." Unpublished report, 1995.

———. "FY 2008 Annual Performance Report." 2008. http://www.nsf.gov/publications/pub_summ.jsp?ods_key=nsf0922.

———. "National Science Foundation Announces Graduate Research Fellows for 2008." Press release, April 15, 2008. http://www.nsf.gov/news/news_summ.jsp?cntn_id=111452.

———. "Survey of Doctorate Recipients." 2008. http://www.nsf.gov/statistics/srvydoctoratework/.

———. "Survey of Graduate Students and Postdoctorates in Science and Engineering." webCASPAR, 2008. https://webcaspar.nsf.gov/Help/dataMapHelpDisplay.jsp?subHeader=DataSourceBySubject&type=DS&abbr=GSS&noHeader=1&JS=No.

———. "Survey of Earned Doctorates." 2011. http://www.nsf.gov/statistics/srvydoctorates/.

National Science Foundation, Division of Science Resources Statistics. *Characteristics of Doctoral Scientists and Engineers in the United States: 2006*. Detailed Statistical Tables, NSF 09–317. 2009. http://www.nsf.gov/statistics/nsf09317/.

———. *Doctorate Recipients from U.S. Universities: Summary Report, 2007–08*. Special Report NSF 10–309. 2009. http://www.nsf.gov/statistics/nsf10309/.

———. *Graduate Students and Postdoctorates in Science and Engineering: Fall 2007*. Detailed Statistical Tables, NSF 10–307. 2010. http://www.nsf.gov/statistics/nsf10307/.

———. *Science and Engineering Degrees: 1966–2006*. Detailed Statistical Tables, NSF 08–321. 2008. http://www.nsf.gov/statistics/nsf08321/.

Neumann, Anna. *Professing to Learn: Creating Tenured Lives and Careers in the American Research University*. Baltimore, MD: Johns Hopkins University Press, 2009.

Nock, Stephen L. *Marriage in Men's Lives*. New York: Oxford University Press, 1998.

Noonan, Mary C. "The Long-Term Costs of Women's Work Interruptions." Unpublished paper, Department of Sociology, University of Iowa, 2005.

"Oh the Guilt." *Academic Aspirations (blog). LabSpaces*, October 25, 2010. http://www.labspaces.net/blog/profile/611/Dr__O.

O'Laughlin, Elizabeth M., and Lisa G. Bischoff. "Balancing Parenthood and Academia: Work/Family Stress as Influenced by Gender and Tenure Status." *Journal of Family Issues* 26 (2004): 79–106.

O'Neil, Robert M. "Ending Mandatory Retirement in Two State Universities." In *To Retire or Not? Retirement Policy and Practice in Higher Education*, ed. R. L. Clark and P. B. Hammond, 122–127. Philadelphia: University of Pennsylvania Press, 2001.

O'Neill, June E., and Dave M. O'Neill. "What Do Wage Differentials Tell Us about Labor Market Discrimination?" Working paper 11240, National Bureau of Economic Research, Cambridge, MA, 2005. http://www.nber.org/papers/w11240.pdf.

Ono, Hiromi. "Husbands' and Wives' Resources and Marital Disruption." *Journal of Marriage and the Family* 60 (1998): 674–689.

Parker-Pope, Tara. "Genius, Madness, and Tenure." *New York Times,* February 22, 2010.

Paul, Christopher, William M. Mason, Daniel McCaffrey, and Sarah A. Fox. "A Cautionary Case Study of Approaches to the Treatment of Missing Data." *Statistical Methods and Applications* 17 (2008): 351–372.

PayScale. www.payscale.com.

Pearce, Diane. "The Feminization of Poverty: Women, Work, and Welfare." *Urban and Social Change Review* 11 (1978): 28–36.

Pencavel, John. "Faculty Retirement Incentives by Colleges and Universities." Paper prepared for the TIAA-CREF Institute conference "Recruitment, Retention, and Retirement: The Three R's of Higher Education in the 21st Century," New York, April 2004. http://www.tiaa-crefinstitute.org/ucm/groups/content/@ap_ucm_p_tcp_docs/documents/document/tiaa02029363.pdf.

Perna, Laura W. "The Relationship between Family Responsibilities and Employment Status among College and University Faculty." *Journal of Higher Education* 72 (2001): 584–611.

Petty, Laurie M. "Department Chairs and High Chairs: The Importance of Perceived Department Chair Supportiveness on Faculty Parents' Views of Departmental and Institutional Kid-Friendliness." Master's thesis, Department of Sociology, University of Kansas, 2011.

Philipsen, Maike Ingrid. *Challenges of the Faculty Career for Women: Success and Sacrifice.* With Timothy B. Bostic. San Francisco: Jossey-Bass, 2008.

Philipsen, Maike Ingrid, and Timothy B. Bostic. *Helping Faculty Find Work-Life Balance: The Path toward Family-Friendly Institutions.* San Francisco: Jossey-Bass, 2010.

Piotrkowski, Chaya S., et al. "The Experience of Childbearing Women in the Workplace: The Impact of Family-Friendly Policies and Practices." Women's Bureau, Department of Labor, Washington, DC, 1993. http://www.eric.ed.gov/PDFS/ED364683.pdf.

Press, Julie E., and Eleanor Townsley. "Wives' and Husbands' Housework Reporting: Gender, Class, and Social Desirability." *Gender and Society* 12 (1998): 188–218.

Potter, Claire. "I Will Go Voluntarily at 67." *New York Times,* August 16, 2010.

Powers, Daniel A., and Yu Xie. *Statistical Methods for Categorical Data.* San Diego, CA: Academic Press, 2000.

Preston, Anne E. *Leaving Science: Occupational Exit from Scientific Careers.* New York: Russell Sage, 2004.

Raymo, James M., and Megan M. Sweeney. "Work-Family Conflict and Retirement Preferences." *Journal of Gerontology: Social Sciences* 61B (2006): S161–S169.

Rimer, Sara. "Rift Deepens as Professors at Harvard See Remarks." *New York Times,* February 19, 2005.

Rossi, Alice, and Peter Rossi. *Of Human Bonding: Parent-Child Relations across the Life Course.* New York: Aldine de Gruyter, 1990.

Roth, Benita. *Separate Roads to Feminism: Black, Chicana, and White Feminist Movements in America's Second Wave.* New York: Cambridge University Press, 2003.

Rudd, Elizabeth, Emory Morrison, Joseph Picciano, and Maresi Nerad. "Finally Equal Footing for Women in Social Science Careers?" CIRGE Spotlight on Doctoral Education 1. CIRGE, University of Washington, Seattle, 2008. http://depts.washington.edu/cirgeweb/c/wp-content/uploads/2008/07/1-finally-equal-footing-for-women1.pdf.

Rusconi, Alessandra. "Academic Dual-Career Couples in the U.S.: Review of the North American Social Research." Working paper, Die Junge Akademie, Berlin, Germany, 2002.

Schaffer, Walter T. "Women in Biomedical Research." National Institutes of Health, Washington, DC, 2008. www.womeninscience.nih.gov/bestpractices/docs/WalterSchaffer.pdf.

Schiebinger, Londa, Andrea Davies Henderson, and Shannon K. Gilmartin. *"Dual-Career Academic Couples: What Universities Need to Know."* Report, Michelle R. Clayman Institute for Gender Research, Stanford University, 2008. http://www.stanford.edu/group/gender/Publications/index.html.

Schwartz, F. N. "Management Women and the New Facts of Life." *Harvard Business Review,* January–February 1989, 65–76.

Schuster, Jack H., and Martin J. Finkelstein. *The American Faculty: The Restructuring of Academic Work and Careers.* Baltimore, MD: Johns Hopkins University Press, 2006.

Science Council of Japan. "Japan Vision 2050: Principles of Strategic Science and Technology Policy." 2005. http://www.scj.go.jp/en/vision2050.pdf.

Seltzer, Mildred M., and Jane Karnes. "An Early Retirement Incentive Program." *Research on Aging* 10 (1988): 342–357.

Shelton, Beth Anne, and Daphne John. "The Division of Household Labor." *Annual Review of Sociology* 22 (1996): 299–322.

Shriver, Maria, and the Center for American Progress. *The Shriver Report: A Woman's Nation Changes Everything.* Ed. Heather Boushey and Ann O'Leary. Center for American Progress, Washington, DC, 2009. http://www.americanprogress.org/issues/2009/10/pdf/awn/a_womans_nation.pdf.

Smith, Gilia C., and Jean A. Waltman. "Designing and Implementing Family Friendly Policies in Higher Education." Report, Center for the Education of Women, University of Michigan, Ann Arbor, 2006. http://www.cew.umich.edu/sites/default/files/designing06.pdf.

Smith, Roger G. "Remembering Nils Wessell." Letter. *Tufts Magazine,* Summer 2007. http://www.tufts.edu/alumni/magazine/summer2007/departments/letters.html.

South, Scott J., and Glenna Spitze. "Housework in Marital and Nonmarital Households." *American Sociological Review* 59 (1994): 327–347.

Stacy, Angelica, Sheldon Zedeck, Marc Goulden, and Karie Frasch. "Report on the University of California, Berkeley Faculty Climate Survey." Report, University of California, Berkeley, 2011. http://vpaafw.chance.berkeley.edu/Images/Faculty_Climate_Survey_Report_2011.pdf.

Stephenson, Betsey, and Justin Wolfers. "Marriage and Divorce: Changes and Their Driving Forces." *Journal of Economic Perspectives* 21 (2007): 27–52.

Suitor, J. Jill, Dorothy Mecom, and Ilana S. Feld. "Gender, Household Labor, and Scholarly Productivity among University Professors." *Gender Issues* 19 (2001): 50–67.

Springer, Kristen W., Brenda K. Parker, and Catherine Leviten-Reid. "Making Space for Graduate Student Parents: Practice and Politics." *Journal of Family Issues* 30 (2009): 435–457.

Summers, Lawrence H. "Remarks at NBER [National Bureau of Economic Research] Conference on Diversifying the Science and Engineering Workforce." Office of the President, Harvard University, 2005. http://www.harvard.edu/president/speeches/summers_2005/nber.php.

Teachman, Jay D., Karen Polonko, and John Scanzoni. 1999. "Demography of the Family." In *Handbook of Marriage and the Family,* ed. M. Sussman, S. Steinmetz, and G. Peterson, 39–76. New York: Plenum, 1999.

Thornton, Arland, and Linda Young-DeMarco. "Four Decades of Trends in Attitudes toward Family Issues in the United States: The 1960s through the 1990s." *Journal of Marriage and Family* 63 (2001): 1009–1037.

Thornton, Saranna. "Implementing Flexible Tenure Clock Policies." *New Directions for Higher Education,* Summer 2005, 81–90.

"Thoughts about Women In Science." *The Prodigal Academic* (blog), June 1, 2010. http://theprodigalacademic.blogspot.com/.

Thurgood, Lori, Mary J. Golladay, and Susan T. Hill. *U.S. Doctorates in the 20th Century*. National Science Foundation, Division of Science Resources Statistics, NSF 06–319. 2006. http://www.nsf.gov/statistics/nsf06319/pdf/nsf06319.pdf.

Thurow, Lester C. "The Optimum Lifetime Distribution of Consumption Expenditures." *American Economic Review* 59 (1969): 324–330.

Tierney, William G., and Estela Mara Bensimon. *Promotion and Tenure: Community and Socialization in Academe*. Albany: State University of New York Press, 1996.

Tong, Rosemarie. *Feminist Thought*. Boulder, CO: Westview Press, 1989.

Toth, Emily. *Ms. Mentor's Impeccable Advice for Women in Academia*. Philadelphia: University of Pennsylvania Press, 1997.

Trower, Cathy A. "Amending Higher Education's Constitution." *Academe*, September–October 2008, 16–19.

Umbach, Paul D. "Gender Equity in College Faculty Pay: A Cross-Classified Random Effects Model Examining the Impact of Human Capital, Academic Disciplines, and Institutions." Paper presented at the annual meeting of the American Educational Research Association, New York, March 2008.

———. "How Effective Are They? Exploring the Impact of Contingent Faculty on Undergraduate Education." *Review of Higher Education* 30 (2007): 91–123.

United States Census Bureau. *America's Families and Living Arrangements: 2006*. 2007. Table FG8. http://www.census.gov/population/www/socdemo/hh-fam/cps2006.html.

———. Current Population Survey Demographic Supplement, March 2004. http://www.census.gov/cps/methodology/techdocs.html.

———. *Educational Attainment in the United States: 2008*. http://www.census.gov/population/www/socdemo/education/cps2008.html.

———. "Public Use Microdata Sample (PUMS)." 2003. http://www.census.gov/main/www/pums.html.

———. *Statistical Abstract of the United States: 2008*. 128th ed. Washington, DC: U.S. Government Printing Office, 2008.

———. *Statistical Abstract of the United States: 2010*. 130th ed. Washington, DC: U.S. Government Printing Office, 2010. http://www.census.gov/prod/www/abs/statab.html.

———. "Table MS-2. Estimated Median Age at First Marriage, by Sex: 1890 to Present, 2004." http://www.census.gov/population/socdemo/hh-fam/tabMS-2.pdf.

———. "U.S. Census Bureau Reports Men and Women Wait Longer to Marry." Newsroom, November 10, 2010. http://www.census.gov/newsroom/releases/archives/families_households/cb10–174.html.

United States Department of Agriculture. *Expenditures on Children by Families*. 2009. http://www.cnpp.usda.gov/expendituresonchildrenbyfamilies.htm.

United States General Accounting Office. *Women's Earnings: Work Patterns Partially Explain Difference between Men's and Women's Earnings*. GAO-04-35. 2003. http://www.gao.gov/assets/250/240547.pdf.

University of Rhode Island. "Dual Career Guidelines." http://www.uri.edu/advance/work_life_support/dual_career_guidelines.html.

Valian, Virginia. *Why So Slow? The Advancement of Women*. Cambridge, MA: MIT Press, 1998.

van Anders, Sari M. "Why the Academic Pipeline Leaks: Fewer Men than Women Perceive Barriers to Becoming Professors." *Sex Roles* 51 (2004): 511–521.

Vicker, Lauren A., and Harriette J. Royer. *The Complete Academic Search Manual: A Systematic Approach to Successful and Inclusive Hiring*. Sterling, VA: Stylus, 2006.

Vogel, Gretchen. "A Day in the Life of a Topflight Lab." *Science*, September 3, 1999, 1531–1532.

Waite, Linda J., and Maggie Gallagher. *The Case for Marriage: Why Married People Are Happier, Healthier, and Better Off Financially*. New York: Doubleday, 2000.

Waldfogel, Jane. "The Effect of Children on Women's Wages." *American Sociological Review* 62 (1997): 209–217.

Ward, Kelly, and Lisa Ellen Wolf-Wendel. "Academic Motherhood: Managing Complex Roles in Research Universities." *Review of Higher Education* 27 (2004): 233–257.

———. "Work and Family Perspectives from Research University Faculty." *New Directions for Higher Education,* Summer 2005, 67–80.

Wasserman, Elga. *The Door in the Dream: Conversations with Eminent Women in Science.* Washington, DC: Joseph Henry Press, 2000.

Welch, Michael R., and Stephen Lewis. "A Mid-decade Assessment of Sex Biases in Placement of Sociology Ph.D.s: Evidence for Contextual Variation." *American Sociologist* 15 (1980): 120–127.

West, Martha S. "Gender Bias in Academic Robes: The Law's Failure to Protect Women Faculty." *Temple Law Review* 67 (1994): 67–178.

West, Martha S., and John W. Curtis. *AAUP Faculty Gender Equity Indicators, 2006.* American Association of University Professors, Washington, DC. http://www.aaup.org/NR/rdonlyres/63396944-44BE-4ABA-9815-5792D93856FI/0/AAUPGenderEquityIndicators2006.pdf.

Widnall, Sheila E. "AAAS Presidential Lecture: Voices from the Pipeline." *Science* 241 (1988): 1740–1745.

Williams, Joan. *Unbending Gender: Why Family and Work Conflict and What to Do about It.* New York: Oxford University Press, 2000.

Williams, Wendy, and Stephen J. Ceci. "When Scientists Choose Motherhood." *American Scientist* 100 (2012): 138–145. http://www.americanscientist.org/issues/feature/2012/2/when-scientists-choose-motherhood.

Wilson, Robin. "The Law of Physics." *Chronicle of Higher Education,* November 11, 2005. http://chronicle.com/article/The-Laws-of-Physics/35304.

———. "Working Half Time on the Tenure Track." *Chronicle of Higher Education,* January 25, 2002. http://chronicle.com/article/Working-Half-Time-on-the/27272.

Winship, Christopher, and Larry Radbill. "Sampling Weights and Regression Analysis." *Sociological Methodology and Research* 23 (1994): 230–257.

Wolfinger, Nicholas H., Mary Ann Mason, and Marc Goulden. "Alone in the Ivory Tower." *Journal of Family Issues* 31 (2010): 1652–1670.

———. "Problems in the Pipeline: Gender, Marriage, and Fertility in the Ivory Tower." *Journal of Higher Education* 79 (2008): 388–405.

———. "'Stay in the Game': Gender, Family Formation, and Alternative Trajectories in the Academic Life Course." *Social Forces* 87 (2009): 1591–1621.

Wolf-Wendel, Lisa Ellen, Susan B. Twombly, and Suzanne Rice. *The Two-Body Problem: Dual-Career-Couple Hiring Practices in Higher Education.* Baltimore, MD: Johns Hopkins University Press, 2003.

Wolf-Wendel, Lisa Ellen, and Kelly Ward. "Academic Life and Motherhood: Variations by Institutional Type." *Higher Education* 52 (2006): 487–521.

Wyden, Ron. "Title IX and Women in Academics." *Computing Research News* 15 (2003): 1–8.

Xie, Yu, and Kimberlee A. Shauman. *Women in Science: Career Processes and Outcomes.* Cambridge, MA: Harvard University Press, 2003.

Yang, Yang, and S. Philip Morgan. "How Big Are Educational and Racial Fertility Differentials in the U.S.?" *Social Biology* 51 (2004): 167–187.

Zahed, Sofia Katerina Refetoff. "Parsimony Is What We Are Taught, Not What We Live." In *Motherhood, the Elephant in the Laboratory: Women Scientists Speak Out,* ed. Emily Monosson, 187–193. Ithaca, NY: Cornell University Press, 2008.

INDEX

The letter f *following a page number denotes a figure; the letter* t *denotes a table.*

ABOUT THE AUTHORS

MARY ANN MASON is Professor of the Graduate School and Faculty Codirector of the Berkeley Law Center on Law and Social Policy, the University of California, Berkeley. From 2000 to 2007, she served as the first woman dean of the Graduate Division at UC Berkeley, with responsibility for nearly ten thousand students. During her tenure, she championed diversity in the graduate student population, promoted equity for student parents, and pioneered measures to enhance the career-life balance for all faculty. Her most recent book is *Mothers on the Fast Track: How a New Generation Can Balance Family and Careers* (Oxford University Press, 2007).

NICHOLAS H. WOLFINGER is Associate Professor in the Department of Family and Consumer Studies and Adjunct Associate Professor of Sociology at the University of Utah. He is the author of *Understanding the Divorce Cycle* (Cambridge University Press, 2005) and the coeditor of *Fragile Families and the Marriage Agenda* (Springer, 2005).

MARC GOULDEN studies the life course of academics at the University of California, Berkeley. His research projects include Do Babies Matter and the UC Faculty Family Friendly Edge. In 2005, Goulden was profiled by the *Chronicle of Higher Education* as one of higher education's next generation of thinkers.